THE CATHOLIC UNIVERSITY OF AMERICA
CANON LAW STUDIES
No. 116

THE RADICAL SANATION OF INVALID MARRIAGES

AN HISTORICAL SYNOPSIS AND COMMENTARY

A DISSERTATION

Submitted to the Faculty of Canon Law of the Catholic University of America in Partial Fulfillment of the Requirements for the Degree of

DOCTOR OF CANON LAW

BY

REV. ROBERT J. HARRIGAN, M.A., S.T.B., J.C.L.
Priest of the Diocese of Reno

THE CATHOLIC UNIVERSITY OF AMERICA
WASHINGTON, D. C.
1938

Nihil Obstat:

VALENTINUS T. SCHAAF, O.F.M., J.C.D.
Censor Deputatus

Washingtonii, die VI Junii, 1938

Imprimatur:

† THOMAS K. GORMAN, D.D.,
Episcopus Renensis

Reno, die VI Junii, 1938

PRINTED IN THE UNITED STATES OF AMERICA
BY THE WATKINS PRINTING CO., BALTIMORE

TO

HIS EXCELLENCY

THE MOST REVEREND THOMAS K. GORMAN, D.D.,

D. Sc. Hist. et Moral.,

First Bishop of Reno, Nevada

With esteem and gratitude

TABLE OF CONTENTS

CHAPTER III

CHAPTER IV

CHAPTER V

CHAPTER VI

INTRODUCTION

It is the purpose of the present work to offer a study of the extraordinary mode of convalidating invalid marriages. In the Code of Canon Law this mode of convalidation is called *"Sanatio in radice."* But throughout this study it will be called *"radical sanation."* In the use of this English phrase it will be possible to maintain the very significant meaning that is attached to the Latin phrase and at the same time to avoid the unwieldy repetition of the Latin terminology. It is in the interest of accuracy of meaning that the Latin word *"retrotractio"* has been rendered *"retrotraction"* throughout the study.

The study consists of two distinct parts. The first part is an historical synopsis of the origin, the use and the legislation governing this mode of convalidation up to the promulgation of the Code. The second part consists of a commentary of the canons which directly concern radical sanation, that is, of Canons 1138-1141. Following the commentary on these canons is a consideration of the faculties for radical sanation that are granted to the Apostolic Delegate to the United States, local Ordinaries in this country and certain Ordinaries in Mission territories. Finally an inquiry is made into the scope of Canons 81, 1043 and 1045 in relation to the granting of radical sanation.

The writer takes this opportunity to acknowledge his deep appreciation to the Most Reverend Thomas K. Gorman, D.D., Bishop of Reno for according him the privilege of making advanced studies. He further wishes to express his gratitude for the kindly assistance that has been afforded him by the Reverend Members of the Canon Law Faculty, members of the University Library staff and others whose aid and encouragement has made this study possible.

CHAPTER I

PRELIMINARY NOTIONS OF RADICAL SANATION

Radical sanation presents an instance of the exercise of the plenitude of the Papal power. It is not restricted to the convalidation of invalid marriages, but extends to all those things that fall under the positive law of the Church. Thus it is possible to have a sanation of invalid professions in a religious institute and of invalid receptions into confraternities. Furthermore, the invalid erection of Religious Institutes, the invalid erection of the Stations of the Cross, the invalid alienation of Church property and invalid judicial sentences can all be rendered valid by the healing effects of radical sanation.[1]

A dispensation in its generic concept, radical sanation represents the most ancient form of dispensation, namely, the *post factum* dispensation. In fact, Perrone[2] sees the first traces of the *sanatio in radice* in certain *post factum* dispensations contained in some conciliar enactments of the early sixth century. Whether or not this is true will be considered later, but it is certain that today the radical sanation of marriages is clearly a *post factum* dispensation, because it is granted only after a marriage has been invalidly contracted. Its very nature excludes its use prior to marriage, that is to say, it is never granted *ad contrahendum matrimonium.*

In the Code of Canon Law, four separate canons are devoted to the subject of convalidating marriages by means of radical sanation. The first of these four canons is divided into three

[1] "Quaesitum de momento quo sanatio operetur," *Periodica,* XV (1926-1927), (54); "Acta summatim relata," *op. cit.,* XVII-XVIII (1928-1929), 206, n. 79; *Analecta Ord. Min. Cappucc.,* T. 44., p. 178; Cleary, *Canonical Limitation on The Alienation of Church Property,* (Washington, 1936), p. 110; Canon 586, § 3; Schäfer, *De Religiosis,* nn. 72, 81, 91, 223, 282, 542, 617 and 634.

[2] *De Matrimonio Christiano,* II, 88.

sections. In the first section one finds a definition of sanation and an enumeration of its principal elements. It is with this section that the present chapter will deal. It is placed ahead of the chapter which treats of the historical development of this mode of convalidation in order that the historical synopsis may be better understood. The remaining commentary will follow the historical synopsis.

Canon 1138, § 1.—Matrimonii in radice sanatio est eiusdem convalidatio, secumferens, praeter dispensationem vel cessationem impedimenti, dispensationem a lege de renovando consensu, et retrotractionem, per fictionem iuris, circa effectus canonicos, ad praeteritum.

Art. I. The Nature of Radical Sanation

A. Nominal Definition

The name by which this extraordinary mode of convalidation is commonly known is easily understood when one has a clear notion of the manner in which it operates. The phrase *"sanatio in radice"*, which is used in the Code, is literally translated as a *"healing in the root"*. The healing or sanation refers to the curative work done by the Church in respect to the root of the marriage, which is the consent of the parties.[3] In resorting to this particular mode of convalidation the Church looks first to the nature of the consent exchanged by the parties when they entered the union under consideration. If it is sufficiently established that the parties entered their marriage with a consent that was, of itself, naturally sufficient for marriage, the Church then looks to the removal of the obstacle or obstacles which vitiated and diseased that consent and rendered it juridically inefficacious.[4] In proceeding thus to the convalidation of the union through radical sanation, the Church departs from the

[3] Canon 1081, § 1. "Matrimonium facit partium consensus inter personas iure habiles legitime manifestatus; . . ."

[4] Payen, *De Matrimonio in Missionibus*, (Zi-ka-wei, 1929), n. 2595.

usual mode of convalidation and does not require the parties, or at least one of the parties, to observe the law which usually requires a renewal of the marriage consent.[5] In the place of this customary renewal of consent the Church accepts the consent, originally given, as sufficient to constitute a valid marriage, when the invalidating impediment has been removed or a dispensation from the required form has been given.[6] Consequently it is really the first consent that is being rendered juridically effective, through a fiction of the law, by which the Church draws the dispensation back to the beginning of the union, or to some intermediate point, and heals the marriage at its root. As the canons under consideration are further analyzed and explained, it will become thoroughly evident why this mode of convalidation is expressed most completely and accurately by the phrase "radical sanation".

B. Real Definition

The foregoing will serve for what may be termed a nominal definition of radical sanation. But this is of less importance than the real definition of radical sanation as it is found in the Code, where it is stated that "Radical sanation of a marriage is the convalidation of the same which carries with it not only a dispensation or cessation of the impediment and a dispensation from the law requiring a renewal of consent, but also a reaching back to the past by a fiction of the law, in respect to its canonical effects."

It is clear from the words of this canon that radical sanation is above all things a convalidation of marriage. The word "convalidation" denotes the restoration of validity to an act that has hitherto been null and void. An act is null in Canon Law when "it lacks those things that essentially constitute it, or the solemnities which the sacred canons require under pain of invalidity".[7]

[5] Canons 1133-1137.

[6] Feije, *De Impedimentis Et Dispensationibus Matrimonialibus,* n. 766; Putzer, *Commentarium In Facultates Apostolicas,* n. 224; Vecchiotti, *Institutiones Canonicae,* III, 277.

[7] Canon 1680, § 1.

Brennan,[8] explains that the term *"convalidation"* is preferable to the word *"validation"*, because it connotes the idea of giving validity to an act that already had the appearance of validity the first time it was performed. This is true, however, as Brennan admits, only if this appearance of validity was present. For, if the invalidity is clear from the beginning, it cannot be said to be convalidated in the strict usage of that term. But the Code does not use the word in its strictest sense, since it evidently speaks of the convalidation of marriages which were manifestly invalid from the beginning. Therefore it is in this broader sense that radical sanation is called convalidation.

It is equally clear from this canon that radical sanation is not simple convalidation. In other words, it is not simply a second type of ordinary convalidation. For, it carries with it a dispensation or cessation of the impediment and a dispensation from the law requiring the renewal of consent. Finally, it has a retrotractive force that is in no way a part or element of simple convalidation. It is only when these three points are considered together that one has a true vision of radical sanation and is able to appreciate the fact that radical sanation is truly an extraordinary mode of convalidation. A more extensive delineation of the points of similarity and difference which exist between simple convalidation and radical sanation will be set forth as the work of explaining the three essential elements of the latter mode of convalidation develops.

Art. II. The Three Elements of Radical Sanation

A. Dispensation or Cessation of the Impediment

If it is possible to conceive of degrees of priority among the various elements which constitute this mode of convalidation, it would seem that the dispensation or cessation of the impediment must rank first. It is mentioned first in the canon itself. Furthermore it appears to be first, in sequence of time, among the sev-

[8] *The Simple Convalidation of Marriage,* (Washington, 1937), pp. 1-2.

eral dispensations necessary to effect the radical sanation of an invalid marriage. The reason for attributing this priority to the dispensation or cessation of the impediment is clear from the fact that it effects the primary object of radical sanation, namely, the removal of the nullifying obstacle. If the impediment is not dispensed or if it has not ceased in some other way, it would be of no avail to dispense from the renewal of consent or to speak of a reaching back to the beginning of the marriage, for these two elements of themselves, without the dispensation or cessation of the impediment, would not effect a convalidation or sanation of the marriage.

The dispensation or cessation of the impediment refers to the nullifying obstacle which, at the time of the first celebration of the marriage, rendered the naturally sufficient consent of the parties juridically ineffective. There are two possible nullifying forces. The first of these forces is that group of impediments which are known as diriment or nullifying impediments.[9] The second legal force that can produce a nullifying effect on a marriage is the lack of juridical form of marriage that must be observed for validity.[10] If either of these two legal forces was present at the first celebration of the marriage, it constitutes the impediment spoken of in this Canon. For the word "impediment" is used in this canon in its most general sense as referring to any legal obstacle, whether it be a diriment impediment or simply a lack of juridical form.[11]

The canon speaks of a *"dispensatio vel cessatio"* of the impediment. The Latin word *"vel"* is here used in its disjunctive sense and consequently the words dispensation and cessation are mutually exclusive and refer to two distinct ways in which the obstacle nullifying the marriage may be removed. An impediment is removed by a dispensation when there has been "a relaxation of the law in a special case granted by the founder of the law, by his successor or superior or by one to whom any of the foregoing have conceded the faculty of dispensing.[12] But

[9] Canons 1067-1080.
[10] Canon 1094.
[11] Cappello, *De Sacramentis,* III, n. 850, 3.
[12] Canon 80.

an impediment is removed by cessation in one or the other of two ways. It will, in a manner of speaking, cease to exist of itself, either through the passage of time or by the elimination of the circumstance which caused a certain person or persons to be bound by it. Thus the impediment of age will cease to bind when, by the passage of time, the canonical age will have been attained. The impediment of *ligamen* will cease upon the death of one of the parties to the first marriage or through the legitimate dissolution of the marriage.[13] An impediment can also cease by the abrogation of the law which established it. Instances of such cessation are readily found among such one-time diriment impediments as have now been abrogated by the Code. It is to be recalled at this point that the mere cessation of an impediment is not, of itself, sufficient to effect the convalidation or sanation of a marriage.[14]

The cessation of the impediment must be accompanied by at least *one* other element in order to effect *simple convalidation,* namely, the renewal of consent. Thus, if a marriage is invalid because of the impediment of disparity of worship and the impediment ceases through the conversion of the unbaptized party, the marriage can be convalidated through the renewal of consent by both parties in the juridical form to be observed in the convalidation of marriage.[15] In order to effect the *radical sanation* of a marriage, the cessation of the impediment must be accompanied by *two* other elements, namely, a dispensation from the renewal of consent and a retrotraction to the past. Thus, if the impediment of age has ceased, but one of the parties refuses to renew his or her consent according to the norms of simple convalidation, the marriage can be sanated by a dispensation from the renewal of consent and a retrotraction to the past by which, through a fiction of the law, the Church acts as if she had drawn the dispensation from the renewal of consent back to the beginning of the marriage.[16]

[13] Canons 1118-1127.

[14] Pont. Comm. Intr., 3 June, 1918—AAS, X (1918), 346, n. 7.

[15] Canons 1133, § 1 and 1135, § 1.

[16] Gasparri, *De Matrimonio* (edition of 1932), n. 1211.

B. Dispensation from the Renewal of Consent

In attributing a certain priority to the dispensation or cessation of the impediment, it must not be supposed that this is anything more than a logical priority. It would not appear congruous to attribute to it a priority of importance, for, as it has already been pointed out, the mere cessation or dispensation of the impediment is of little avail for the purposes of simple convalidation or radical sanation, unless it is at the same time accompanied with a renewal of consent for the former and unless it is similarly accompanied with a dispensation from the renewal of consent and a retrotraction to the past for the latter. Hence, it is clear that these two elements, the dispensation from the renewal of consent and the retrotraction, are of equal importance with the dispensation or cessation of the impediment and must therefore be as fully explained if a complete picture of radical sanation is to be had.

The dispensation from the law requiring the renewal of consent is one of the features of radical sanation which definitely distinguishes it from simple convalidation. It is a distinguishing feature of major importance, requiring as it does a separate dispensation from a second general and invalidating law of the Church. In simple convalidation the renewal of consent is always required. This is true whether the marriage is invalid because of a diriment impediment, because of defect of consent or because of defect of form. Furthermore, this renewal of consent is always required by ecclesiastical law for the sake of validity and not only for the purpose of licitness.[17] Consequently nothing excuses from it, neither *epikeia*,[18] nor ignorance of the law.[19] But there are always some marriages to be dealt with in which this renewal of consent cannot be conveniently obtained for a variety of reasons. This inconvenience may be due to the

[17] Canon 1133, § 2.

[18] Vermeersch-Creusen, *Epitome Iuris Canonici*, (quarta editio, 1933), I, n. 117.

[19] Canon 16, § 1.

moral or physical impossibility of locating the parties to a marriage for which an invalid dispensation has been granted or for which the officiating priest did not have the proper authorization. It may also be due simply to a persistent refusal of one of the parties to renew his or her consent at a time when the other party, for the peace of conscience or the legitimation of offspring, may be anxiously seeking to procure the convalidation of the marriage.

There are, of course, other reasons which may make it necessary to grant a dispensation from the renewal of consent. But for the present these more ordinary examples suffice to illustrate the point that, although the renewal of consent is always required by the common law of the Church, there are times when it will be impossible to obtain it. In these cases, given the other necessary conditions and circumstances to be dealt with later on, the Church can and does grant a dispensation from this law. It must never be lost sight of, however, that in dispensing from the law requiring the *renewal* of consent the Church is not by any means dispensing or pretending to dispense from the *necessity* of marital consent. For, as it has been noted, marital consent is the very root of marriage. Without it there is nothing upon which the Church can exercise a sanative influence. In like manner, it is equally important to remember that, in dispensing from the renewal of consent, the Church is not attempting to supply for the consent which "cannot be supplied by any human power".[20]

What the Church actually does is to examine the consent exchanged by the parties at the time they began their invalid union. If it was of a marital character and if of itself it was naturally sufficient for marriage in the event that there had been no nullifying obstacle to its effect, the Church accepts it and dispenses from the necessity of repeating the exchange of this consent at the moment of convalidation. It does not seem that it is safe to designate the dispensation from the renewal of consent as the one feature of radical sanation which, more than any other, makes this mode of convalidation the extraordinary means of rectifying invalid marriages. For, when considered from this angle, the third

[20] Canon 1081, § 1.

element of radical sanation, namely, the retrotraction to the past, seems to be of equal importance as a feature which marks radical sanation as the extraordinary mode of convalidation. The basis for this statement is found in the fact that it is possible to have radical sanation if one or the other of these two elements is present, that is, either the dispensation from the renewal of consent or the retrotraction to the past. But it is impossible to have more than a simple convalidation if both of these elements are lacking.

C. *Retrotraction to the Past*

Of the three elements which constitute radical sanation, the third element, which is a "reaching back to the past by a fiction of the law in respect to the canonical effects of marriage", seems at first sight to be the one which is most difficult to comprehend. There is really no difficulty in analyzing this particular element, if it is clearly borne in mind that this retrotraction or reaching back to the past is merely a legal fiction, and not an objective reality.[21] A legal fiction "is a rule of law which assumes as true, for a just cause, something which is false, but not impossible".[22] In the radical sanation of marriages the Church assumes as true, for a just cause, something which is actually false, but not impossible. The Church assumes as true that the dispensation from the nullifying impediment was given at the first, though invalid, celebration of the marriage and that the consent of the parties was never rendered juridically ineffective and that consequently the canonical effects of the marriage were never vitiated or invalidated.[23] Some authors in the past were apparently unable to grasp this concept of the use of legal fiction and were misled into teaching that the Church claimed that the invalid marriage was rendered valid from its very beginning, that is, that through radi-

[21] Canon 1138, § 1; Benedict XIV, instr. *"Cum super,"* 27 Sept., 1755, n. 7—*Bullarii Romani Continuatio,* IV, 291.

[22] This is Alciati's definition quoted by Cicognani, *Canon Law,* (Philadelphia, 1935), pp. 535-536.

[23] Cappello, *De Sacramentis,* III, n. 851; Gasparri, *De Matrimonio,* (edition of 1932), nn. 1208-1209.

cal sanation the marriage obtained an objective validity *ex tunc.*[24] This opinion was rejected by the majority of canonists and the erroneousness of it will be completely manifested in the article dealing with the effects of radical sanation.

ART. III. OTHER NOTIONS OF RADICAL SANATION

A. Its Division

In order to avoid confusion in the articles and chapters which are to follow, it seems advisable to point out at once that, although the Code speaks of radical sanation only in general terms, it is not to be presumed that this mode of convalidation does not admit of a division. In fact, unless this division is clearly set forth, it would be difficult, if not impossible, to understand the question of radical sanation in a satisfactory and useful way. The authors do not follow a uniform method of establishing a division of radical sanation, although they generally use the same terminology. In other words they usually divide radical sanation into *perfect* and *imperfect,* or into *total* and *partial.*[25]

But there is a variation among the authors in respect to what constitutes the perfect or total and the imperfect or partial sanation. In any event, even a passing glance at the way in which these authors divide radical sanation will show that they do not sufficiently indicate the very essential difference between radical sanation which both convalidates marriage and legitimates children and the radical sanation which legitimates children without convalidating the marriage.

[24] Giovine, *De Disp. Matrimon.,* consult. 23, sect. 326, n. I; Aichner, *Compendium Juris Ecclesiastici,* p. 661; Vecchiotti, *Institutiones Canonicae,* III, 277; Scavini, *Theologia Moralis Universa,* III, 1050; De Angelis, *Praelectiones Juris Canonici ad Methodum Decretalium Gregorii IX Exactae,* lib. IV, tit. 17, n. 3.

[25] Cappello, *De Sacramentis,* III, n. 850, 4; Gasparri, *De Matrimonio,* n. 1212; Wernz-Vidal, *Ius Canonicum,* V, n. 659; Chelodi, Ius Matrimoniale, (3a ed. 1921), n. 167.

In view of this fact, it seems advisable for the purposes of this work to subscribe to the division given by Payen and to maintain it throughout the succeeding chapters.[26] Payen speaks of radical sanation *properly so called* and of radical sanation *improperly so called.* Then the same author subdivides sanation properly so called into *perfect* and *imperfect* sanation. This division, as it will be seen, takes into account the fact that there is a wide difference in effect between sanation (properly so called) which effects both convalidation and legitimation and radical sanation (improperly so called) which brings about merely the legitimation of children. Furthermore, the subdivision of sanation properly so called makes adequate provision for the variations which are possible in the operation and the effects of this mode of convalidation. Radical sanation is *perfect,* that is, complete when all the elements mentioned in Canon 1138 are present and if it results in both the convalidation of the marriage and the legitimation of the children.[27] It is *imperfect* or partial, if: (1) the dispensation from the impediment is lacking; (2) a renewal of consent is required of at least one of the parties; (3) the retrotraction extends back only to some intermediate point; (4) the offspring is not legitimated.[28] If this division is to serve a useful purpose it will be necessary to keep in mind that the *perfect* and the *imperfect* sanation are merely subdivisions of radical sanation in its proper sense and are not to be confused with radical sanation in its improper sense. For the term "radical sanation" used in its improper sense actually comprehends nothing more than the legitimation of the children. It is, as Wernz expresses it, only a mild shadow of radical sanation used in its proper sense.[29] It is not idle to place great stress on the difference in the two uses of the term "radical sanation", for a failure to comprehend this difference would result in a failure to appreciate the true but somewhat varied character of this extraordinary remedy.

[26] Payen, *De Matrimonio in Missionibus,* nn. 2607-2608.

[27] Payen, *op. cit.,* n. 2608, 1.

[28] Payen, *op. cit.,* n. 2608, 2; Gasparri, *De Matrimonio,* n. 1212.

[29] *Ius Decretalium,* IV, n. 655.

B. Radical Sanation and Simple Convalidation

From what has already been set down regarding radical sanation and the elements that constitute it, it is evident that there is more than a passing difference between this mode of convalidation and that which is known as "simple convalidation". It is true that for the most part both seek the same end, namely, the convalidation of an invalid marriage. But the manner in which each attains its end is the chief point of difference between the two methods of convalidation. It has been said that simple convalidation depends on the cooperation of the parties, whereas radical sanation depends on the operation of the superior.[30] There is a further difference between the two in the effects produced by each. For the sake of further clarifying the nature of radical sanation and of distinguishing it from simple convalidation, these differences can be set down briefly at this point, without attempting an extensive treatment of the ordinary mode of convalidation, which has already been accorded special consideration.[31]

Considered from the angle of their respective modes of operation, it can be noted that the essential difference between simple convalidation and radical sanation is centered around the question of the renewal of consent. In simple convalidation the renewal of consent is always required, no matter whether the marriage is invalid because of defect of consent, defect of form or a diriment impediment.[32] In radical sanation this renewal of consent is entirely dispensed with whenever a perfect radical sanation is granted, and at least one party will be dispensed from renewing consent whenever there is a question of an imperfect sanation. In simple convalidation, if the marriage is invalid because of defect of form, the form prescribed by the law will have to be observed.[33]

[30] Sipos, *Enchiridion Iuris Canonici,* p. 651.

[31] Cf. Brennan, J. H., *The Simple Convalidation of Marriage,* (Catholic University of America, Canon Law Studies, No. 102, Washington, D. C., 1937).

[32] Canon 1133.

[33] Canon 1137.

In radical sanation, if the marriage is invalid because of defect of form the observance of the form will be waived.[34] If the marriage is invalid because of a diriment impediment, the impediment must have ceased to exist or must be removed by dispensation before it can be convalidated by simple convalidation or radical sanation. But if the marriage is invalid because of a defect of consent that has been present since the first celebration of the marriage and has not been remedied, there can be no radical sanation of the marriage. But if the marriage is invalid because there was a defect of consent at the first celebration of the marriage radical sanation can be granted if, at some point between the first celebration of the marriage and the granting of the sanation, this defect of consent was remedied by the placing of a valid consent. In respect to a marriage that is invalid because of a defect of consent, the mode of operation in the simple convalidation of that marriage is not always the same. Thus, if the marriage is invalid because of a defect of consent that has not become public, the simple convalidation of the marriage will be effected by a private renewal of consent. But if the original defect of consent was of a public character, the norms of simple convalidation require that the renewal of consent be made according to the juridical form of marriage prescribed by Canon 1094.

In respect to the effects produced there is no difference between the two modes of convalidation as far as the actual convalidation of the marriage is concerned. For in either case the marriage is actually rendered valid from the moment when the norms of simple convalidation have been observed or from the moment when sanation has been granted. But in relation to the legitimation of children there are several differences. It is impossible, for instance, to have legitimation of children by means of simple convalidation unless there is at the same time an actual convalidation of the marriage. But by means of radical sanation it is possible to obtain the legitimation of the children without there being any convalidation of the marriage, if one or both parties to the marriage are dead or perpetually insane. Legitimation of

[34] Canon 1139, § 1.

the offspring follows as an essential effect of radical sanation. But legitimation will follow as an essential effect of simple convalidation only when the child is capable of legitimation by the subsequent marriage of its parents,[35] or when a dispensation has been granted in accordance with the norm of Canon 1051.

A schema setting forth the differences between simple convalidation and radical sanation will further clarify these points.[36]

[35] Canon 1116.

[36] Cf. Appendix I.

CHAPTER II

AN HISTORICAL SYNOPSIS OF RADICAL SANATION

PART I

RADICAL SANATION AND ROMAN LAW

In order to ascertain the presence or absence of this or a similar process in Roman Law, it seems necessary to consider the provisions which that legal system made for the convalidation of marriage and the legitimation of children.

ARTICLE I. CONVALIDATION OF MARRIAGE

There is no definite or precise treatment of marriage convalidation in Roman Law. There is, however, evidence that the practice of convalidation was not unknown. This is true in spite of the fact that the terms "valid" and "invalid" were not used in relation to marriages. The terms in use were ***"nuptiae iustae"*** and *"nuptiae iniustae"*. The terms *"matrimonium iniustum"* and *"matrimonium non legitimum"* were also current[1]

"Nuptiae iustae" designated a marriage contracted between persons having *"Connubium"* or the capacity for civil marriage.[2] This capacity for civil marriage belonged to Roman citizens as one of the rights of citizenship and it was granted to others by way of a privilege.[3] This capacity was unrestricted for the majority of Roman citizens and for them

[1] Corbett, *The Roman Law of Marriage* (Oxford, 1930), pp. 102-103; Leage, *Roman Private Law* (London, 1932), p. 98.

[2] G. (1.56; 67; 76); D. (38.11) 1; Inst. (1.10) pr.

[3] Muirhead, *Roman Law,* p. 59; Corbett, *op. cit.,* pp. 24 ff; Leage, *op. cit.* p. 98.

it was considered to be absolute. In those cases where capacity for civil marriage was restricted, it was considered to be relative. The law contained various obstacles to an absolute capacity and one of these forbade intermarriage between persons of one class of citizens with persons of another class of citizens. In other words, the capacity of certain citizens to enter a civil marriage was only a relative capacity, for there was a class of citizens whem they were forbidden to marry. If persons who were forbidden to intermarry did so in spite of the law, their marriages were null.[4]

"Nuptiae iniustae" designated a marriage contracted between two persons, neither of whom, or only one of whom, had the capacity for civil marriage.[5] Such a marriage was valid indeed, but it was not productive of those specifically civil effects that followed from *"nuptiae iustae"*, namely *"manus"* and *"patriapotestas"*.[6] Although there could be *"nuptiae iniustae"* between some persons who did not have *"connubium"*, or between persons of whom only one had *"connubium"*, it does not follow that all persons without *"connubium"* could enter into *"nuptiae iniustae"*. There were some classes, e. g., slaves, who not only did not have *"connubium"*, but who were not allowed to marry at all.[7]

"Connubium" or the capacity for civil marriages was not a requisite for a valid marriage. In fact, it was merely an additional requirement for *"nuptiae iustae"* and played no part in the validity or invalidity of *"nutiae injustae"*. Of itself it would not serve to render a marriage valid if there were also present any of those prohibitions or impediments that rendered both *"nuptiae iustae"* and *"nuptiae iniustae"* invalid. Thus, marriages that might otherwise have been *"nuptiae iustae"* or *"nuptiae iniustae"* would be rendered null and void if the parties had not given their consent, if they were below the required age, if they were related

[4] Buckland, *A Textbook of Roman Law* (Cambridge, 1932), p. 105.

[5] D. (50.1) 37.2.

[6] Buckland, *op. cit.*, p. 105; Corbett, *The Roman Law of Marriage*, p. 103.

[7] Ulp. (5.5); Corbett, *op. cit.*, p. 30; Buckland, *op. cit.*, p. 105; Leage, *Roman Private Law*, p. 103.

within the forbidden degrees or if they belonged to those classes of persons between whom marriage was prohibited.[8]

These various laws were not so rigorously enforced that they did not admit of dispensations which would permit the marriage to be contracted. Likewise, these same laws made provision for the convalidation of marriages that had been contracted contrary to the law. In some cases the marriage was convalidated when the impediment ceased, provided the parties were still cohabiting as man and wife. Such was the case when marriage had been attempted before the parties reached the required age, the convalidation being effective at the moment they attained the proper age.[9] It was likewise the case in a marriage that was invalid because of defect of consent, for the marriage became valid only from the time that consent was actually and validly given.[10]

The laws which placed a restriction on marriage between certain classes of persons also provided for the convalidation of marriages that had been attempted contrary to these laws. Thus, a marriage between a tutor or curator and his ward became valid if the parties were still living together as man and wife at the time that the guardianship ended in accordance with the provisions of the law governing that subject.[11]

Again, if a senator while in office married a freed-woman to whom he was not betrothed before entering upon his office, the union was invalid, but would be convalidated if they were still living as man and wife after he had ceased to hold or exercise that office.[12] The same was true when a magistrate or his son married a woman of the province over which he was magistrate, the marriage became valid only at the time that the official had completed his tenure of office, provided they were persevering in their marriage at that time.[13]

[8] Declareuil, *Rome, The Law-giver* (New York, 1926), p. 105; Buckland, *A Textbook of Roman Law*, pp. 113 ff.

[9] D. (23.2) 4.

[10] D. (23.2) 16.

[11] D. (23.2) 64.1.

[12] D. (23.2) 27.

[13] D. (23.2) 27.

The formalities which may have accompanied these various instances of convalidation are not contained in the sources. The silence of the law on the question of formalities in connection with the process of convalidation may indicate that there were none. But, granting the fact that convalidation was accomplished without a definite renewal of consent and without recourse to any definite act on the part of the parties themselves or of the civil authorities, it seems safe to say that Roman Law convalidation did not represent any process like radical sanation. In fact, everything seems to point to the fact that continued cohabitation after the cessation of the impediment sufficed to convalidate a marriage, without any further act on the part of the superior or even of the parties.

Article II. The Legitimation of Children

Three methods of legitimating children are most commonly mentioned by writers on this subject. They were legitimation by subsequent marriage, by dedication to the Curia and by a rescript of the Emepror.[14] Each of these methods of legitimation had its own formalities; but with the exception of the first, they had no direct connection with marriage or its convalidation. Legitimation by subsequent marriage was allowed by the Emperor Justinian, provided certain conditions were fulfilled. In the first place, it was necessary that the marriage should have been possible at the time the child had been conceived, or at least when it was born. Thus, children born of an adulterous union or of a union entirely prohibited by law could not enjoy the favor of this privilege. In the second place, there had to be a proper marriage settlement, known as the *"instrumentum dotis"*. Finally, it was necessary for the child or children to consent to this legitimation, because as illegitimate children they were *sui juris,* whereas legitimation would bring them under *potestas.*[15]

Legitimation by imperial rescript provided for cases in which

[14] Buckland, *op. cit.,* sect. XLVI; Leage, *op. cit.,* p. 80; Sherman-Robinson, *Readings in Roman Law,* pp. 17-19.

[15] Nov. (89.11) pr.; C. (5.27) 8, 10, 11; C. (5.18) 11.

legitimation by subsequent marriage was impossible, either because the mother was dead or because the father would not marry her.[16] This rescript was granted only on petition of the father. He could make this petition while still living or it could form a part of his last will and testament.

Legitimation by dedication to the Curia was a peculiar provision of Roman Law and came into being as a result of the difficulty in getting anyone to accept the office of *Decurio,* to which great personal liability was attached.[17] Under the Emperor Justinian it was provided that if a man dedicated his illegitimate son to the office of *Decurio,* the son fell under *patriapotestas* and was considered legitimate in respect to the father. But his legitimacy was not extended to the father's relatives, with whom he did not become agnate or cognate.

This brief consideration of the most common forms of legitimation in Roman Law seems sufficient to lead one to believe that they did not bear any resemblance to legitimation by radical sanation in Canon Law. In none of these instances are the children considered as if they had been born of a valid marriage in view of a radical sanation of the prior invalid marriage.

PART II

RADICAL SANATION IN CANON LAW

Article I. Origin of Radical Sanation

The origin and early history of radical sanation is still so uncertain that there is no unanimity of opinion among the authors on this point.[18] By general admission it has been

[16] Nov. (74.1) 2; Nov. (89.9) 1.

[17] Nov. (89.2) 1; Inst. (3.1) 2; Inst. (1.10) 13; C. (5.27) 9, 11.

[18] Freisen, *Geschichte des canonischen Eherechts bis zum Verfall der Glossenliteratur,* p. 403 ff; 528 ff; Leitner, *Lehrbuch des katolischen Eherechts,* p. 486; Esmein, *Le mariage en droit canonique,* II, 352 ff.

acceptable to adopt the opinion that the first recorded instance of radical sanation occurred in 1301.[19] It would not be correct, however, to accept this statement without reservation, or to conclude from it that there were no dispensations of this kind granted prior to that date. The fact is that there is not sufficient proof available to make any positive statements for or against this fact. Nevertheless, Perrone[20] and Giovine,[21] do not hesitate to declare that they see the first traces of radical sanation in certain conciliar enactments of the sixth century. Their claims are not, in all probability, without some foundation and are, therefore, worthy of more than a passing mention.

Both of these authors find these traces of radical sanation in Canon 10 of the Third Council of Orleans, celebrated in the year 538.[22] Using practically the same words to express their ideas they seem to wish to place their claims beyond all question of a doubt by asking if this canon can be anything else than radical sanation. The canon in question is similar to other canons that had been enacted at earlier councils and at one later council.[23] It prescribed that those who had in bad faith contracted marriage within the forbidden degrees of consanguinity, that is, with

[19] Rigantius, *Commentaria in Regulas Cancellariae,* tom. 4, reg. 49, nn. 10-11; reg. 50, n. 107.

[20] *De Matrimonio Christiano,* II, 163.

[21] *De Dispensationibus Matrimonialibus,* I, consult. XXIII, sect. 323, n. 7.

[22] "De incestis coniunctionibus ita quae sunt statuta serventur, ut his qui aut modo ad baptisum veniunt, aut quibus patrum statuta sacerdotali praedicatione in notitiam non venerunt, ita pro novitate conversionis ac fidei suae credidimus consulendum, ut contracta hucusque huiusmodi coniugia non solvantur, sed in futurum quod de incestis coniunctionibus in anterioribus canonibus interdictum est observetur; id est, ut ne quis sibi sub nomine coniugii sociare praesumat relictam patris, filiam uxoris, relictam fratris, sororem uxoris, consobrinam, aut sobrinam, relictam avunculi vel patrui."—Mansi, IX, 14-15.

[23] Council of Agde (506), can. 61—Mansi, VIII, 335; Council of Epaon (517), can. 30—Mansi, VIII, 562-563; Fourth Council of Orleans (541), can. 27—*Monumenta Germaniae Historica, Legum Sectio* III, *Concilia,* T. I., 93.

full knowledge of the laws forbidding such marriages, were to be separated. But it likewise provided that those who had contracted the same kind of marriages in good faith, that is, in ignorance of the laws due to the recentness of their conversion, as well as those who had contracted these marriages prior to their baptism, were not to be separated. Giovine points out that the *"statuta patrum"* had declared such marriages invalid. He further calls attention to the fact that ignorance of invalidating laws does not excuse from their observance and, finally, that in this enactment the Fathers of the Council did not require a renewal of consent. From these three facts he says that it is to be inferred that the Fathers of the Council were granting radical sanation for these marriages.[24]

Without affirming or denying this view, Wernz says that it is possible that the Fathers of the Council acted on the theory which at one time was held by some, namely, that ignorance of invalidating laws excused from them.[25] If this were actually the case, it is needless to point out that the marriages in question were already valid and needed neither convalidation nor an application of radical sanation and that the canon was no more than a declaration to this effect. However, the wording of the canon does not seem to offer any basis for such an interpretation and it seems clear that the Fathers actually followed the more acceptable principle that ignorance of invalidating laws does not excuse from them.

The argument advanced by Giovine in support of his claim, namely, that the Council validated these marriages without making any mention of the necessity of renewing consent, is scarcely conclusive in face of the statements of those who testify that explicit renewal of consent in the convalidation of marriage did not become a definite requirement of canon law until the thirteenth century.[26] Moreover, it is to be noted that it is not certain, though

[24] *De Dispensationibus Matrimonialibus,* I, consult. XXIII, sect. 323, n. 7.

[25] *Ius Decretalium,* IV, n. 654, footnote 14.

[26] Scherer, *Handbuch des Kirchenrechts,* II, 501; Wernz, *Ius Decretalium,* IV, n. 610, note 20; Brennan, *The Simple Convalidation of Marriage* (Washington, 1937), p. 12-13.

Giovine would seem to indicate it as certain, that the Council validated these marriages at all. In fact, the canon merely uses the words *"non solvantur"*, which could just as easily imply that the Fathers deemed it advisable to leave the parties to such marriages in good faith because of the grave difficulties that might arise from disturbing those who were still novices in the Christian religion.

In view of the uncertainty surrounding the interpretation of this canon, it cannot be categorically denied that it represented some form of convalidation. But, if it did represent an early instance of marriage convalidation, it cannot be said with the definiteness of Giovine and Perrone that it was nothing else but radical sanation. It would rather seem to be an instance of convalidation by the natural law, which does not require an explicit renewal of consent, unless the marriage is invalid because of the lack of consent. Furthermore, such a form of convalidation seems to be more in line with the fact that legitimation, which, in the beginning was the primary note of radical sanation, did not become an object of the Church's concern and legislative enactments until a much later date. Whatever may be said for or against the claims of these two authors, this much seems certain, that their claims are based on an uncertain interpretation of this canon. Consequently it seems necessary to look to a later date for the origin of radical sanation and, until such time as more light is shed on the interpretation of these canons, to regard them as instances of convalidation by the natural law.

In attempting to establish the beginnings of radical sanation, it is to be noted that no mention of this extraordinary dispensation is to be found in the Decretals. It is to be found, however, in the writings of Joannes Andreae, a canonist of great note of the fourteenth century.[27] Before attempting to explain the circumstances which led this canonist to propose and defend this doctrine, of which he has been called the inventor, it must be pointed out that radical sanation was not always considered in the same light as it is today. In the beginning this dispensation was

[27] Esmein, *Le Mariage En Droit Canonique,* II, 358; Joannes Andreae, *glossa, v. Pro infectis;* c. 13, X, *qui filii sint legitimi,* IV, 17.

considered to be primarily a means of legitimation. It was only at a later date, probably at the beginning of the seventeenth century, that it came to be regarded first as a mode of convalidating marriages and secondly as a means of legitimation.[28] A thorough search of the older authors reveals the fact that they considered it and spoke of it as *"legitimatio plenissima"*, or as the means of obtaining the most complete legitimation. Accordingly, in their commentaries and treatises they dealt with this dispensation in that section of Decretal Law which provided for legitimation.[29]

The necessity for such an institute as radical sanation seems to have risen in large part from various laws that were enacted to govern the question of legitimacy. Celestine III (1191-1198) promulgated some of these laws,[30] which were modified somewhat by Pope Innocent III at the Fourth Lateran Council in 1215. At this Council, this latter Pontiff, issued stringent regulations concerning the publication of the banns of marriage. To these regulations he added very severe sanctions, one of which concerned the legitimacy of children. He declared that any marriages which were contracted without the publication of the banns would not enjoy the character of putative marriages and that consequently, if they were invalid because of some impediment, their children would be illegitimate.[31]

At this period in history the question of the legitimacy of children was of great importance, because it was a requirement in both civil and ecclestiastical law for obtaining offices, dignities and inheritances. As a result of the canonical legislation governing the legitimacy of children born of invalid mariages, there was proposed to Innocent III a question that was at once delicate and

[28] Esmein, *op. cit.*, II, 354.

[29] Corradus, *Praxis Dispensationum Apostolicarum,* lib. VIII, c. III; Sanchez, De Sancto Matrimonii Sacramento, tom. III, lib. VIII; Gonzalez Tellez, C. XIII, X, *qui filii sint legitimi,* n. 23 sq.; Panormitanus, C. XIII, X, *qui filii sint legitimi,* n. 22 sq; Alexander de Nevo, C. XIII, X, *qui filii sint legitimi,* n. 18.

[30] CC. 4, 6, 10, 11, X, *qui filii sint legitimi,* IV, 17.

[31] C. 3, X, *de clandestina desponsatione,* IV, 3.

intricate. The Pontiff was asked to legitimate certain children so that they would be eligible to obtain certain temporal offices and successions in territories that were not subject to the temporal power of the Pope.[32]

The text of the Pontiff's response clearly indicates that he was well aware of the difficulty which confronted him, because of the danger of appearing to usurp the power of civil authorities in territories that were not his own. After carefully distinguishing between the powers of the Church and State and showing the separation between these two societies he replied that the Pope could freely legitimize children in lands that were subject to the Church; but that in other lands he could legitimize them directly only in respect to those things which were spiritual in nature. In reference to temporalities he added that the Pope could legitimize only indirectly and as a consequence, so to speak, of another action.

This celebrated decretal became the center of considerable discussion as the canonists of that period sought to explain how the Pope could effect this indirect legitimation of which Innocent III had spoken. In their anxiety to defend the powers that this Pope had affirmed were proper to the Papacy, the canonists produced a variety of opinions and explanations, some of which fell far short of the goal that their authors sought to attain. One of these, Joannes Teutonicus, disregarded the rights of the temporal powers by holding that the legitimation which the Pope would grant for spiritual things would carry with it legitimation for temporal things, because the spiritual order, being higher than the temporal order drew the temporal order up to it.[33] In maintaining such an opinion, Tuetonicus asserted precisely what Innocent III had denied, namely, that the Pope did not have

[32] C. 13, X, *qui filii sint legitimi*, IV, 17.

[33] "Ad hoc dixit Joannes quod dominus papa non habet potestatem legitimandi in temporalibus; sed, eo ipso quod legitimat aliquem quoad spiritualia, per consequens legitimat eum quoad temporalia quae sunt minus digna, et sic legitimat per consequentiam sed non directe: saepe enim permittitur aliquid indirecte quod non permittitur directe."—*Glossa*, C. XIII, X, *qui filii sint legitimi*, IV, 17, *v. Habeat Potestatem.*

the power to legitimate children directly for temporal things in territories not subject to the temporal power of the Holy See..

Another opinion, held by such canonists as Laurentius, Vincentius and Tancredus, suggested that the Pope could legitimize only for spiritual things and that this legitimation had no civil effects properly so called. Nevertheless it sought to defend the power of the Pope by claiming that the legitimation produced a certain effect in public law and that, as a consequence, the children could seek those temporalities which required legitimate birth or legitimation after birth.[34]

Bernard de Botone, apparently seeing that the foregoing opinion was not a satisfactory solution to the problem, declared that the Pope could legitimize only for spiritual things and not for temporal offices.[35]

None of these opinions explained in a satisfactory manner the power which had been claimed by Innocent III for the Papacy. The canonists were not willing to renounce this power and their study of this decretal was productive of two further opinions. The first of these was sponsored by Hostiensis and came closer than any of the earlier ones to solving this problem. But it remained for Joannes Andrae to discover and elucidate the doctrine

[34] "Tamen quidam extendunt legitimationem ad honores saeculares unde per hoc intelligitur legitimatus ut possit esse iudex et habere huiusmodi honores temporales quos alias habere non posset. Et in hac sententia fuerunt Laurentius, Vincentius et Tancredus."—*Glossa,* C. XIII, X, *qui filii sint legitimi,* IV, 17, *v. Habeat postestatem.*

[35] "Propter hoc tamen quod legitimat aliquem in spiritualibus non probatur quod habeat iurisdictionem in temporalibus. Legitimare enim pertinet ad voluntariam iurisdictionem; item quia papam nihil spectat de temporalibus; et sic videtur quod papa quoad temporalia legitimare non possit ubi non habet iurisdictionem temporalem . . . Sed contrarium credo scilicet, quod dominus papa non potest legitimare aliquem quantum ad hoc ut succedat in haereditate, tamquam legitimus haeres, qui non sit, dico, de sua iurisdictione temporali. Sic enim esset mittere falcem in messem alienam, et usupare alienam iurisdictionem, quod esse non debet, et privare aliquem iure succedendi, unde credo quod non possit legitimare nisi quoad actus spirituales."—*Glossa,* C. XIII, X, *qui filii sint legitimi,* IV, 17, *v. Habeat potestatem.*

that was to settle the difficulty and was to earn for him the name of being the inventor of radical sanation.[36]

In his opinion Hostiensis went straight to the source of legitimacy, namely, a valid marriage and then pointed out that a marriage was valid or invalid according as it did or did not conform to the laws of the Church. Therefore, he reasoned, if the Church could render children illegitimate by placing a diriment impediment to the marriage of its parents, it could also give back the legitimacy, of which its laws had deprived the children. In doing this, Hostiensis felt, the Church would not be usurping the power of civil authorities, because in thus legitimizing the children it would be exercising a recognized power over an effect of marriage, which all admitted was in the Church's proper domain. The weakness of this opinion lay in the fact that the Church in so acting would be dealing with an effect of marriage apart from the marriage itself and would be dealing with it only for the purpose of rendering the children eligible for those things requiring legitimacy.[37]

It remained for Joannes Andreae, a layman and skilled canonist, to avoid the mistakes of others by declaring that it was necessary to make the papal will extend back to the very source of filiation, namely, the marriage itself. For, according to his theory,

[36] Genestal, *Histoire De La Legitimation Des Enfants Naturels En Droit Canonique,* p. 214; Esmein, *Le Mariage En Droit Canonique,* II, 358.

[37] "Salva reverentia aliorum, mihi videtur dominum papam habere potestatem legitimandi quoad spiritualia et temporalia et ipsum solum. Cum enim causa matrimonialis spiritualiter pertineat ad Ecclesiam, adeo quod saecularis iudex de ipsa cognoscere non possit etiam si inciderit, nec de legitima filiatione, multo fortius dispensatio . . . Dicas tamen quod imperator legitimat, id est, tamquam legitimum etiam spurium ad haereditatem suam admittere potest, et etiam in hoc potest cum filio suo proprio, non tamquam filio, sed tamquam subdito dispensare. Sed papa vere legitimat et illegitimat. Cum enim secundum leges filii duorum fratrum rite contrahant et etiam secundum legem divinam quam iudaei servant, de fidelibus papa huiusmodi matrimonium illegitimum fecit, et sic filii suscepti ex tali matrimonio hodie secundum legem et secundum canonem ab haereditate repelluntur. Multae enim personae prohibentur lege canonum contrahere quae lege divina non prohibentur. Si vero illegitimos facit, quanto magis poterit legitimare."—*Summa Aurea Hostiensis,* C. XIII, *qui filii sint legitimi,* IV, 17, n. 11.

if one could admit that the Pope, by granting a dispensation from the diriment impediment to the marriage, could efface and erase the effects which the impediment had produced in the past, there would be given to the Pope an indirect, but sure means of legitimizing children born of this marriage. To this canonist, who "is to be regarded as the Father of the History of Canon Law",[38] this did not seem impossible, because there existed documents that showed that certain Popes had abrogated laws and that their abrogation carried with it a retroactivity which erased all the effects which the laws had produced.[39]

In the light of these facts and in view of the apparent readiness with which other noted canonists[40] adopted this doctrine of Joannes Andreae, it would seem that this now famous theory was the solution to what had become a great canonical question. Without sacrificing the power which had been claimed by Innocent III for the Papacy and without disregarding any rights of the temporal powers, it definitely established a mode of action whereby the Pope could legitimize children directly in respect to spiritual affairs and indirectly in respect to civil affairs. For in this manner of legitimizing the offspring of an invalid marriage, the invalid marriage itself became the object of the Pope's direct action, with legitimation following as a consequence of the retrotractive force which he would attribute to his action and thus becoming only the indirect object of the papal action.

Before moving on to a consideration of the first recorded instance of radical sanation and to the history of this institution up to the time of the Code of Canon Law, it seems safe to say in conclusion that, if the doctrine proposed by Joannes Andreae is not the exact origin of radical sanation, it is at least the first definite point in the history of Canon Law at which this insti-

[38] Cicognani, *Canon Law,* p. 258.

[39] Joannes Andreae, C. *Per Venerabilem,* n. 26 Sq.

[40] Panormitanus, C. XIII, X, *qui filii sint legitimi,* n. 22; Alexander de Nevo, C. XIII, X, *qui filii sint legitimi,* n. 18; Gonzalez, C. XIII, X, *qui filii sint legitimi,* n. 23; Corradus, *Praxis Dispensationum Apostolicarum,* lib. VIII, cap. III; De Justis, *De Dispensationibus Matrimonialibus,* lib. I, cap. VIII; Navarrus, *Opera Omnia,* (Consilia et Responsa), lib. IV, consil. 2.

tution was accorded special treatment. This does not by any means exclude the possibility of the principles on which it is founded, having been known and used at an earlier date in reference to other affairs of the Church. The fact, however, that the first recorded instance of its use in respect to marriage occurred only in 1301 seems to add weight to the view that prior to that time it had not been used as a means of convalidating marriages or legitimating children.

Article II. History of the Use of Radical Sanation

Pope Boniface VIII, on September 8, 1301, granted what is generally accepted as the first recorded instance of radical sanation. His favor was extended to Maria, widowed Queen of Sancius IV, King of Castile. The marriage of this royal couple had been invalid because of the multiple impediment of consanguinity, affiinity and spiritual relationship. In this instance the favor was one of radical sanation improperly so called, inasmuch as the King being dead, the only effect that it could produce was the legitimation of the children, one of whom, Ferdinand IV, had succeeded to the throne of his father. Soon after, however, this same Pontiff granted a perfect sanation for the marriage of Ildephonse III, King of Portugal, whose marriage was likewise null because of consanguinity.[41]

The rescript for the radical sanation granted to Maria in behalf of her children is included here, in full, because of its historical value and its evident worth as a connecting link between the days when radical sanation was still a novel practice and today when it has become a well defined institution of Canon Law.

> Mariae relictae quondam Sanctii nati Alfonsi regis Castellae ac Legionis.
>
> Sensus hominis proni ab adolescentia sua in malum, plerumque sic efficiunt lubricos actus parentum, quod ii in copulam legitimam delinquentes, illegitimitatis rubi-

[41] Rigantius, *Commentaria in Regulas Cancellariae*, reg. 49, nn. 10-11; reg. 50, n. 107.

gine ortum maculant filiorum. Veruntamen sic genitos, quod propriae virtutis decorat auxilium, geniturae vitium minime decolorat, quia decus virtutis maculam abstergit in filiis et pudicitia morum pudor originis aboletur. Quapropter Apostolicae Sedis circumspecta benignitas, qualitates negotiorum et merita personarum diligenti circumspectione prospiciens, nonnullis ex huiusmodi generis, quibus virtutes et merita suffragantur, consuevit interdum favoribus opportunis assistere ac donum gratiae liberaliter impertiri. Mira enim Regis aeterna benignitas honore multiplici sponsam suam Romam Ecclesiam insignivit: sed in hoc potissime ipsam honorabilem fecit, et felici statu fulgentem, quod in clavium collatione caelestium illam eidem tribuit plenitudinem potestatis, ut non solum personis humilibus, sed quantumcumque generis excelsi solemnitate conspicuis in iis possit adesse magnifice, per quae clari nominis titulum assequantur, et incrementum famosae potentiae prosequantur.

Sane petitio tua per solemnes nutios, ad hoc specialiter ad Sedem Apostolicam destinatos, nuper nobis exhibita continebat, quod quondam Sanctius natus clarae memoriae Alfonsi regis Castellae ac Legionis consors tuus et tu, tertio consanguinitatis gradu vobis mutuo attinentes, necnon et alias tertio affinitatis gradu coniuncti, ex eo quod idem Sanctius cognoverat carnaliter Mariam Alfonsi de Uzero, tibi tertio gradu consanguinitatis conjunctam, quorum etiam Sanctii et Mariae Alfonsi filiam quamdam tu de sacro fonte levaveras: vivente quoque tunc quondam Guillelma nata Gastonis de Beart, quam idem Sanctius per verba de praesenti receperat in uxorem, et a qua non fuit sententialiter separatus, licet inter ipsos Sanctium et Guillelmam carnalis non fuerit copula subsecuta; de facto matrimonium, seu potius contubernium, invicem contraxistis, et dilectos filios nobiles viros Fernandum, Petrum et Philippum fratres, ac dilectas in Christo filias nobiles mulieres Isabellam et Beatricem sorores eorum, tuos et ipsius Sanctii natos, huiusmodi contubernio procreastis.

Cum autem ex iis iidem Fernandus, Petrus et Philippus, ac Isabella et Beatrix defectum, quinimo defectus natalium patiantur, nobis humiliter supplicasti, ut pio tibi et eis compatientes affectu, et agentes misericorditer dignaremur. Nos igitur, attendentes quod sicut fide dignorum testimonio accepimus, tu demum per laudabilis et honestae conversationis, et vitae meritum super iis a te maculam commendabiliter expiasti; quodque praefati Fernandus, Petrus et Philippus, ac Isabella et Beatrix huiusmodi defectum natalium supplent virtute laudabilium meritorum, redimentes favore prudentiae quod ortus odiosus ademit, sicque prosapiam regalis generis morum elegantia. et operibus virtutum adornant; dignum reputamus et congruum, ut eos praecipuis gratiis et favoribus attollamus.

Tuis itaque supplicationibus inclinati eosdem Fernandum, Petrum et Philippum, ac Isabellam et Beatricem legitimationis titulo decorantes, ut iidem Fernandus, Petrus et Philippus ac Isabella et Beatrix, huiusmodi defectu seu defectibus natalium non obstantibus, ad omnes honores omnesque dignitates, Ecclesiasticos et mundanos, religiosos et saeculares, etiam statui regio congruentes, et quoslibet actus legitimos, prout eorum cuilibet obvenerint, vel quomodolibet provenire possunt, assumi et admitti licite valeant; ipsique illos et illas assequi libere modi illegitimitatis maculam non obstarent; cum ipsis, et eorum quolibet de speciali gratia et Apostolica plenitudine potestatis dispensamus: sperantes, quod tu et ipsi tantae gratiae magnitudinem memoriae signaculis taliter alligetis, quod veniatis in dilectionem omnium Conditori per vitae virtuosae studium, et sanctae matri Ecclesiae per sincerae devotionis augmentum placere iugiter studeatis. Nulli ergo etc., nostrae legitimationis et dispensationis, etc., Datum Anagniae, VIII id. Septembri, anno VII.[42]

After the time of Boniface VIII the Roman Pontiffs continued the practice of granting radical sanation. The practice, however, has not always been uniform. At first it was granted solely for reasons of the greatest necessity and public good and only at a later date was it granted in individual cases for reasons of a private nature. Since the end of the eighteenth century this favor has been granted much more frequently and today it is conceded quite readily.[43]

Although it is impossible to give anything like a complete list

[42] Baronius, *Annales Ecclesiastici*, tom. 23, p. 287, nn. 18-19.

[43] Cappello, *De Sacramentis*, III, n. 858.

of either the general or particular concessions of radical sanation, some instances may be pointed out because of their historical significance. It seems that Pope Julius III, in January of the year 1554, granted the first general sanation for many marriages, when he permitted Cardinal Pole, his Legate to England, to grant such a favor to all those persons who had contracted invalid mariages during the troublous reign of Henry VIII. This favor was granted in order to facilitate the work that was being done by Mary Tudor in her attempt to bring England and its people back to their former Faith.[44]

The next general sanation of note was granted by Clement VIII, about 1595, for the marriages of certain Greek Catholics that were invalid because they had been contracted within the fourth degree of consanguinity.[45] Benedict XIV (1740-1758), records that other concessions of radical sanation were made by Gregory XIII (1572-1585), Clement XI (1700-1721) and Clement XII (1730-1740).[46] This testimony is particularly important in regard to Gregory XIII, because those who have sought to impugn the power of the Sovereign Pontiff to grant sanation, have based their claims to some extent on the assertion that Gregory once said that he could not grant such a dispensation.[47] Regarding this assertion Benedict XIV made the comment that, if it was made by Gregory XIII, it must be explained and understood to mean that in some certain case he could not and would not grant the favor, because the circumstances of the case did not warrant such a favor.[48] Pichler[49] was of the same opinion, asserting that, if the statement imputed to Gregory were true, it must be interpreted as

[44] Cappello, *op. cit.*, III, n. 858; Wernz, *Ius Decretalium*, IV, n. 654, note 18; Dodd and Tierney, *History of England*, II, append., p. cx; Haile, *The Life of Reginald Pole*, p. 455.

[45] Cappello, *op. cit.*, n. 858.

[46] Benedict XIV, *Quaest. Can. et Moral.*, n. 174; *De Syn. Dioec.*, lib. XIII, cap. XXI, n. 7.

[47] Cf. Wernz-Vidal, *Ius Canonicum*, (Rome, 1928), V, 799, note 20.

[48] *Quaest. Can. et Moral.*, Qu. 174.

[49] *Ius Canonicum*, I, lib. 4, n. 18.

referring to a defect of sufficient cause for the dispensation and not a deficiency of power to grant it. He added that this assertion was not contained in the edition of the *Consilia* of Navarrus that he used. In spite of this statement of Pichler regarding the edition of Navarrus that he used, the assertion regarding Gregory XIII can be found in other editions of that work.[50]

It must be interpreted in the same way as Benedict XIV and Pichler have done, because Navarrus himself apparently did not attach much importance to the assertion, inasmuch as he defended the power of the Roman Pontiffs to grant this dispensation. Furthermore, it is to be remembered that Gregory could not have been unmindful of the fact that Julius III had already granted a general sanation in 1554 or that its principles had been applied by Clement V in reference to affairs concerning ecclesiastical benefices, when at the Council of Vienne (1311-1312) he revoked the constitution *"Clericos laicos"* of Boniface VIII.[51]

Besides the radical sanation that was granted by Clement XI in his letter *"Apostolicae Dignitatis"*, issued April 2, 1701,[52] there was a general sanation granted by Clement XII in his brief *"Cum dudum"* given on September 9, 1734, and sent to the Provincial of the Jesuits doing missionary work in the East Indies.[53] Instances such as this may account in part for the fact that today the faculties from the Sacred Congregation of the Propagation of the Faith to missionaries carry the notation that if the missioners through inadvertence use the fac-

[50] "Notandum Gregorium XIII, mense Novembris, 1584, negasse petitam hanc dispensationem: ac addidisse non posse."—Navarrus, *Operia Omnia* (Venetiis, 1621), tom. 6, lib. IV, consil. 2.

[51] Cap. un. *de immunitate ecclesiarum*, III, 17 in Clem.

[52] Benedict XIV, *De Syn. Dioec., lib.* XIII, cap. XXI, n. 7; *Institutiones,* LXXXVII, n. 80.

[53] *Bullarium Romanum,* XXIV, p. 5-8. The purpose of this concession was to convalidate those marriages which were invalid because the faculties, which had been granted first by Pius IV and were later renewed by Clement XI, to dispense from certain impediments had lapsed and through an oversight had not been again renewed, although the missioners continued to grant the dispensations.

ulties after their expiration the dispensations and concessions will nevertheless be valid.[54]

At the time that Benedict XIV began his reign in 1740 many decisions of the Rota as well as Resolutions of the Sacred Congregation of the Council had made the granting of radical sanation a well established practice of the Holy See. A question has been raised, however, concerning the famous Benedictine Declaration,[55] in which it was decreed that the marriages that had been entered into between Catholics and heretics in Holland and Belgium without the observance of the Tridentine form were to be held valid and that neither party could contract a new marriage until the other spouse had died. Wernz is of the opinion that this declaration was at least a partial radical sanation and he argues from the fact that the Sacred Congregation of the Council in several cases that had been presented to it prior to the declaration had declared marriages null. Thus he concludes that it was only in virtue of the declaration that they became valid.[56] This conclusion is difficult to understand in view of the wording of the declaration, wherein it is plainly stated that the Holy Father was aware of the fact that the Sacred Congregation of the Council had, in certain circumstances, called some of these marriages invalid and that it was only after a more mature investigation that the Pope declared these marriages must be held valid.

The preservation of peace among royal families and the necessity of safe-guarding the salvation of other individuals has always prompted the Roman Pontiffs to exercise their supreme power in the matter of invalid marriages. Therefore, Clement XIII (1758-1769) and Pius VI (1775-1799) did not hesitate to grant radical sanation for marriages that were invalid because dispensations for these marriages had been invalidly granted by certain bishops of France who had assumed the power to grant

[54] Vermeersch-Creusen, *Epitome Iuris Canonici,* I, p. 646.

[55] S. C. C. *Declaratio "Matrimonia,"* 4 Nov. 1741—*Bull. Rom. Benedict. XIV,* I, pp. 111-113.

[56] *Ius Decretalium,* IV, n. 654, note 18.

dispensations without the proper faculties from the Holy See.[57] Further general concessions of this dispensation were made by Pius VII on August 14, 1801, and again on February 8, 1809, for those marriages that were contracted invalidly during the Revolution in France.[58] Later in the same century Pius IX, on March 17, 1856, granted a general sanation for certain invalid marriages in Austria. Soon after the beginning of the present century Pius X in his constitution *"Provida"*, given on January 18, 1906, granted a general sanation for invalid marriages in the German Empire.[59] This was later extended to Hungary through a decree of the Sacred Congregation of Sacraments on February 27, 1909.[60]

As has already been noted, there were many concessions of radical sanation in particular cases as well as on occasions when general sanations were required. It is likewise to be pointed out that the Sovereign Pontiffs have not refused to delegate the power of granting radical sanation to others. The practice of delegating this faculty to Apostolic Delegates, to Bishops and to Missionaries has been in use at least since the seventeenth century. It is not certain just when this faculty was first delegated, but it appears to have been granted to certain missioners by the Sacred Congregation of the Propagation of the Faith on February 28, 1644.[61]

A notable concession of the faculty to grant radical sanation is found in the Instruction of Cardinal Caprara, given by him to the Bishops of France, on April 25, 1803.[62] Similar concessions of this faculty were made by the Holy See to the Archbishop and three bishops of a certain country, each of whom was delegated to act as an Apostolic Delegate of the

[57] Perrone, *De Matrimonio Christiano,* II, 157.

[58] Wernz, *Ius Decretalium,* IV, n. 654, note 18; Cappello, *De Sacramentis,* III, n. 858, note 5.

[59] *Fontes,* n. 670.

[60] AAS, I (1909), 516-517.

[61] Perrone, *De Matrimonio Christiano,* II, 156.

[62] Zitelli, *De Dispensationibus Matrimonialibus,* p. 175-179.

Holy See, to grant radical sanation for marriages that were invalid because the Tridentine form had not been observed or because dispensations from the impediment of disparity of worship had not been obtained. These four bishops were also empowered to subdelegate their faculties to other worthy priests.[63] This concession of the power to grant radical sanations has been more generally made to bishops, especially those of North America, since before the end of the last century and is continued to the present day.

Although in the centuries when radical sanation was still something new in matrimonial dispensations its concession was made by the reigning Pontiff himself, it has long been a part of the work of certan Congregations to grant this dispensation Thus, the Sacred Congregation of the Council has granted radical sanation for individual marriages for several centuries.[64] The same power was also shared by the Sacred Congregations of the Propagation of the Faith and the Holy Office, the former having jurisdiction in missionary countries. In his constitution *"Sapienti Consilio"*, which was issued on June 29, 1908, and in which he reorganized the Roman Curia, Pius X committed to the Sacred Congregation of the Sacraments competence in all things pertaining to the Sacraments and dispensations from matrimonial impediments,[65] without, however, changing the authority of the Holy Office in respect to the impediments of mixed religion and disparity of worship and the right to grant sanations for invalid marriages involving either of these two impediments.[66]

[63] Instruction of the Secretary of State, 27 Mar. 1830—*Collect. S. C. de Prop. Fid.*, n. 1426.

[64] Pallottini, *Collectio Omnium Conclusionum et Resolutionum Apud Sacram Congregationem Cardinalium S. Concilii Tridentini*, v. Dispensatio, § XI, Dispensatio in radice matrimonii putativi, p. 534 ff.

[65] *Fontes*, n. 682.

[66] *Ordo servandus in S. Congregationibus, etc.*, 29 Sept. 1908, *pars* II, *Normae Peculiares, cap.* VII, *art.* III, n. 11 a; *cap.* VII, *art.* 1—AAS, I (1909), 87.

Article III. Legislation Governing Radical Sanation

Radical sanation is substantially the same today as it was in the days of Joannes Andreae. One change, however, that may be noted is in the title which this institution bears. In the beginning and until late in the nineteenth century canonists spoke of it as the *"dispensatio in radice"*. This same title was given to it in pontifical documents until the latter part of the eighteenth century, when the Sacred Congregation of the Propogation of the Faith in one of its rescripts used the term *"sanatis in radice matrimoniis"*.[67] In his instructions to the bishops of France, Cardinal Caprara used a double terminology, namely, *dispensatio in radice seu sanatio in radice"*.[68] From that time on the term *"sanatio in radice"* became canonized by its continual use in pontifical documents, to the exclusion of the older term *"dispensatio in radice"*. Today it is known by no other name, having been incorporated into the Code of Canon Law by that title.[69] It has already been noted that, whereas in the beginning this dispensation was regarded primarily as a means of legitimation, it later came to be regarded as primarily a mode of convalidating marriages.

This institution has been marked by little change or development in the legislation governing it from the fourteenth century to the Code. A study of the writings of the canonists and of pontifical documents, in which this dispensation was granted, shows that it has been the constant practice of the Church to restrict this favor to marriages that were invalid because of an impediment of the ecclesiastical law.[70]

It was repeatedly stated by the authors that it was not given

[67] July 5, 1788—*Fontes*, n. 4622.

[68] Zitelli, *De Dispensationibus Matrimonialibus*, p. 175.

[69] Canons 1138-1141.

[70] Panormitanus, C. 13, X, *qui filii sint legitimi*, n. 23; Gonzalez Tellez, C. 13, X, *qui filii sint legitimi*, n. 22. Sanchez, *op. cit.*, tom. III, disp. VII, lib. VIII, n. 8; Benedict XIV, epist. *"Redditae Nobis,"* 5 Dec. 1744—*Fontes*, n. 350; instr. *"Cum super,"* 27 Sept. 1755—*Bull. Rom. Contin.* IV, 291; *De Synodo Dioecesano*, lib. XIII, cap. XXI, n. 7.

for marriages that were invalid because of an impediment of the divine or natural law. The Sacred Penitentiary, however, seemed to break with this constant practice of the Church when, on April 25, 1890, it granted radical sanation for a marriage that had been invalid because of the impediment of *ligamen,* after that impediment had ceased to exist. The rescript, which is given here because of its unusual character, clearly indicates that this exception was only a partial or imperfect sanation, inasmuch as it refused to grant legitimation to those children who had been born while the impediment existed and who were, therefore, adulterine offspring.

N. mulier Catholica dioecesis Parisiensis exponit, quod ipsa anno 1867 matrimonium rite contraxerat cum X, sed ab illo atrociter verberata, obtento divortii sententia in sui favorem . . . in Helvetia a. 1872, in eadem civitate contractum mere civilem inivit cum H., viro catholico, at ab omni praxi religiosa alieno, vivente adhuc priore conjuge. E vivis erepto X (prior conjux) oratrix praefata a H (secundo conjuge) obtinere studuit ut coram Ecclesia consensum renovarent, sicque praevideretur legitimationi matrimonii, sed frustra; nam ille affirmabat contractum mere civileme sibi sufficere, constanterque renuit comparere coram sacerdote. Hisce adjunctis nihil oratrici restat, nisi ad S. V. recurere ad ut suae miserae conditioni per sanationem in radice providantur, ita ut Ecclesiae sacramentis participare valeat.

S. poenitentiariae de speciali et expressa Apostolica auctoritate Parisiensi facultatem concedit, praevia sive per se sive per aliam idoneam ecclesiasticam personam ab eo specialiter deputandam praedictae mulieri absolutione a praemissis cum congrua poenitentia salutari, praefatum matrimonium sic, uti praefertur, nulliter contractum, dummodo consensus perseveret, Apostolica auctoritate in radice sanandi, prolemque sive susceptam, non tamen in adulterio conceptam, sive suscipiendam exinde legitimam decernendi ac respective nuntiandi. Praesentes autem litterae, cum attestatione imperitae exsecutionis, in cancellaria episcopali diligenter custodiantur, ut pro quocumque futuro eventu de matrimonii validitate et prolis legitimitate constare possit, imposita mulieri praedictae obligatione prudenter monendi virum de

> huiusmodi sanatione obtenta, ad hoc ipse sciat se in legitimo versari, necnon remoto scandalo, quod occasione simillum sanationum oriri potest" . . .[71]

It is evident that this concession on the part of the Sacred Penitentiary, as well as any others it may have granted, was truly an exception to the established practice of the Holy See from the fact that the Holy Office declared in the early part of the present century that radical sanation could not be granted for a marriage that was invalid because of an impediment of the divine or natural law.[72] In this connection it is interesting to note that the code merely states that the Church *does not grant* radical sanation after impediments of the divine or natural law have ceased.[73] Gasparri and others objected to the response of the Holy Office on the grounds that it deprived the Church of a power that had been attributed to it by canonists and theologians of great authority. Therefore, in his capacity of President of the Commission for the Codification of the Law, Gasparri again proposed the question to Pius X and pointed out that this response of the Holy Office, having already obtained great authority, would receive an even greater authority, amounting to a dogmatic definition according to some theologians, if it were included in the Code. This argument, according to Gasparri himself, led to the use of the moderate wording found in the Code today.[74]

In respect to this point of law, it is interesting to note that in the beginning the canonists were in doubt about the power of the Pope to grant radical sanation for marriages that were invalid because of the impediment resulting from Sacred Orders or Solemn Religious Profession.[75] Later canonists, however, agreed that this was not beyond the power of the Roman Pontiff,

[71] *Le Canoniste Contemperain,* XIV (1881), 61 ff.

[72] 2 Mart. 1904—*Fontes,* n. 1270.

[73] Canon 1139, § 2.

[74] Gasparri, *De Matrimonio* (edition of 1932), nn. 1216-1218.

[75] Joannes Andreae C. XIII, X, *qui filii sint legitimi,* n. 30; Panormitanus, C. XIII, X, *qui filii sint legitimi,* n. 12.

since these impediments were of merely ecclesiastical origin.[76] Nevertheless, it apparently has not been granted for such cases, if the impediment involves the order of priesthood, at least not in individual cases nor for private cause. This favor may have been extended to such marriages in the general sanation granted by Julius III in 1554. It is claimed, however, that permission to grant radical sanation in such cases has not been given even in the most complete faculties.[77] This statement is correct, if these authors meant that faculties had not been given for marriages invalid because of priesthood; but, if they included the orders of Subdiaconate and Diaconate then their statement is not correct, because present-day faculties grant such powers.

Another requirement governing the concession of radical sanation that has been constant and unchanging since the very beginning is the necessity of marital consent at the beginning of the marriage or at some time prior to the concession of sanation. But the factor that determined the presence of such consent has not been as constant and unvarying. Prior to the Council of Trent marital consent, or consent naturally sufficient for marriage, was presumed to be present in clandestine marriages as well as in marriages that were contracted publicly, even if there had been knowledge of some impediment.[78] There is also evidence that sanation was granted for marriages that were clandestine.[79]

The decree *"Tametsi"* enacted by the Council of Trent made it imperative that marriages be contracted in the presence of a priest and two witnesses, in those places where it was promulgated.[80] As a result of this decree it became necessary to prove the

[76] Sanchez, *De Sancto Matrimonii Sacramento,* tom. III, disp. VII, lib. VIII, n. 9.

[77] Wernz, *Ius Decretalium,* IV, n. 657; Feije, *De Dispensationibus Matrimonialibus,* n. 769.

[78] Carberry, *The Juridical Form of Marriage* (Washington, D. C., 1934), p. 4; Wernz-Vidal, *Ius Canonicum,* V, n. 523.

[79] Pyrrhus Corradus, *Praxis Dispensationum Apostolicarum,* lib. VIII, cap. III, nn. 46-49; De Justis, *De Dispensationibus Matrimonialibus,* lib. I, cap. VIII, n. 271.

[80] Sess. XXIV, *de ref. matr.,* c. 1.

existence of marital consent in the case of clandestine marriages and undoubtedly this caused Benedict XIV to declare that radical sanation would not be granted for marriages that did not have the *"species vel figura matrimonii"*, that is, for marriages which were not contracted according to the prescribed form, or unions which were *"manifeste fornicaria"*, that is, unions entered into without marital intent.[81]

This requirement of the *"species matrimonii"* naturally gave rise to the question of what action the Church would take in respect to civil marriages. In the early days following the publication of the decree *"Tametsi"*, it is certain that clandestine marraiges, that is, marriages which were not contracted according to the prescribed form, did not enjoy the presumption of law that they had formerly enjoyed in regard to the presence of marital consent.[82] Later on, however, there seems to have been some relaxation on this point, for there is evidence that the Holy See, on several occasions, granted a general sanation for civil marriages that had been contracted in France during the Revolution. This did not signify that the Church was again giving these marriages that presumption of law which clandestine marriages formerly enjoyed. This seems clear from the fact that in his allocution of September 27, 1852, Pius IX termed these civil marriages mere concubinage.[83] Although the Church does not now generally speak of these marriages in such a way, it has not altered its views regarding them when there is question of persons bound to the canonical form.[84] Consequently the fact that the Holy See grants radical sanation for civil marriages merely signifies a less rigorous stand on this point of law, in view of the ever increasing number of such unions.[85] The Code no longer requires the *"species vel figura matrimonii"*, being content to accept the consent given at

[81] Epist. *"Redditae Nobis,"* 5 Dec. 1744—*Fontes*, n. 350; *De Syn. Dioec.*, lib. XIII, cap. XXI, n. 7; *Quest. Can. et Moral.*, qu. 174.

[82] Manning, *Presumptions of Law in Marriage Cases* (Washington, D. C., 1935), p. 44.

[83] *Fontes*, n. 515.

[84] Maroto, "Animadversiones"—*Apollinaris*, II (1929), 248-249.

[85] Feije, *De Disp. Matrimon.*, n. 768; Wernz, *Ius Decretalium*, IV, n. 657, note 28; Gasparri, *De Matrimonio*, n. 1225.

the time of the marriage, provided it was marital and still endures.[86]

The necessity of the perseverance of consent in the parties to the marriage did not receive special treatment and sometimes was not even mentioned by the early canonists. The very obvious necessity of this element probably accounts for this fact. Later, when the question was accorded special treatment by the authors, it was universally admitted to be absolutely essential for the concession of radical sanation.[87] This same condition has been repeatedly expressed in papal rescripts.[88] In conformity with this condition, namely, that the consent endure in the parties, it seems certain that the Holy See is not accustomed to grant radical sanation when one or both parties know of the impediment and do not wish to continue in the marriage.[89]

In the early days it was the opinion of several canonists that the renewal of consent, when radical sanation was granted, was required for the validity of the dispensation.[90] The practice of the Holy See, however, has been to require the renewal of consent only if it could be obtained. Generally it has not refused to grant radical sanation in cases where the renewal of consent could not be obtained, provided the first consent still endured.[91]

[86] Canon 1139, § 1.

[87] Aichner, *Compendium Iuris Ecclesiastici,* p. 661, n. 4; Feije, *op. cit.,* n. 771; Ojetti, *Synopsis Rerum Moralium et Juris Pontificii,* "Sanatio in Radice."

[88] S. C. S. Officii, 11 Mart. 1868—*Fontes,* n. 1004; 22 Aug. 1906, ad 4—*Fontes,* n. 1278; 12 Apr. 1899—*Fontes,* n. 1219.

[89] Vecchiotti, *Institutiones Canonicae,* n. 115; Wernz, *Ius Decretalium,* IV, n. 659; Giovine, *De Disp. Matrimon., consult.* XXIII, sect. 328, n. 6; Secret. Status instruct., 27 Mart. 1830—*Collect. S. C. de Prop. Fide,* n. 1426; Benedict XIV, Instr., *"Cum Super,"* 27 Sept. 1755—*Bull. Roman. Cont.,* IV, 291.

[90] Sanchez, *De Sancto Matrimonii Sacramento,* tom. III, disp. VII, lib. VIII, n. 4; Pirhing, *Ius Canonicum,* lib. IV, tit. 17, n. 42.

[91] S. C. S. Officii, 11 Mart. 1868—*Fontes,* n. 1004; 9 Dec. 1874—*Fontes,* n. 1036; 11 Sept. 1878, ad 1—*Fontes,* n. 1057; 12 Apr. 1899—*Fontes,* n. 1219; 22 Aug. 1906 ad 4—*Fontes,* n. 1278; S. C. de Prop. Fide, 5 Jul. 1788—*Fontes,* n. 4622; 17 Jan. 1836 ad 1—*Fontes,* n. 4760; 1 Jun. 1845—*Fontes,* n. 4812.

The necessity of a grave and urgent cause for the concession of this dispensation has never been questioned by any canonist and has been required by the Church, even when it was granted in an individual case.[92]

The prescription of Canon 1141, that the concession of this favor belongs to the Apostolic See alone, is likewise found in a declaration of Benedict XIV in which he states that only the Roman Pontiff can grant this dispensation and establish the conditions for its validity.[93]

[92] Sanchez, *op. cit., loc. cit.*, n. 5; Benedict XIV, epist. "*Redditae Nobis,*" 5 Dec. 1744—*Fontes*, n. 350; instr. "*Cum super,*" 27 Sept. 1755—*Bull. Roman. Cont.*, IV, 291; *De Syn. Dioec.*, lib. XIII, cap. XXI, n. 7.

[93] Instr. "*Cum Super,*" 27 Sept. 1755—*Bull. Roman. Cont.*, IV, 291.

CHAPTER III

THE EFFECTS OF RADICAL SANATION

The effects of radical sanation are essentially two: the convalidation of marriage and the legitimation of any children born of the previously invalid marriage. These effects form the substance of the matter contained in the second paragraph of Canon 1138.

Canon 1138, § 2.—Convalidatio fit a momento concessionis gratiae; retrotractio vero intelligitur facta ad matrimonii initium, nisi aliud expresse caveatur.

ARTICLE I. THE CONVALIDATION OF MARRIAGE

A. The Time of Convalidation

The moment when the favor of radical sanation is granted is also the time at which the hitherto invalid union is convalidated. Moreover, this convalidation is effected *only* for the future and *only* from the moment of the granted sanation.[1] In other words, it is effective, as canonical writers express it, *ex nunc,* and not *ex tunc,* as several authors of note formerly claimed. The distinction noted here is one of major importance. For, if one were to hold that the convalidation took place *ex tunc,* it would be necessary to attribute to the Church the power to do something that is utterly impossible, namely, to render valid from its very beginning a marriage that was certainly invalid. This the Church cannot do and no present day writer makes this unusual claim. Consequently it seems useless to repeat again

[1] Gasparri, *De Matrimonio* (edition of 1932), n. 1211; Cappello, *De Sacramentis,* III, n. 851, 2, 1; Payen, *De Matrimonio in Missionibus,* n. 2599, 2.

the arguments for and against the proposal that radical sanation renders a marriage valid *ex tunc.*

As it has already been stated, radical sanation achieves its end in respect to an invalid marriage by first removing the legal obstacles which had rendered this naturally sufficient consent juridically ineffective,[2] and then accepting the marital consent which was given at the beginning of the marriage. This, at least, is the process in the case of the perfect radical sanation of a marriage.[3] For in this case, because of one reason or another, both parties will be dispensed from the necessity of renewing their marriage consent in the prescribed form. But in this instance of perfect radical sanation the exact moment when convalidation occurs will depend on the manner in which this favor is granted. There are two ways of granting favors: one is known as the *forma commissoria,* in which an executor is needed to bring about the ratified application of the favor; the second way is known as the *forma gratiosa,* in which no such executor is required.[4] If, then,, the favor is granted *in forma commissoria,* convalidation will occur only at the moment when the appointed executor has fulfilled all the conditions set forth in the rescript and has applied the dispensation in due manner.[5] On the other hand, if the rescript of sanation is granted *in forma gratiosa* and there is no need of an executor, the convalidation of the marriage will occur at the very moment when the rescript is granted.[6] This suffices to show when convalidation takes place in a case of perfect radical sanation. But it is also necessary to point out at what moment convalidation occurs in a case of imperfect (partial) radical sanation. In respect to convalidation, radical sanation will be imperfect if one or both parties are required to renew

[2] Feije, *De Imped. et Disp. Matrim.,* n. 766; Giovine, *De Disp. Matrim.,* I, consult. 23, sect. 322, n. 1.

[3] Canon 1138, § 1.

[4] O'Neill, *Papal Rescripts of Favor* (Catholic University of America, Canon Law Studies, No. 57, Washington, D. C., 1930), p. 156.

[5] Payen, *De Matrimonio,* nn. 2599, 2 and 2601, 2; De Smet, *De Sponsalibus et Matrimonio,* (Brugis, 1909), n. 346, 4.

[6] Payen, *op. cit.,* nn. 2599, 2; 2601, 1; De Smet, *op. cit.,* n. 346, 4.

consent. When this is the case, and it frequently happens, the marriage will be convalidated at the moment when, after the dispensation has been granted, the party or parties renew their marital consent.[7]

B. *The Force of this Convalidation*

The effects of the convalidation produced by radical sanation are the same effects as those which would have been produced had the union been valid from the beginning. Thus, if the marriage convalidated by radical sanation is a union between two baptized persons it acquires a sacramental character, for it is only at the moment of convalidation that the sacrament begins to exist.[8] The sacrament, like the convalidation itself, is present only *ex nunc* and for the future. It can in no respect be referred to the period prior to the convalidation. For just as it is metaphysically impossible for the Church to cause convalidation to cover a period in which the union was certainly invalid, so also it is equally impossible for the Church to cause the sacrament to exist during a period when it was juridically impossible for it to be present. At the same moment when the marriage is convalidated, the parties acquire all the rights and duties proper to the marital state. But here, too, it is to be noted that these rights and duties are conferred for the future only and have no retrotractive effect. Consequently, the convalidation of the union with its accompanying bestowal of all marital rights, privileges and duties merely makes the use of these rights lawful for the future and does not in any way whatsoever absolve the parties of any sins of which they may have been guilty by the illicit use of these rights prior to the convalidation of their union.[9]

This statement does not contradict or alter the fact that in radical sanation properly so called there is a retrotraction to the

[7] Wernz-Vidal, *Ius Canonicum,* V, n. 670.

[8] Canon 1012, § 2.

[9] Gasparri, *De Matrimonio,* n. 1208.

past, by a fiction of the law, in respect to canonical effects. On the one hand it is stated that the marital rights and duties are established for the future only and that their accomplished establishment is not and can not be recognized as an actuality that existed in the past. Consequently the sins committed before the convalidation of the marriage remain sins subject to absolution after convalidation as well as before. On the other hand it is stated that in radical sanation there is a force which operates in retrospect, effecting juridically a retrotraction to the past in the canonical effects that flow from a valid marriage. This simply means that the Church cherishes, approves and confirms the juridical attitude that looks upon the newly convalidated marriage as if it had been valid from the beginning and therefore accords to it, for the past as well as for the present, such effects as are equal in juridical value and extent to the genuine juridical perogatives of a valid matrimonial union.

The Church knows positively and definitely that previously the marriage was invalid and that none of the canonical effects consequent upon a valid union were present in the past. But the Church is also ready, upon the act of convalidation, to supply for the canonical deficiencies which attached to the past juridical aspect of the marriage. And once the Church has employed this legal discretion, the marriage is set free of all its former legal disabilities and juridical obstructions.[10]

A marriage convalidated by means of radical sanation does not imply a denial of past actualities; it merely enshrines the disposition of the law in virtue of which the legal restrictions of the past are lifted. It is the fiction of the law and not the consciousness of fact that stamps the marriage with its newly enfranchised character. This recourse to legal fiction by an act of the law's benevolent dissimulation does not change the objective truth of things, but it does alter the juridic view which the Church takes in regard to sanated marriages. For by the Church's own recognition and approval the sanation effects the fullest legi-

[10] Benedict XIV, instr. *"Cum Super,"* 27 Sept. 1755.—*Bull. Rom. Cont.*, IV, 291.

timation of the offspring of the marriage. And in this precisely consists the second effect of radical sanation.[11]

Article II. The Retrotraction of Radical Sanation

A. Preliminary Notions

It has already been explained that the element of retrotraction is one of the distinguishing features of radical sanation.[12] It is a result of a fiction of the law, to which the Church has recourse for a just cause in order that she may assume as true something which is not actually true. In other words, the dispensations which the Church grants in radical sanation are, by a fiction of the law, made to reach back as it were to the beginning of the marriage, so that the Church may act as if the marriage had never been invalid, at least in respect to its canonical effects. This retrotractive force of radical sanation does not alter the objective validity of the marriage for the past, for the reason that the Church cannot cause something not to be which already is.[13] But the Church can, in virtue of its supreme legislative power, erase the detrimental effects which have followed from some act that is subject to her legislation.[14] Consequently, by having recourse to legal fiction the Church causes the dispensations of radical sanation to reach back to the past so that the marriage will obtain the appearances of validity from its beginning and thus will erase the hurtful legal effects that have followed from the invalid marriage.

Such an action on the part of the Church is neither impossible nor at variance with any principles governing the common good. It is not impossible, for it is not outside the realm of any supreme

[11] Benedict XIV, epist. *"Redditae Nobis,"* 5 Dec. 1744—*Fontes,* n. 350; *Quaest. Canon. et Moral.,* n. 174.

[12] Cf. supra, pp. 9-10.

[13] Sanchez, *De Sancto Matrimonii Sacramento, tom.* III, *disp.* VII, *lib.* VIII, n. 2-3; Gasparri, *De Matrimonio,* n. 1208.

[14] *Cap. un., de immunitate ecclesiarum,* III, 17, *in Clem.*

legislative authority, civil or ecclesiastical, to erase the harmful effects which have followed from any act which has been performed either in accord with, or contrary to, any law enacted by that supreme authority.[15] For all practical purposes it implies neither more nor less than a mode of conduct by which the supreme legislative authority, in a given case acts as if these baneful effects had never existed. Such an action, moreover, is not at variance with any principles governing the common good, because the common good is injured in no way whatsoever if, in a certain case, the supreme authority of Church or State should for a just and reasonable cause see fit to dispense from the laws which it has enacted or to erase the effects which have resulted from the violation of law. It is true, of course, that this is an extraordinary procedure and one not to be followed to the extent of promoting laxity on the part of supreme authorities. But radical sanation is an extraordinary process and the Church makes use of it only when the extraordinary and urgent circumstances of certain given cases seem fully to warrant it.

The second paragraph of Canon 1138, after indicating the moment at which convalidation occurs, goes on to state that "the retrotraction [of radical sanation] is understood to extend back to the beginning of the marriage, unless the contrary is expressly stated "in the rescript". Thus it is evident that the *terminus ad quem* of the retrotraction will not always be the same. Unless otherwise expressly stated the element of retrotraction will reach back to the very beginning of the marriage, that is, to the time when the parties first exchanged their marital consent. This will always be the case in the perfect radical sanation of a marriage.[16] On the other hand it will sometimes happen that the retrotraction will extend back only to some intermediate point after the first invalid celebration of the marriage. When this happens the sanation will *be imperfect* or *partial*.[17] The circumstances which

[15] Gonzalez, lib. IV, tit. 17. *qui filii sint legitimi*, n. 22; De Justis, *De Dispensationibus Matrimonialibus*, lib. I, cap. VII, n. 277.

[16] Gasparri, *De Matrimonio*, n. 1212.

[17] Gasparri, *op. cit.*, n. 1212; Cappello, *De Sacramentis*, III, n. 851, 5.

will necessarily limit retrotraction and at the same time designate the point of time beyond which it will not extend are those mentioned in Canon 1140, §2.[18] This canon is concerned with a case which true marital consent was at first lacking in one or both parties, but was later supplied on their part. In such a case, retrotraction will be limited by the time of the giving of the proper marital consent and therefore will not extend back beyond the moment when that consent was actually given. The reason for this limiting of the retrotractive force of radical sanation is evident, namely, the absence of any root or basis of marriage up to the moment that the consent was eventually given. For, until consent was given there was no root to be healed and no field in which radical sanation could operate.

This retrotractive force of radical sanation represents an outstanding instance of the benevolence which the Church exercises towards those of her children who have erred or who have been wayward in respect to her legislation on marriage. For the Church, not satisfied solely with the convalidation of the marriage, also wishes to erase the detrimental effects which followed from the prior invalid union. The effects of marriage to which this retrotractive force of radical sanation is applied are twofold: those that concern the parties themselves and those that concern their offspring.[19]

The canonical effects of marriage are set forth in Canons 1110-1117 inclusively. In respect to the parties themselves the principal effect is the validity and indissolubility of their marriage, together with the various rights and duties that accompany it in virtue of these properties. In respect to the children the principal effect of marriage is the legitimacy which they enjoy as a result of being born in lawful wedlock. It has been pointed out that as a result of radical sanation the Church acts as if these effects actually had been present from the very beginning of the union. But inasmuch as the marriage is actually rendered ob-

[18] "Quod si consensus ab initio quidem defuerit, sed postea praestitus fuerit, sanatio concedi potest a momento praestiti consensus."

[19] Payen, *De Matrimonio,* n. 2600; Wernz-Vidal, *Ius Canonicum,* V. n. 670.

jectively valid only then when radical sanation is granted, that is to say, *ex nunc,* it follows that for practical purposes the legitimation of the offspring is the principal fruit of the retrotractive force of radical sanation and that it is likewise the second and last effect of sanation. This erasure of the children's illegitimacy which followed from their having been born of the invalid union of their parents is of sufficient practical importance to warrant special consideration.

B. The Legitimation of the Children

Legitimacy has been definied as a juridic quality proper to a person who has been conceived or born of a valid or a putative marriage, unless the parents of the child, at the moment of its conception, were prohibited the use of marriage, previously validly contracted, because of a solemn religious profession or a sacred order.[20] Because, although the marriage just referred to may have been valid, a child conceived in such circumstances will be illegitimate and will therefore be lacking that juridic quality of legitimacy which ordinarily belongs to a child born or conceived of a valid or putative marriage.[21] All children not born of a valid or putative marriage are illegitimate and therefore lacking in the juridic quality of legitimacy. Now, it is of great importance that this state of things should not remain unaltered throughout the child's life, for illegitimacy is not merely a negative item, namely the lack of a juridic quality, but it is also something positive inasmuch as it entails various disabilities, not the least of which is irregularity.[22] By reason of the one an illegitimate child is marked as having been born out of lawful wedlock. By reason of the other the child labors under a disability which is described by the Code as one of the perpetual impediments which renders him incapable of certain things for which the law requires legitimacy.[23] Now, inasmuch as illegitimacy results from a certain positive

[20] Payen, *De Matrimonio,* n. 2160.
[21] Canon 1114.
[22] Canon 984.
[23] Canon 983.

disposition of the positive law, it will require another positive act of law to remove it. This remedial act of law is known as the process of legitimation.

The process of legitimation has been variously defined. Payen calls it "the juridic restoration of legitimacy".[24] Vermeersch-Creusen in their commentary speak of it as "a benefit of the law or law-giver, by which some or all of the rights and honors of legitimacy are conferred on an illegitimate child".[25] These definitions agree in substance and adequately indicate that legitimation is an act performed in accordance with a positive and definite prescription of the law or law-giver, acting either personally or through a delegate. There are four distinct ways in which legitimation can take place: (1) by the subsequent marriage of the parents; (2) by a dispensation; (3) by a rescript of the Roman Pontiff; (4) by radical sanation. That these four modes of legitimation are truly distinct, not only in their manner of operation but also in their scope and efficacy, will be evident from a summary consideration of each.

1. *Legitimation by Subsequent Marriage of the Parents*

Canon 1116. Per subsequens parentum matrimonium sive verum sive putativum, sive noviter contractum sive convalidatum, etiam non consummatum, legitima efficitur proles, dummodo parentes habiles extiterint ad matrimonium inter se contrahendum tempore conceptionis, vel pregnationis, vel nativitatis.

An illegitimate child will be legitimated by the subsequent marriage of its parents, provided that the parents were capable of contracting marriage, that is, were not hindered by a diriment impediment, at the moment of the child's conception, or during the period of gestation, or at the moment of the child's birth. This does not mean that they must have been capable of contract-

[24] *De Matrimonio*, n. 2171.

[25] *Epitome Iuris Canonici*, (Ed. 5a, 1934), II, n. 419.

ing marriage at all three of these stated times in order that the child could be legitimated by their subsequent marriage.[26] The legitimation will result from subsequent marriage regardless of whether the parents were free from every diriment impediment at all three times, or only at one of the three times. Thus, the parents may have been laboring under the diriment impediment of age at the moment of the child's conception and during the period of pregnancy, but may have been free from it at the moment of the child's birth. In this case their subsequent marriage will legitimate the child. On the other hand, the parents may have been free from every diriment impediment and therefore capable of contracting marriage at the moment of the child's conception, but may not have been free at the moment of its birth. Thus, if one of the prospective parents were to contract marriage with another person before the child's birth, the child's parents would be hindered from contracting a valid marriage because of the impediment of *ligamen*. But if, upon the dissolution of this bond of marriage, the child's parents were to contract a valid or putative marriage between themselves, the child would be legitimated by reason of this marriage, because at the moment of its conception the child's parents were free to contract this marriage. The subsequent marriage by which a child is legitimated may be either a valid or a putative marriage, newly contracted or convalidated, consummated or unconsummated. There are two essentials necessary: (1) that the marriage take place between the parents themselves, for the marriage of one of the parents with a person who is not the other of the parents will not suffice to effect the legitimation of the child; (2) that the child be a *proles naturalis,* that is, a *natural child.* A *natural* child is one whose parents were free to contract a valid marriage at the moment of its conception, during the period of gestation or at its birth. For, if the parents were not capable of contracting marriage at one of these three times, the child will belong to the class of spurious progeny. For this class of illegitimates subsequent marriage of the parents does not effect legitimation.[27]

[26] Gasparri, *De Matrimonio,* n. 1118; Cappello, *De Sacramentis,* III, n. 750.

[27] Gasparri, *De Matrimonio,* n. 1121.

2. *Legitimation by Dispensation*

In the preceding paragraph it was noted that only *natural* children are legitimated by the subsequent marriage of their parents. *Spurious* illegitimates must obtain the benefit of legitimation in one of the three remaining modes of legitimation. The term *"spurious"* is a general one and is applicable to any children born of parents who, because of a diriment impediment, were not free to contract marriage either at the time of the child's conception, during the pregnancy or at the child's birth.[28] But, according to the specific nature of the diriment impediment which rendered the parents incapable of contracting marriage, *spurious* children may be: (1) *Merely spurious;* (2) *Adulterine;* (3) *Sacrilegious;* (4) *Incestuous;* (5) *Nefarious.* This classification of *spurious* offspring is not established in the Code nor is it the only classification to be found among canonical writers. But it has found sufficient acceptance among recent authors to warrant its use in this work.[29]

The classification is developed in the following manner: (1) *Merely spurious* children are those whose parents were hindered from contracting a valid marriage by such diriment impediments as age, disparity of worship, abduction, crime, public propriety, spiritual or legal relationship. This is to say any diriment impediment which in its juridical effect will not place the offspring in any of the following groups will have the effect of branding the offspring as *merely spurious.* (2) *Adulterine* children are those whose very conception implies a concomitant act of adultery on the part of their parents. The parents were incapable of intermarrying at the time of the child's conception because an already existing bond of marriage held each of them, or one of them, to some third person. (3) *Sacrilegious* children may be thus designated for one or the other of two reasons: (a) they may have been born of an attempted marriage between parents who were not free to marry because of the impediment arising

[28] Payen, *De Matrimonio,* n. 2162.

[29] Payen, *De Matrimonio,* n. 2162; Wernz-Vidal, *Ius Canonicum,* V, n. 608; Gasparri, *De Matrimonio,* n. 1112.

from sacred orders or the impediment resulting from solemn religious profession; (b) they may have been born of a valid marriage from parents who were forbidden the use of their marriage because of subsequent sacred orders or solemn profession, at the moment of the child's conception. (4) *Incestuous* children are those whose conception is traceable to parents who are related in the collateral line of consanguinity within the degrees which constitute a canonical basis for matrimonial impediments, or also to parents who are related in either the direct or collateral line of affinity within the degrees which effect similar matrimonial impediments. (5) *Nefarious* children are those whose parents are related by consanguinity in the direct line. In a pejorative sense such children might also be called *incestuous,* but they are singled out by the more specific name of *nefarious,* because of the odium which is attached to this marriage which is forbidden by the natural law, over which the Church can not exercise any powers of dispensation.

The various classes of *spurious* children having been thus established it will be easier to attend to the various ways in which they can be legitimated. It has already been noted that no *spurious* child obtains the benefit of legitimation through the subsequent marriage of its parents. Therefore, the next mode of legitimation to be considered is that provided for in Canon 1051.

Canon 1051. Per dispensationem super impedimento dirimente concessam sive ex potestate ordinaria, sive ex potestate delegata per indultum generale, non vero per rescriptum in casibus particularibus, conceditur quoque eo ipso legitimatio prolis, si qua ex iis cum quibus dispensatur iam nata vel concepta fuerit, excepta tamen adulterina et sacrilega.

In this canon it is expressly stated that a dispensation from a diriment impediment carries with it the legitimation of any offspring already born or merely conceived, unless that offspring be *sacrilegious* or *adulterine.* A necessary condition for the effectiveness of this dispensation, however, is set down in this same canon. The condition concerns the person of the one granting the dispensation, for the canon states that the dispensation must be granted by one having ordinary power or one having power delegated through a general indult. It is further stated that legitimation does not accompany a rescript in particular cases. This latter condition refers to a special faculty that has been conceded to someone whereby he may dispense an individual or some few determinate persons. This may be stated in another fashion. If a bishop, acting in virtue of the ordinary powers granted in Canons 1043 and 1045, grants a dispensation from a diriment impediment, this dispensation will carry with it the legitimation of the offspring. In like manner if a bishop, acting in virtue of his quinquennial faculties, grants a dispensation from a diriment impediment, this dispensation will also carry with it the legitimation of the offspring. But if a bishop, in a particular case, applied to the Holy See for the faculty to dispense from a diriment impediment, the rescript conceding this faculty would not necessarily carry with it the legitimation of the offspring. Certainty in regard to the matter of legitimation could be obtained only by a careful scrutiny of the actual rescript conceding the faculty to dispense in the particular case.[30]

Two things in particular are to be noted concerning this second mode of legitimation. First, in virtue of this canon legitimation is provided for by the law and will accompany the dispensation from a diriment impediment, even if legitimation is not expressly sought, and even if the one granting the dispensations does not advert to that phase of the matter.[31] Secondly, this canon provides a means of legitimation for those *spurious* children who have been designated as *merely spurious* or *incestuous*. In the case of *incestuous* children, however, it is to be noted that this canon does not provide a means of legitimation if the parents are related in the first degree of consanguinity in the collateral line, since persons who are thus related can never obtain a dispensation. In like manner this canon does not provide a means of legitimation for those children who have been termed *nefarious*. The canon does not expressly

[30] Cappello, *De Sacramentis*, III, n. 291, 4; Ayrhinac-Lydon, *Marriage Legislation in the New Code of Canon Law*, n. 83.

[31] Cappello, *op. cit.*, III, n. 291, 3.

exclude them for the very obvious reason that such an exclusion was wholly unnecessary inasmuch as their parents can never obtain a dispensation to marry since the impediment binding them is one of the natural law.[32]

The canon does, however, make two exclusions. It first excludes *adulterine* children from the benefits of legitimation. Secondly, it excludes *sacrilegious* children. In respect to the *adulterine* children the following distinction is necessary. If an *adulterine* child is actually born at a time in which his parents were still bound by the impediment of *ligamen* he will be excluded from the benefits of legitimation in virtue of Canon 1051, if at some date subsequent to his birth his parents become free to marry and obtain a dispensation from the diriment impediment of crime. The will of the Church in this matter is the sole reason for this fact. If, on the other hand, an *adulterine* child conceived while the parents were bound by the impediment of *ligamen* was actually born when the parents were free to contract a valid marriage, the child will be legitimated by the fact of the parents' subsequent marriage.[32a] As far as *sacrilegious* children are concerned, the exclusion must be attributed to the express will of the Church which does not wish to confer the benefit of legitimation by this means on such children. Therefore, even if a dispensation is granted in this latter case for the impediments of Canons 1072 and 1073, legitimation will not result from the dispensation. For *adulterine* children who were born during an adulterous union and *sacrilegious* children recourse must be had to one of the remaining modes of legitimation.

3. *Legitimation by Rescript of the Pope*

Legitimation by a rescript of the Roman Pontiff is, in itself,

[32] Canon 1076, § 1.

[32a] Gasparri *(De Matrimonio,* 1932 edition, n. 1117) makes a contrary statement and in so doing he establishes an exception to the law of the Code as found in Canon 1116. No reasons are advanced for such an exception by Gasparri. The opinion does not seem tenable if one invokes the rule of law which states that when the law does not distinguish neither should we distinguish.

the widest mode of legitimation in the sense that no class of illegitimates is beyond the power of the Pope. Its utility is, therefore, quite evident. In the first place it offers a means of legitimation to *natural* children whose parents do not contract a subsequent marriage. In the second place it offers a means of legitimation to those who are expressly excluded by law from enjoying the benefits provided in other modes of legitimation.

Legitimation by a rescript of the Roman Pontiff is obtained only when it is specifically requested.[33] This specific request may accompany a petition to the Holy See for the faculty to grant a dispensation in a particular case.[34] But apart from any question of petitioning for the faculty to grant a dispensation, it is also possible for an illegitimate person to petition the Holy See, directly or indirectly, for the favor of legitimacy. Such a rescript of legitimation is sometimes necessary for a person wishing to receive sacred orders. It is to be noted that the Pope could, if he wished, by a rescript, confer legitimation on any illegitimate person, whether that person be a *natural* child or a *spurious* one. However, it is certain that the Roman Pontiff is not accustomed to confer legitimacy on *nefarious and sacrilegious* offspring.[35] This does not mean that the petition should not be made in such cases. The granting of the favor depends entirely on the will of the Sovereign Pontiff who will be guided in his decision by the circumstances attending the particular case.

4. *Legitimation by Radical Sanation*

There now remains to be considered the fourth and last means of legitimation, namely, radical sanation. It is proposed to give a more extensive treatment to this mode of legitimation than could be accorded to the three modes already considered. It has already been sufficiently explained that this mode of legiti-

[33] Wernz-Vidal, *Ius Canonicum,* V, n. 615.

[34] Cappello, *De Sacramentis,* III, n. 291, 4.

[35] Gasparri, *De Matrimonio,* n. 1231; Wernz-Vidal, *op. cit.,* V, n. 663; Vlaming, *Praelectiones Iuris Matrimonii,* II, n. 685.

mation is made possible through the retrotractive force which the Church has given to radical sanation. It seems sufficient, therefore, to confine the treatment of this subject to a consideration of the force, the scope and the effects of this legitimation by radical sanation.

A. Force of Radical Sanation

Legitimation by radical sanation, like all others, depends ultimately on the will of the law-giver who established it and from whom it draws its force and effectiveness. But, as it has been noted, in the case of radical sanation it is the will of the legislator that, by a fiction of the law, the dispensations will reach back to the beginning of the marriage. The actual results of this retrotraction to the past is that the marriage is considered as if it had been valid from the beginning and the children are regarded as if they had been born of a valid marriage. The practical result is that the children obtain their legitimation by the mere operation of radical sanation. Nothing further is required in order that this mode of legitimation produce its effects.[36] In the first place it is not necessary for the one seeking the favor of sanation specifically to request legitimation in order that it be obtained. It is an essential effect of radical sanation and not a separate concession. In the second place its concession is so intimately connected with radical sanation that there is no cause for concern, even if it is not specifically mentioned in the rescript, although mention of it ought not to be omitted in the petition, since it constitutes another reason for granting the request. In the third place legitimation of the offspring through radical sanation produces its effects even in a case where the parents, the offspring himself, or some third party would not be desirous or would possibly even be unwilling that the favor of legitimation be granted.

The power of radical sanation as a mode of legitimation is nowhere better exemplified than in the case of a child being

[36] Gasparri, *De Matrimonio*, n. 1231.

legitimated in this manner, even when the marriage of its parents is not convalidated. When this happens the favor is one of radical sanation improperly so called,[37] for, lacking the effect of convalidation, it is scarcely more than a shadow of true radical sanation and would be considered little more than a mere rescript of legitimation, if it were not for its mode of operation. This type of radical sanation is possible in two instances. It is possible first of all when there can be no question of convalidating the marriage, because one or both of the parties has become insane.[38] In such a case the Church is accustomed not to convalidate the marriage, particularly if the insanity is perpetual. But this practice of the Church is also followed for cases of temporary insanity at least for the period during which the insanity perdures. In the second place this type of sanation is possible and useful in a case where one or both of the parties to the marriage have died. The Code does not make any distinction between radical sanation in its proper and improper sense. Indeed there is no need of the Code making any distinction, for the mode of operation is identical and only the effects which are produced are different.[39] As it has been previously noted, the first recorded instance of radical sanation was one in which one of the parties to the marriage had died and legitimation was the only effect desired and produced.

The fact that there can be no convalidation of the marriage in either of the two cases noted in the foregoing paragraph, does not in any way nullify the power of the Roman Pontiff to grant legitimation through radical sanation. The death or insanity of one or both of the parties would, it is true, make it impossible for radical sanation to produce its first and chief effect, namely, convalidation. In order that there be a convalidation of marriage it is necessary that there be a marriage to convalidate. But there is no marriage to convalidate if one of the parties has died. It

[37] Payen, *De Matrimonio*, n. 2607.

[38] Gasparri, *De Matrimonio*, n. 1222; Wernz-Vidal, *Ius Canonicum*, V. n. 659.

[39] Gonzalez lib. IV, tit. XVII, n. 23; De Justis, *De Dispens. Matrim.*, lib. I, cap. VII, n. 296.

is also necessary for convalidation that the parties be persevering in their marital consent at the moment the favor of radical sanation is granted. But this consent is virtually or actually extinct in a party who is insane.[40] On the other hand, however, since there is no question of convalidating a marriage or of contracting a new marriage, there is nothing to prevent the Roman Pontiff from granting the favor of radical sanation to the union as it existed prior to the death or insanity of the parties. This is true because in this case, as in all other cases of radical sanation, the dispensations will reach back to the beginning of the marriage and thus, by a fiction of the law in respect to its canonical effects, the marriage will be considered as if it had been valid at the time the children were born. They in turn will be regarded as if they had been born in lawful wedlock and thus they are legitimated.

B. *Its Scope*

Legitimation through radical sanation extends only to the offspring already conceived or born of the marriage which is being convalidated by the sanation.[41] But radical sanation does not extend back beyond the time when the parties exchanged true marital consent. Therefore, if the parties had lived in concubinage, that is, without any exchange of marital consent, and a child had been born to them during that period, the child would not be legitimated in virtue of any radical sanation that might take place at some future time after the parties had exchanged true consent. This sanation will extend back only to that moment in which the parties exchanged marital consent and will have no effect on the period during which they lived in concubinage. Therefore another means of legitimation must be sought for such a child.

Two cases offer themselves for solution. The first is the case of a *natural* child, that is, one born of parents who were capable

[40] Wernz-Vidal, *Ius Canonicum,* V, n. 657, footnote 14.

[41] De Justis, *De Disp. Matrim.,* lib. I, cap. VII, n. 294; Corradus, *Praxis Disp. Apost.,* lib. VIII, cap. III, n. 54.

of marriage either at the child's conception, during the period of gestation or at its birth. If this child were born after the parents had exchanged true but juridically ineffective marital consent, it would have a twofold title to legitimation if the marriage of the parents were convalidated by radical sanation. The first title would be that which comes from the subsequent marriage of the parents, and the second title would be that which follows from the retrotractive force of radical sanation. But, if the child was born while the parents were living in concubinage, it would have only one title to legitimation if the marriage of the parents was later convalidated by radical sanation. That sole title would be the one flowing from the subsequent marriage of the parents. There would be no title of legitimation by reason of the sanation, because the sanation would not reach back to the time the child was born, namely, before the parents exchanged marital consent. The second case concerns a *spurious* child, that is one born of parents who were not capable of marriage at the child's conception, during the period of gestation or at its birth. If the child was born after the parents exchanged marital consent, it will be legitimized by radical sanation. But if it was born before the parents exchanged marital consent, it will not be legitimized by the retrotractive force of radical sanation, because that force will not extend back to the time when the child was born. Neither will it be legitimized by reason of the subsequent marriage of the parents, for it is not a *natural* child. It remains to be seen, then, whether or not it is possible for such a child to obtain legitimation in virtue of the provisions of Canon 1051 or whether recourse must be had to a rescript of the Roman Pontiff.

As it has already been pointed out in the consideration of Canon 1051 *sacrilegious* and *adulterine* children never obtain legitimation in virtue of the provisions of this canon. Consequently for them, recourse must be had to legitimation through a rescript of the Pope. But having excluded these, there still remain those children who are *merely spurious* or who are *incestuous*. Illegitimates of both these classes are born of parents who are laboring under impediments that are dispensable and whose marriage can be convalidated by radical sanation, because the sanation will carry with it a dispensation from the diriment impediment under consideration. But the question is, will the dispensation that accompanies sanation also carry with it the legitimation of the child which was born before the parties exchanged their marital consent? If it does, the legitimation will be for the future only, that is, not for the time prior to the granting of the dispensation, and will not be as full as that legitimation that results from radical sanation. If it does not, then recourse must be had to the Holy See for a rescript of legitimation.

It seems safe to say that the answer to this question is in the affirmative. The very wording of Canon 1051 seems to lend support to this opinion, for it is stated there that legitimation is conceded by a dispensation from a diriment impediment, if it is granted in accordance with the law. No distinction is made regarding the purpose for which this dispensation is granted, that is, it does not seem to make any difference, as far as legitimation is concerned, whether the dispensation is granted for the purpose of a simple convalidation or for the sake of a radical sanation. Consequently it seems certain that a *merely spurious* or *incestuous* child, which was born prior to the exchange of marital consent on the part of its parents, will be legitimated at the time the parents receive the favor of radical sanation. But in this case the legitimation will be an effect of the dispensation from the diriment impediment, in accordance with the provisions of Canon 1051. It will not be an effect of the retrotractive force of radical sanation.

The foregoing matter was concerned with the classes of illegitimates who are not and who cannot be legitimated by radical sanation. It is now necessary to consider those who can be legitimated in this manner. In brief, it may be stated that the scope of radical sanation extends to all those children who are born or who are yet to be born of the marriage which is receiving the sanation. By this is meant all the children born or conceived after the parents exchanged marital consent. It does not matter how old these children are, for, by reason of the retrotractive force of radical sanation which reaches back to the moment when the parties exchanged their consent, these children will enjoy the benefit of legitimation as from the time of their birth. Therefore, *natural* children and those who are *merely spurious* as well as those who are *incestuous* will be legitimated by the retrotractive force of radical sanation provided they were born after their parents exchanged marital consent. Concerning children who are *sacrilegious, nefarious* and *adulterine*, special notice must be taken of each class.

Sacrilegious children fall into two separate groups. In the first group will be those children who were born of a valid marriage, but whose parents were forbidden the use of marriage at the time of the child's conception.[42] This prohibition to use the marriage, which still continues as a valid union, may have arisen from the obligations imposed either by solemn religious profession, by sacred orders or by simple pofession in the Society of Jesus.[43] For the children born in these circumstances there will be no possibility of legitimation by radical sanation, inasmuch as the marriage from which they were born was already valid. Consequently they must seek legitimation through a rescript of the Roman Pontiff.

In the second group of *sacrilegious* children will belong all those who have been born of a marriage attempted by those who were already incapable of contracting marriage because of sacred orders, because of solemn religious profession or because of simple profession in the Society of Jesus. Is it possible for these children to be legitimized by radical sanation? At an earlier period this was a debated question, some canonical writers feeling that it was at least doubtful whether the Roman Pontiff could grant radical sanation for marriages contracted with the diriment impediments arising out of sacred orders or solemn profession.[44] Their doubt was founded on their opinion that these marriages were rendered invalid by divine law because of the vows.

[42] Canon 1114.

[43] Canon 1073. In respect to simple profession in the Society of Jesus it is to be noted that by an Apostolic privilege the same obligations arise from their simple profession as would otherwise arise only from solemn profession. Cf. Gregorius XIII, Const., *"Ascendente Domino,"* 25 Maii, 1584, § 22—*Fontes,* n. 153.

[44] Joannes Andreae, C. XIII, X, *qui filii sint legitimi,* n. 30; Panormitanus, C. XIII, X, *qui filii sint legitimi,* n. 12.

This opinion was rejected at an early date and today there is no question raised concerning the power of the Pope to grant radical sanation for these marriages.[45] Therefore it must be answered in the affirmative that sacrilegious children can be legitimated through the radical sanation of their parents' marriage. But this does not mean that it is customary for the Church to extend this favor to such children. Consequently it would seem that for them recourse to the Holy See for direct legitimation is the only alternative.

In regard to the two remaining classes of ***spurious*** children, namely, ***nefarious*** and ***adulterine*** children, it may be said at once that neither will benefit from legitimation by radical sanation. The ***nefarious*** children cannot obtain this benefit. Inasmuch as they are born of parents who are related by consanguinity in the direct line, the effects of radical sanation can in no way reach them, since the marriage of their parents is one which the Church never convalidates or permits. It cannot permit or convalidate such a marriage if the parents are related in the first degree of consangunity in the direct line, because all theologians acknowledge that this is an impediment of the divine natural law.[46] For the cases in which the parents are related in other degrees of consanguinity in the direct line the Church has never, as far as can be ascertained, granted a dispensation for the marriage, since it is not only possible, but strongly probable, that such a marriage is also forbidden by the divine law.[47] For ***nefarious*** children, therefore, the only hope for legitimation is in having recourse to the Holy See for this favor.

Adulterine children, finally, cannot hope for legitimation through radical sanation. In the first place they cannot hope for it if their parents are still laboring under the diriment impediment of *ligamen*. Because this impediment, being an enactment of the divine natural and positive law, cannot be removed by a dispensa-

[45] Sanchez, *De Sancto Matrimonii Sacramento,* tom. III, disp. VII, lib. VIII, n. 9.

[46] Cappello, *De Sacramentis,* III, n. 518, 1; Gasparri, *De Matrimonio,* n. 702.

[47] Cappello, *op. cit.,* III, n. 518, 2; Payen, *De Matrimonio,* n. 1440, 2.

tion of the Church, for the Church has no power over the effects of the divine law. In the second place they cannot hope for legitimation through radical sanation even if the impediment of *ligamen* has ceased and the parents are now free to marry. For the Code definitely states that it does not grant radical sanation for such marriages after the impediment has ceased, not even for the time subsequent to the cessation of the impediment.[48] For *adulterine* children, then, as for *nefarious* and *sacrilegious* children, the only hope for legitimation is to have recourse to the Holy See for a rescript of legitimation.

The scope of legitimation by radical sanation also includes those children who are already legitimate by reason of having been born of a putative marriage. Thus, by means of sanation these children acquire legitimacy by a second title.[49] This concludes the list of those who come within the scope of legitimation by radical sanation, as well as those who are excluded from it. It now remains to be seen what are the canonical effects of legitimation by radical sanation.

C. *Its Effects*

The canonical effect of legitimation is the restoration of that juridic capacity which is proper to those who are born in lawful wedlock.[50] But the extent of this restoration depends on the means by which legitimation is conferred. In other words, a fuller restoration of this juridic capacity will be obtained by one means than by another. For this reason, the legitimation that is conferred by a rescript of the Roman Pontiff is called *minus plena*.[51] That which is conferred *ipso iure* is called *plena*.[52] That which is affected by radical sanation is frequently termed *plenissima*.[53] It is according to this threefold division that one must

[48] Canon 1139, § 2.
[49] Wernz-Vidal, *Ius Canonicum*, V, n. 671.
[50] Payen, *De Matrimonio*, n. 2171.
[51] Cappello, *De Sacramentis*, III, 751, 3.
[52] Payen, *De Matrimonio*, n. 2172.
[53] Payen, *op. cit.*, n. 2600.

determine the measure of juridic capacity which has been conferred on the legitimated person.

Legitimation *per rescriptum pontificis* is termed *minus plena* because the person legitimated in this manner may not enjoy complete juridic capacity for those offices, honors and dignities which require legitimacy. Such a person will obtain only that measure of capacity which is conferred on him expressly in the rescript. Therefore the wording and tenor of the rescript must be interpreted and applied in strict accordance with its intended import.[54]

Legitimation which is conferred *ipso iure* is termed *plena,* because according to the law such persons are made equal to those who are born legitimate, in all things, unless the law expressly states otherwise in certain specific instances. The law expressly states otherwise in respect to the requirements for the cardinalitial dignity, the episcopacy and the offices of Abbot and Prelate *Nullius*.[55] Therefore, even those who enjoy the legitimation which is termed *plena* are nevertheless excluded by law from these three dignities. In all other things they enjoy the same capability as those of legitimate birth. Thus, those who obtain legitimation *ipso iure* are considered to be legitimate children in the sense of Canon 1363 and are therefore eligible for admission to the seminary.[56]

Legitimation by means of radical sanation, although it is granted *ipso iure,* is spoken of as *legitimatio plenissima,* because this type of legitimation is effective *ex tunc,* that is, from the moment when the first marriage celebration took place. Therefore, any children legitimated by radical sanation, whether they be *natural, merely spurious, sacrilegious* or *incestuous* children, are regarded as having been born of a valid marriage. However, if the fact that the children are regarded as having been born of a valid marriage is the only reason for calling it *legitimatio plenissima,* it would not seem to deserve this special title, unless these children also enjoy a greater juridic capacity than *natural* children

[54] Cappello, *op. cit.,* III, n. 751, 3.

[55] Canons 232, § 2, 1°; 320, § 2; 331, § 1, 1°.

[56] Pont. Comm. Interpr. 13 Jul., 1930—AAS, XXII (1930), 365.

who are legitimated by the subsequent marriage of their parents,[57] for they too are regarded, by a fiction of the law, as having been born of a valid marriage. In brief, unless the children who are legitimated by radical sanation are thereby eligible for all ecclesiastical honors, offices and dignities including the cardinalate, the episcopacy, and the offices of Abbot and Prelate Nullius, this legitimation differs little, if any, from that which is termed *legitimatio plena*.

The question to be considered at this point is not whether the Sovereign Pontiff could confer on those who are legitimized through radical sanation the eligibility for the three offices mentioned in the previous paragraph. It is absolutely certain that he could, for the qualifications for these offices are a matter of ecclesiastical law. But the question is one of fact, namely, whether this eligibility is an effect of legitimation by radical sanation. Payen states that it seems more reasonable to accept the affirmative view and gives as his reasons: (1) that inasmuch as the dispensation from the impediment is regarded as having been granted before the marriage, the offspring is looked on as having been born of a valid marriage; (2) that it is not certain that the canons in which the qualifications for these offices are set down are any obstacle to this view.[58] Cappello merely makes the general statement that those who are legitimated by radical sanation are not bound by the exceptions contained in Canon 1117.[59] Other authors, without specifically mentioning this question in relation to these particular offices, also state in general terms that those who are legitimated by radical sanation are thereby rendered *"habiles quoad omnes effectus canonicos"*.[60] But neither the reasons advanced by Payen nor the very general and unconvincing statements by Cappello and others seem sufficient to permit one to

[57] Payen, *De Matrimonio*, n. 2177, 3; Cappello, *De Sacramentis*, III, n. 750.

[58] *De Matrimonio*, n. 2600.

[59] *De Sacramentis*, III, n. 857.

[60] Gasparri, *De Matrimonio*, n. 1213; Wernz-Vidal, *Ius Canonicum*, V, n. 671; Vromant, *Ius Missionariorum*, V, *De Matrimonio*, n. 248.

overlook certain arguments that might be adduced in support of a negative view on this question.

In the first place, although it is altogether reasonable to hold fast to the view that legitimation by radical sanation renders the legitimated person *habilis quoad omnes effectus,* inasmuch as he is considered as having been born of a valid marriage, nevertheless it does not seem to be in accord with the mind of the legislator to say that such a person is not bound by the exceptions of Canon 1117. For, even granting the fact that *per se* and by its very nature radical sanation is capable of producing the fullest legitimation and therefore of restoring the fullest juridic capacity, it does not follow that the Sovereign Pontiff has not actually limited this effect. The very wording of Canon 1117 seems to contain a very clear and explicit declaration of the mind of the legislator on the effect of legitimation and at the same time to set a limit to the extent of eligibility conferred by legitimation. But to say that the limitation of this canon does not apply to those legitimated by radical sanation would seem to defeat the very purpose of the limitation therein contained.

In the second place it does not seem entirely correct to say that the canons which prescribe the qualifications necessary for Cardinals, Bishops, and Abbots and Prelates *Nullius* do not offer any obstacle to the view that those legitimated by radical sanation are thereby rendered eligible for these various dignities and offices. These canons do not contain all new legislation, but for the most part renew the legislation that has been in force for centuries. Therefore, in accordance with the norm established in Canon 6, 3°, those things which agree with the old law must be judged according to the old law. Now, in respect to the requirement of legitimate birth for the dignity of the Cardinalate, Canon 232, §2, 1°, renews the law enacted by Pope Sixtus V on December 3, 1586.[61]

[61] Const. *"Postquam,"* § 12.—"Praeterea, qui Cardinales creandi erunt, legitimis, et honestis sint exorti natalibus, neque ulla prorsus labe, aut illegitimorum natalium suspicione quovis modo laborent, sed omni macula, et impuritate careant, alioquin ad tam eminentem dignitatis gradum, penitus inhabiles, et illius incapaces sint, et esse censeantur. . . . Ideo ut puriori dignitati puriores natales respondeant, quoscumque illegitime natos, . . .

But it is evident from the prescriptions of this constitution that Pope Sixtus V required absolute and not merely juridic legitimacy of those who were to be raised to the dignity of the Cardinalate. It is true, he specifically deals with those who are legitimated by the subsequent marriage of their parents and positively excludes them from the ranks of the Cardinals. But it seems idle and inconsequent to suggest that his detailed mention of those who are legitimated by the subsequent marriage of their parents and his consequent positive exclusion of them from the dignity of the Cardinalate can be urged to show that his less specific mention of those who are legitimated in a way other than that effected by the parents' subsequent marriage (including therefore the case of legitimation by radical sanation) implies their non-exclusion from the Cardinalitial rank. Pope Sixtus V certainly was not unaware or unmindful of the operation and effects of radical sanation when he published his constitution. Yet he concedes no particular privilege and makes no specific grant in favor of this mode of legitimation. On the contrary, he seems definitely to exclude *all* classes of legitimated persons by his use of general and comprehensive clauses when pointing to other modes of legitimation than that which is effected by the parents' subsequent marriage. The text of the constitution reveals that even such persons who had received a papal dispensation, in whatsoever way it may have been granted, were still to be considered permanently disqualified for obtaining promotion to the Cardinalate.

In view of this ruling by Pope Sixtus V along with the fact that Canon 232, §2, 1° does not incontestably change the ruling set up by this Pope it would appear that there is little, if any, support for the opinion which holds that the final clause of Canon

etiam genitos ex soluto, et soluta, inter quos tunc Matrimonium constare poterat, ac postea per subsequens Matrimonium, etiam rite, et solemniter in facie Ecclesiae contractum, vel alias legitimatos, et quomodolibet habilitatos, et natalibus restitutos, ac quorumvis bonorum capaces effectos, etiam si cum eis, ut hanc ipsam dignitatem obtinere valeant, super defectu natalium fuerit expresse, et in specie auctoritate Apostolica quomodolibet dispensatum, nihilominus praedictae Cardinalatus dignitatis prorsus incapaces, et ad eam obtinendam perpetuo inhabiles decernimus, ac declaramus.—*Fontes,* n. 159.

1117, which provides for the maintenance of all expressly exceptional norms, nevertheless leaves intact a person's qualification for the dignity of the Cardinalate, provided only his legitimation was effected by radical sanation and not by his parent's subsequent marriage.

But if persons, though they be legitimated by means of radical sanation, are none the less bound by the exception of Canon 232, §2, 1°, in reference to the Cardinalate, then these same persons are bound by the similar exceptions safeguarded in Canon 1117 in reference to the Episcopate and the offices of Abbots and Prelates *nullius*.[62] These canons are parallel in structure as well as in their canonical import with the canon prescribing the qualifications required in persons who are to be appointed to the dignity of the Cardinalate. Furthermore, the factor of legislative consistency encourages the legal presumption that the legislator is desirous of setting the standard of qualifications in reference to legitimacy of birth on an altogether unimpeachable basis for the Episcopate as well as for the Cardinalate. It does not at all seem likely that in this respect he would enhance the juridical prestige of the Cardinalate which is of ecclesiastical institution, to the possible relative detriment of the innate dignity ofthe Episcopate which is of divine foundation.

It is true that the former legislation, which set forth the requisite qualifications for persons who were to be invested with the dignities and offices of episcopal and inferior prelates, did not contain the same strong and direct wording concerning the exclusion of legitimated persons as that contained in the prescriptions in reference to the Cardinalate. If, then, the present law substantially reechoes the legal dictates of the past, must it be acknowledged that the law of the Code is less determinate and by consequence less exacting, in its statements of the personal requirements of legitimacy of birth in relation to bishops and inferior prelates than in reference to Cardinals? The answer must still remain in the negative, for, in addition to what has already been submitted in support of this conclusion, it must also be

[62] Canons 331, § 1, 1° and 320, §2.

remembered that in the former law the legislator required in reference to even lower dignities and offices than those of the bishops and the inferior prelates a status of absolute and not merely juridic legitimacy.[63] Surely, unless there be express legislation to the contrary, it is eminently reasonable to assume that no less was required of prospective bishops and inferior prelates than of those who ranked below them. For both classes, then, the requirement was one of absolute and not merely juridic legitimacy. And in this connection one cannot ignore the fact that legitimation by radical sanation confers nothing more than a juridical status of legitimacy. It is metaphysically impossible that radical sanation confer an absolute legitimacy or that it restore to a person a status he has never enjoyed—that of objective legitimacy. Absolute and objective legitimacy is proper only to those who were conceived or born of a valid or putative marriage and to no others as it is evident from the norm established in Canon 1114.

Two other questions are usually considered in respect to the effects of legitimation by radical sanation. The first concerns the prejudice that may be offered by means of this legitimation to the rights of a third party. The second question concerns the effects of this legitimation upon matters which are subject to the civil law. Neither question is of any great practical value today and therefore they can be accorded a very summary treatment. The first question, namely, the one relative to the prejudice that may be offered to the rights of a third party, deals with the right of succession and inheritance that would ordinarily belong to the first legitimate child born of the marriage.[64] It is the accepted doctrine that the Roman Pontiff by his act of legitimation in virtue of radical sanation can confer on a person the right to any succession and inheritance that would have been his if he had been born legitimate, even if by such an action the right of a third

[63] Gregorius XIV, const. "*Onus Apostolicae,*" 15 Maii, 1591, §§ 9 et 12—*Fontes,* n. 171.

[64] Schmalzgrueber, *Ius Ecclesiasticum Universum,* lib. V, (pars IV), tit. XVII, *qui filii sint legitimi,* n. 122.

person seems to be prejudiced.[65] The reason advanced for this doctrine is that the detriment accruing to a third party cannot impede the power of the Pope to legitimize a person in such a way that he will be considered as having been born of a valid marriage and therefore as being eligible for this succession and inheritance. However, it is not to be presumed that the Roman Pontiff wishes to injure the acquired rights of a third person in this manner and therefore, unless this right is expressly conferred in the rescript of sanation, it is not to be presumed.[66]

The second question concerns the effects of legitimation by radical sanation in respect to those things which fall under the civil law. It is now the unquestioned doctrine of canonists that, by radical sanation, the Roman Pontiff can legitimize a person directly for all things spiritual and temporal in the territories belonging to the Church,[67] but that outside the temporal sovereignity of the Church the Roman Pontiff can grant legitimation directly only in reference to spiritual effects and indirectly also in regard to civil and temporal effects by means of radical sanation.[68] Today this power is no longer acknowledged by civil authorities and would have little application unless, by reason of a concordat, certain States would accept these effects of radical sanation as sufficient to fulfill the requirements in their civil law.[69]

[65] Sanchez, *De Sancto Matrimonii Sacramento,* tom. III, disp. VII, lib. VIII, n. 6.

[66] De Justis, *De Disp. Matrimon.,* lib. I, cap. VII, n. 293.

[67] Gasparri, *De Matrimonio.* n. 1213.

[68] Gonzalez, *Commentaria in Decretales Gregorii IX,* lib. IV, tit. XVII, *qui filii sint legitimi,* n. 25.

[69] Cappello, *De Sacramentis,* III, n. 857, 1.

CHAPTER IV

THE DISPENSATION FROM THE RENEWAL OF CONSENT

One of the three elements that constitute radical sanation is the dispensation from the obligation of renewing marital consent. It naturally finds a place only in radical sanation properly so called, for it is only in this type of radical sanation that there is any question of a convalidation of marriage. It does not really find a place in radical sanation improperly so called, for that type of sanation seeks only the legitimation of the children in cases where one or both parties to a marriage are dead or insane. In radical sanation properly so called, if both parties are dispensed from the renewal of consent, the radical sanation is perfect. If only one of the parties is dispensed from this obligation the sanation is only partial or imperfect. But in either case the dispensation remains as one of the features distinguishing radical sanation from simple convalidation. However, in order to have a clear idea of the importance and force of this dispensation, it seems advisable to give a brief consideration to the obligation of renewing consent for simple convalidation before moving on to an explanation of the dispensation itself. For this reason this chapter has been divided into two articles, the first treating of the obligation to renew consent and the second dealing with the dispensation from this obligation.

ARTICLE I. THE OBLIGATION TO RENEW CONSENT

A. Source of the Obligation

A marriage may be invalid because of defect of consent, because of defect of form or because of the presence of a diriment impediment. But whatever be the reason for the invalidity, the marriage must be convalidated. The course of action to be pursued in the convalidation of the marriage will, with but one exception, vary according to the source of the invalidity. The one item that is common to the various ways in which marriages are usually convalidated is the obligation of renewing marital consent. The obligation still binds even if both parties had originally given true marital consent and had never revoked it.[1] The manner, however, in which this obligation must be fulfilled is conditioned upon the nature of the source from which the invalidity of the marriage arises. The obligation differs in its nature and execution in accordance with the different sources from which the nullity of the marriage derives its origin and continued subsistence. These sources are: defect of consent, defect of form, a diriment impediment.

When a marriage is invalid because of defect of consent, it is evident that an essential element of marriage, required by the natural law, is lacking. Therefore, before the marriage can be convalidated, the root of the marriage, namely, the consent, must be supplied. It is evident, then, that in the convalidation of a marriage which is invalid because of defect of consent, the renewal of consent is a requirement that is based on the natural law.[2] This renewal of consent is also an obligation of the ecclesiastical law which interprets and defines the natural law.[3]

When a marriage is invalid because of defect of form, it is altogether possible, and even likely, that the parties have exchanged a marital consent that was of itself naturally sufficient for marriage if it were not made ineffective by the lack of the juridical form. But even in this case the parties will be required to renew their consent in order to convalidate their marriage. However, in this instance the obligation of renewing consent will be one of ecclesiastical law only, without any foundation in the natural law.[4] It is required by the ecclesiastical law in order

[1] Canon 1133, § 2.

[2] Brennan, *The Simple Convalidation of Marriage*, p. 37; Payen, *De Matrimonio*, n. 2555, 1.

[3] Canon 1136, § 1.

[4] Payen, *op. cit.*, n. 2555, 2.

that the Church's law which demands a certain canonical form will be fulfilled. It is not required by the natural law, because the consent already given by the parties is sufficient to fulfill the requirements of that law. The fact that the ecclesiastical law requires that a particular form be observed does not render the first consent of the parties naturally insufficient, but it does render it juridically ineffective.

When a marriage is invalid because of a diriment impediment of ecclesiastical law, the mere cessation or dispensation of the impediment is not of itself sufficient to effect the convalidation of the marriage. There must be a renewal of consent. But in this instance, as in the case of a marriage that is invalid because of a defect of form, the renewal of consent is required merely by ecclesiastical law and not by the divine positive or natural law.[5] For, if the parties have already exchanged true marital consent, the specific demand of the natural law has already been fulfilled and without a specific prescript of the ecclesiastical law demanding a renewal of consent, the marriage would validate itself once the impediment ceased or had been removed by a dispensation. But, whether the marriage was invalid because of an impediment of the divine law or an impediment of ecclesiastical law, it is clear that the ecclesiastical law now requires a renewal of consent for convalidation.[6]

B. *Fulfillment of the Obligation*

The fulfillment of the obligation to renew marital consent is a matter of grave duty, binding even those parties whose marriage is being convalidated at a time when death is imminent.[7] Even for these cases the renewal of consent is required for the validity of the marriage, unless the obligation has been expressly abrogated by a dispensation. The question here to be considered will not include this factor of dispensation; it is concerned for the present with the fulfillment of the obligation of renewing

[5] Payen, *op. cit.*, n. 2555, 3.

[6] Canon 1133, § 1.

[7] Vide Canon 1043.

consent, which every case of simple convalidation presupposes and demands in some form or other. The manner in which the parties are required to fulfill this will differ according to the circumstances governing each particular case. But in any event the renewal of consent must consist of an entirely new act of the will on the part of the one making the renewal of consent.[8] This new act of the will must conform to the dictates of Canon 1081, §2, which declares that: "Matrimonial consent is an act of the will by means of which the contracting parties mutually yield and accept the permanent and exclusive right which each is to have to the other's body for the performance of acts which of their nature are meant and adapted for the procreation of children."

When the marriage is null because of a diriment impediment of ecclesiastical law, two things are required for convalidation. First the impediment must be removed by a dispensation. Secondly there must be a renewal of consent.[9]

If the impediment is public, that is, one that can be proved in the external forum, the renewal of consent must be made by both parties in the juridical form prescribed by the Code, namely, before a priest and two witnesses.[10] Therefore, if it happens that one of the parties is unaware of the nullity of the marriage or of the existence of the impediment, it is necessary that this party be informed of the impediment and of his or her obligation to renew consent.[11]

If the impediment is occult, that is, one that cannot be proved in the external forum, although it is known to both parties, the renewal of consent must be made by both parties, but it can be done privately and secretly.[12] This means that in a case where the legitimate form has already been observed, but the marriage is invalid because of an occult impediment, the parties can make

[8] Canon 1134.

[9] Canon 1133, § 1.

[10] Canon 1135, § 1.

[11] Payen, *De Matrimonio*, n. 2557.

[12] Canon 1135, § 2.

their renewal of consent privately, that is, without any particular ceremony and they can do it secretly, that is, without witnesses and without the knowledge of any other persons.[13] The renewal of consent, however, must consist of an external act manifested by the parties in each other's presence.

The foregoing paragraphs demonstrate the fact that the law requires a renewal of consent for simple convalidation and at the same time illustrates the point that the manner of fulfilling this obligation will vary according to the circumstances governing each case. This is the normal rule and usual practice. However, there do exist certain parties who will refuse to make this renewal of consent and likewise there are times and circumstances when it will be impossible or at least inadvisable to require that this renewal be made. If it be refused in any case where the union is null and void because of a continually defective consent throughout the past, then, of course, even a radical sanation is powerless since the very basis for its operation is lacking. But if the renewal of consent be refused in a case where the marriage is invalid by reason of a defect of form or in view of the obstacle of a diriment impediment of ecclesiastical law, and yet the marital consent originally given by the parties is still persevering, then conditions may arise in which the Church can proceed to the convalidation of the marriage by means of a radical sanation. Such a procedure implies a dispensation from the normally required renewal of consent.

Article II. Dispensation from the Obligation to Renew Consent

Canon 1138, § 3.—Dispensatio a lege de renovando consensu concedi etiam potest vel una tantum vel utraque parte inscia.

The wording and the content of the third paragraph of Canon 1138 offer no special difficulty. It is nothing more than a practical

[13] Brennan, *Simple Convalidation of Marriage*, p. 57.

application of Canon 37. It is to this latter canon, then, that one must appeal in order to understand the force of Canon 1138, §3.

The dispensation from the obligation of renewing consent is a rescript of favor. Like all such rescripts it can be obtained for someone without his consent. This means that a dispensation from some law can be given to a person, even if he himself does not request it and even if he is unaware of the fact that another is requesting it for him. It also means that a dispensation can be given to one who is unwilling to request it or accept it. For the validity of the dispensation depends on the will of the law-giver and not on the will of the person who is dispensed from the law. Therefore, it is easy to understand how a dispensation from the obligation of renewing consent can be granted in radical sanation, even when one or both parties are unaware of the fact that it is being granted. They are merely the recipients of the favor and not the source of the favor; consequently their ignorance or willingness will have no bearing on the matter.

It is to be noted, however, that in a case in which both parties are unwilling to receive the favor of this dispensation the Church generally does not grant the dispensation.[14] There are two possible exceptions in which the Church might nevertheless grant this dispensation, even when both parties are unwilling. The first would be in an instance of a general sanation given for a large group of invalid marriages. The second would be in a case in which the Church, for extraordinary reasons, wishes to legitimize the offspring of the invalid marriage. Generally, however, the unwillingness on the part of both parties to accept the dispensation from the renewal of consent would be a basis for suspecting the perseverence of consent which is necessary for radical sanation.

[14] Cappello, *De Sacramentis*, III, n. 852.

CHAPTER V

CONDITIONS FOR RADICAL SANATION

Canon 1139, § 1.—Quodlibet matrimonium initum cum utriusque partis consensu naturaliter sufficiente, sed iuridice inefficaci ob dirimens impedimentum vel ob defectum formae legitimae, potest in radice sanari, dummodo consensus perseveret.

§ 2.—Matrimonium vero contractum cum impedimento iuris naturalis vel divini, etiamsi postea impedimentum cessaverit, Ecclesia non sanat in radice, ne a momento quidem cessationis impedimenti.

Canon 1140, § 1.—Si in utraque vel alterutra parte deficiat consensus, matrimonium nequit sanari in radice, sive consensus ab initio defuerit, sive ab initio praestitus, postea fuerit revocatus.

§ 2.—Quod si consensus ab initio quidem defuerit, sed postea praestitus fuerit, sanatio concedi potest a momento praestiti consensus.

There are four conditions necessary for the radical sanation of an invalid marriage. If all four conditions are present, the radical sanation of the marriage will be perfect and complete. Two of these conditions concern the consent of the parties, namely, its presence and its perseverance. A third condition pertains to the nullifying obstacle to the marriage and the fourth looks to the cause for granting this favor. The first three conditions are explicitly enumerated in Canon 1139, § 1, while the fourth is evident from the very nature of radical sanation as well as from the law set forth in Canon 84, § 1. The conditions mentioned in Canon 1139, § 1, are further clarified and explained by the provisions of Canons 1139, § 2, and 1140, §§ 1, 2. A consideration of these conditions will indicate which marriages the Church can completely sanate and which ones the church can only partially sanate. It will also be clear from these conditions which marriages the Church does not sanate as well as the ones the

Church cannot sanate. The subject matter of this chapter lends itself to the following division: Article 1. The conditions governing the consent; Article 2. The condition governing the nullifying obstacle; Article 3. Condition governing the cause for radical sanation.

Article I. Conditions Governing Consent

Two conditions, both of which govern the consent of the parties, are necessary for radical sanation. The first of these conditions requires either that the parties have entered their marriage with consent that was naturally sufficient or that they have given this consent later on. The second condition requires that this consent be enduring at the time the radical sanation is granted. These two conditions derive their great importance from the very nature and purpose of radical sanation, which is to convalidate the marriage at its root, that is, to heal the consent which has been diseased.

A. Necessity of Prior Marital Consent

It is of particular importance to note that the Code no longer requires the *"species vel figura matrimonii"* in order that radical sanation be granted. This requirement, which received so much attention from pre-Code authors, seems to have come into being as a result of the decree *"Tametsi"*, which required all marriages to be performed in the presence of a properly authorized priest and of at least two additional witnesses.[1] The effect of this decree, in those places where it was published, was to render invalid any marriages that were not contracted in accordance with its provisions. Moreover, it appears that these marriages not only were invalid because of defect of form, but also lacked the benefit of the presumption that they had been contracted with true marital intent. Consequently they were not only regarded as clandestine marriages, but they were even looked on as unions that were *manifeste fornicariae,* that is, unions that were lacking in marital

[1] Conc. Trident., sess. XXIV, *de ref. matrim.,* c. 1.

consent. This was a new attitude in respect to clandestine marriages, for prior to the decree *"Tametsi"* clandestine marriages were illicit, but they were accepted as valid, inasmuch as it was presumed that they had been contracted with marital intent and that the parties had exchanged a consent that was naturally sufficient.[2] As a result of this presumption in favor of the presence of marital consent in clandestine marriages prior to the decree *"Tametsi"*, the Church did not hesitate to grant radical sanation for any of these marriages that were discovered to be invalid because of a diriment impediment of ecclesiastical law.[2a] On the other hand, following the publication of the decree *"Tametsi"*, many canonists were of the opinion that radical sanation could not be granted for marriages that were invalid because of a diriment impediment or defect of form, unless they had been performed in accordance with the provisions of the *"Tametsi"* in those places where this decree was binding.[2b] The practical result of this attitude of the canonists towards clandestine marriages was seen in their opinion that radical sanation could not be granted for civil marriages that had been contracted in those places where the *"Tametsi"* had been promulgated.

As it has been pointed out in the section of this work which treats of the history of the legislation governing radical sanation, the increase of civil marriages in various nations led to a less rigorous attitude toward such marriages.[3] Instances of radical sanation granted for marriages that were contracted civilly became more and more numerous and the Code makes no mention of the requirement of a *species vel figura matrimonii.* This fact is to be properly understood, however, and is not to be interpreted as an implicit approval of civil marriages nor as a change of attitude on the part of the Church towards them when they are con-

[2] Carberry, *The Juridical Form of Marriage,* (Washington, 1934), p. 6; Manning, *Presumpions of Law in Marriage Cases* (Washington, 1935), p. 44.

[2a] Corradus, *Praxis Dispensationum Apostolicarum,* lib. VIII, cap. III, nn. 46-49; De Justis, *De Disp. Matrimon.,* lib. I, cap. VII, n. 271.

[2b] Wernz, *Ius Decretalium,* IV, nn. 657-658; Giovine, *De Disp. Matrimon.,* I, sect. 327; Gasparri, *De Matrimonio,* (edit. 3a, 1904), n. 1445.

[3] Vide supra, p. 40.

tracted by those who are bound to observe the juridical form prescribed by the Church. For today, as always, the Church refuses to regard civil marriages of Catholics as havng any *"species vel figura matrimonii"* and has several times spoken of it as an *"exitialis concubinatus"*.[4] However, the Church is willing to admit that it is possible, in particular cases, for the element of marital consent to be present even in civil marriages contracted by those who are bound to the juridical form prescribed by Canon Law. In other words, the Church now considers the objective truth concerning the presence or absence of marital consent in the marriage. It no longer demands the *"species vel figura matrimonii"* as it did formerly.[5]

At first sight it may seem contradictory for the Church to consider civil marriages of Catholics as nothing more than concubinal unions and yet be willing to admit the possibility of the presence of marital consent in such unions. Far from being contradictory, the present attitude of the Church is in complete accord with her most fundamental doctrines concerning the marriage of baptized persons. On the one hand she vigorously defends her sole competence to legislate for the marriages of baptized persons while denying the right of the civil authorities to intrude in this sacred province. On the other hand she must admit that her sole competence in this matter is often misunderstood or ignored by many who claim to be Catholics and that there will be some who will, in good faith or in bad, consider it sufficient to exchange their marital consent in the form prescribed by the civil law. For this latter reason the Church has declared in Canon 1086, § 1, that "the internal consent of the will is presumed to correspond to the words or signs used in the celebration of marriage". Consequently it is not to be too readily presumed that marital consent was lacking in the case of a civil marriage. However, it is to be carefully noted that the principle set forth in Canon 1086, § 1, is merely a presumption of law and as such it admits of direct and indirect

[4] Pius IX, allocutio, Sept. 27, 1852—*Fontes,* n. 515; Maroto, "Animadversiones," *Apollinaris,* II (1929), 248-249.

[5] Feije, *De Disp. Matrim.,* n. 768; Wernz, *Ius Decretalium,* IV, n. 657, note 28; Gasparri, *De Matrimonio,* n. 1225.

proof against it. For, since a "presumption is only a probable conjecture about an uncertain thing", it must yield to the truth, inasmuch as the truth alone has any real and objective value.[6]

The objective truth to which this presumption must yield can only be ascertained by determining the intention which the parties had at the time they contracted the marriage. Thus it will be discovered that in some cases a civil marriage is regarded by the parties as a mere ceremony and that at the time they went through this ceremony they did not exchange a truly marital consent, but a merely simulated one, intending to make their true exchange of consent at a later time in the form prescribed by the Church. In this case the root of marriage is lacking and radical sanation cannot be granted. Yet, it is altogether possible to find that the parties exchanged true marital consent in good faith, thus making their marriage putatively valid, or that they did so in bad faith, knowing that their marriage would be invalid because of the lack of the juridical form. In either case radical sanation can be granted validly, since the root of marriage is present.

It is evident from the foregoing that, although the Church no longer requires the *species matrimonii,* the marriage must have been entered into with consent that is naturally sufficient, that is, with consent that would meet the requirements of the natural law. This consent, which is called marital and which cannot be supplied by any human power, is defined in Canon 1081, § 2, as "an act of the will by which each party gives and accepts a perpetual and exclusive right over the body for the exercise of acts which of their very nature are meant and adapted for the procreation of children". If this consent is not present when the parties contract marriage, or rather, what appears to be marriage, their union will be numbered among those that are classified as *manifeste fornicariae* and such a union is expressly barred from the benefits of radical sanation.[7] Companionate marriages and unions of a similar nature are to be classed in this group. A very special consideration as to the presence of marital consent would

[6] Canon 1825, § 1.

[7] Benedict XIV, epist. *"Redditae Nobis,"* 5 Dec. 1744—*Fontes,* n. 350; *De Syn. Dioec.,* lib. XIII, cap. XXI, n. 7.

have to be given in the case of a common-law marriage. "Nearly half the States of this country still recognize as a valid marriage the living together of a man and woman without benefit of clergy. Such a union, based only upon mutual verbal agreement, had its origin in the pioneer conditions of American frontier life."[8] It is possible that even in such marriages there would be a true marital consent.[9] However, the likelihood is that in such marriages the marital consent, if it exists in any measure or fashion at all, is at the same time nullified in one way or another to such an extent that radical sanation can not be granted.

In examining the invalid marriage before petitioning for a radical sanation it is of paramount importance to establish whether or not the consent of the parties was nullified by any condition or circumstance whatsoever. It is not within the scope of this work to deal at length with the subject of conditional matrimonial consent. The following passage, taken from a work in which this subject is ably presented, will serve as a summary of the conditions and circumstances that can nullify marital consent:

> . . . The defects that make a marriage consent null are enumerated in the Code. [Canons 1082, §1, §2; 1083, §1, §2, nn. 1 and 2; 1086, §2; 1087, §1; 1092, nn. 2 and 4.] Some of the essentials of consent (as also the vices) are *ex parte subjecti*: consent must be *versus, liber, absolutus*; others are *ex parte objecti*: the consent must have as its object the substance of marriage and the *tria bona essentialia.* On the part of the *subject* consent is not true by simulation; not free by certain kinds of force and fear; not absolute under certain conditions, honest and possible of the past or present.
>
> On the part of the *object* consent is not valid if marriage itself is excluded by a positive act of the will, or the *jus ad copulam,* or some essential property; unity (*fides*), indissolubility (*sacramentum*). Whether this exclusion is by a substantial ignorance, substantial error or *ex industria* is irrelevant. All these beget nullity and

[8] Nimkoff, *Family Life* (New York, 1934), pp. 238-239.

[9] Woywod, *A Practical Commentary on the Code of Canon Law,* n. 1182.

> actions for the declaration of nullity. The phrase *defectus consensus* is used widely and includes any and all of these vices, this phrase is a *genus* and it should be narrowed down in a given case by singling out the particular species of defective consent. *Total* simulation respects the subject of consent, *partial* simulation the object of consent, e.g., *jus in corpus,* therefore they are of distinct natures.
>
> Defects *ex parte intellectus seu in cognitione* are: lack of reason, insanity, error and ignorance; *ex parte voluntatis seu intentione aut in libertate* are: simulation force and fear. *Vitia consensus* can invalidate the consent and the contract *jure naturae* or *jure positivo.*[10]

A further point to be noted in relation to the presence of marital consent in an invalid marriage is a fact which is established in Canon 1085, where it is declared that "the knowledge or the thought that the marriage will be null does not necessarily exclude matrimonial consent". This means that even if the parties knew, or merely thought, that their marriage would be null in the eyes of the Church because of a diriment impediment or for lack of form, the possibility of their wishing to exchange and of their actually exchanging matrimonial consent is not necessarily excluded. This is not uncommon in cases in which a Catholic attempts marriage with an unbaptized person in a civil ceremony. For the Catholic, knowing that their marriage will be null because of the disparity of worship and lack of form, may simply ignore the laws of the Church and fully intend to exchange true marital consent without having any regard for the juridic consequences or effects of that act. On the other hand, consent will necessarily and undoubtedly be excluded in a case where the parties enter a marriage that they know will be null for one cause or another, when they do so by way of experiment and choose this course with deliberation as a certain means by which they will remain free to contract another marriage if they should desire to do so.

It is now clear that before radical sanation can be granted a true marital consent must exist in the marriage. But the time when this consent began to exist in the union is also of import-

[10] Timlin, *Conditional Matrimonial Consent* (Washington, 1934), p. 228-229.

ance in order that one may determine the effects which are to follow radical sanation. If in the first place marital consent was present from the very beginning of the invalid marriage, a complete radical sanation of the marriage will be possible.[11] But if in the second place marital consent was given at the beginning but later revoked, a radical sanation will not be possible; however, if the revoked consent was again restored, a complete sanation will then be possible.[12] Finally, if the consent was lacking at the beginning of the marriage, but was given later on, a partial radical sanation will be possible, the retrotractive force extending back only to the moment in which consent was actually given.[13] The following examples will illustrate the application of this principle of partial sanation and at the same time indicate the occasions which permit only a partial sanation.

1. A marriage entered into according to the juridical form by two Catholics who are free from all impediments may be invalid because of defect of consent. Such a marriage will require a renewal of consent for its convalidation. But the manner in which this renewal of consent is to be made must be determined according to the norms contained in Canon 1136, as was briefly explained in the article concerning the renewal of consent. Generally the renewal of consent will be made without any special ceremony by the party or parties in whom the defective consent existed.

But there is one instance in which the renewal of consent must be made according to the juridical form of marriage. This will be the case when the defect of consent was not only external but also public, e.g., when a condition contrary to the substance of marriage was placed which can be proved as a fact in the external forum. For the convalidation of such a marriage two things will be required, namely, the exchange of true marital consent and the use of the juridical form. If the parties give a true marital consent by placing a new act of the will which ex-

[11] Canon 1139, § 1.

[12] Canon 1140, § 1; cf. Gasparri, *De Matrimonio*, n. 1222, 2°.

[13] Canon 1140, § 2.

presses their consent, but are unwilling to make this renewal in the presence of a priest and two witnesses, their marriage is still invalid, but a radical sanation could then be granted and thus they would be relieved of their obligation of adhering to the prescribed form. But if radical sanation is granted for this purpose, it will be only a partial sanation and its retrotractive force will extend back only to the moment when they remedied the defect of their consent.

2. A civil marriage attempted by two Catholics, who are free from all impediments, may also be null because of a secret defect of consent known only to one party. If this party later remedies the defect by a secret renewal of consent, the marriage will be still invalid because of the lack of form. If one of the parties refuses to convalidate the marriage by renewing consent according to the form as required by law, the marriage can be convalidated by radical sanation, the retrotractive effect of which will extend back to the moment when the defect of consent was remedied.

3. If a marriage is invalid because of a diriment impediment which is public, the law requires that it be convalidated by a dispensation from the impediment and a renewal of consent in the prescribed form.[13a] If the impediment is one of ecclesiastical law, the marriage can be convalidated by radical sanation. But if there had been a secret defect of consent which was later remedied, the sanation will be only a partial one, inasmuch as its retrotractive force will extend back only to the moment when the defect of consent was remedied. In this case, as in the two preceeding cases, the effects of radical sanation, especially in reference to legitimation, will be circumscribed by the fact that it is a partial, and not a complete, sanation.

B. *The Perseverance of Consent*

The second condition governing the consent requires that the marital consent of the parties still endure at the time radical

[13a] Canon 1137.

sanction is granted. This condition can no longer be questioned. in fact it has been the common doctrine of canonists since the beginning of this practice, that before radical sanation could be granted the parties must be persevering in their marital consent. The opinion of those who maintained that this was not a requirement found little or no favor in any treatment on this subject.[13b] It is to be noted at once, however, that the perseverance of consent is a condition for radical sanation properly so called, for one of the effects of this is the convalidation of the marriage. The perseverance of consent is not a requisite condition for radical sanation improperly so called, because the sole effect of this is the legitimation of the offspring.

The first thing to be noticed in reference to the perseverance of the consent of the parties is that the Code establishes a presumption in favor of it. Canon 1093 explicitly declares that "although a marriage has been contracted invalidly because of an impediment, consent once given is presumed to persevere until its revocation is established." This presumption of law in favor of the perseverance of consent holds for marriages that are invalid because of impediments of the divine or ecclesiastical law and also for those that are invalid for lack of form.[14] This presumption holds also whether or not the parties knew of the nullity of their marriage. This presumption will hold until the revocation of consent is established, that is to say, it will yield only to the truth. Therefore, direct certitude concerning the perseverance of consent is not absolutely required for radical sanation.[15] But certitude that the consent has been revoked destroys the presumption in favor of its perseverance and renders the granting of radical sanation impossible.

Since marital consent is a positive act of the will to give and accept all the rights of marriage, its revocation must also be a positive act of the will by which, explicitly or implicitly, one or

[13b] Scavini, *Theologia Moralis,* III, n. 1050; Perrone, *De Christiano Matrimonio,* II, n. 173.

[14] Payen, *De Matrimonio,* n. 1748.

[15] Payen, *op. cit.,* n. 1749.

both parties take back their own rights and return the other person's rights. This can happen only in an invalid marriage, for the indissolubility of a valid marriage prevents any efficacious revocation of marital consent.[16] The fact that there has been a revocation of marital consent can be established from evidence obtained "either from two trustworthy witnesses, or from one witness whose testimony is unimpeachable and given under oath, or (it can be established) from circumstances which, when joined together, destroy the presumption."[17] It is needless to add that the parties themselves, if they can be approached, can give the best testimony of the perseverence of their consent. But if, after radical sanation has been granted for a marriage, one or both parties claim that they had revoked their consent before sanation was granted, their claims must be rejected, unless they can produce the proof necessary to substantiate these claims. In reference to this question of establishing the revocation of consent, it is necessary to consider a variety of circumstances that will seem to point to such a revocation or that will actually establish it.

First among these circumstances is that which is spoken of as the interpretative will of one or both of the parties. This circumstance is possible only when one or both parties are unaware of the nullity of the marriage. It is rather a state of mind than any positive act of the will. Therefore radical sanation can be granted and in fact this very circumstance is considered to be a cause for conceding radical sanation.[18] This case consists in this that the parties who are ignorant of the nullity of the marriage would revoke their consent if they knew of the invalidity of the marriage. Naturally this state of mind is not to be presumed to exist in every case where one or both parties are ignorant of the nullity of the marriage, but it is to be determined from the circumstances of each specific case.

A second circumstance that might point to the revocation of

[16] Canons 1013, § 2; 1081, § 1; 1118.

[17] Vermeersch-Creusen, *Epitome Iuris Canonici,* II, n. 382.

[18] Gasparri, *De Matrimonio,* n. 1223; Wernz-Vidal, *Ius Canonicum,* V, n. 666, note 34, I.

marital consent, but which does not prove it, is a petition for complete separation from bed, board and habitation because of the discords and other causes for which this separation is generally granted.[19] Separation does not dissolve the marriage bond. Consequently, when recourse is had to this remedy rather than to nullity proceedings, it is clear that the parties intend only to end their common life, but are not revoking their marital consent, which must therefore be presumed to persevere. It is clear, of course, that the marriage in question may actually be invalid, although the parties are unaware of it. For it is safe to say that in a case such as this the parties would, if they were aware of the nullity of their marriage, seek a declaration of nullity rather than be content with a complete separation from each other. In practice, however, it is unlikely that the Church would grant radical sanation.

A third circumstance that might lead one to believe that consent has been revoked is a petition for a declaration of nullity by one or both parties who suspect that their marriage is invalid. But the fact is that, while the suit is still pending, the presumption in favor of the perseverance of consent still holds and therefore radical sanation *could* be granted.[20] But this is merely a juridic *possibility* and not by any means a *probability,* for the Holy See will not grant radical sanation under such circumstances.[21] The reason, it is said, that the presumption still holds is that, inasmuch as the parties merely suspect the nullity of their marriage and are not certain of it, they are presumed to be of the mind that they will not recede from their consent, unless the sentence of the Court is in favor of the nullity of their marriage. On the other hand, if they were certain of the existence of a nullifying impediment and petitioned for a declaration of nullity, it is rather to be presumed that they revoked their original consent, absolutely and unconditionally, even before the sentence in the case was handed down.[21a] There is a threefold reason for the

[19] Wernz-Vidal, *op. cit.,* V, n. 666, note 34, II; Gasparri, *op. cit.,* n. 1223.

[20] Wernz-Vidal, *op. cit.,* V, n. 666, note 34, VI; Gasparri, *op. cit.,* n. 1223.

[21] Cf. infra, p. 87 ff.

[21a] Wernz-Vidal, *op. cit.,* V, n. 666, note 34, VI.

Church refusing to grant radical sanation while a suit for the declaration of nullity is pending. In the first place, a suit for the declaration of nullity instituted by the parties themselves proclaims the fact that one or both parties wish to be free of the marriage, whereas through radical sanation there would be established an indissoluble bond. Secondly, in not a few cases it might happen that while the suit for nullity was pending one or both of the parties would revoke their marital consent in an absolute manner. In such cases the Church would be exposing herself to the danger of violating the divine law if she gave a radical sanation. Finally, it is difficult to reconcile the granting of sanation with the right and freedom of the parties to seek a declaration of nullity.[21b]

A fourth circumstance that might seem to indicate that there has been a revocation of marital consent is the refusal of one of the parties to renew consent in the prescribed form. However, unless this refusal to renew consent is accompanied by signs and circumstances which would prove revocation of consent, the presumption in favor of its perseverance still holds. For it is one thing to refuse to renew consent which one considers sufficient and it is quite another thing to place a positive act of the will revoking the prior consent. It frequently happens that non-Catholics cannot be persuaded to renew their consent in the juridical form prescribed by the Church, although they are perfectly willing and fully intent upon continuing in the marriage by reason of their prior marital consent. The same thing may be true, of course, when both parties are Catholics, but one of them is so ignorant of the laws of the Church or so obstinate in his refusal to observe them that he will not renew consent in the presence of a priest and two witnesses.

A fifth circumstance which will give rise to a question concerning the revocation or perseverance of consent is the final sentence in a suit for the declaration of nullity.[22] If the parties themselves or at least one party, seek the declaration of nullity

[21b] Wernz-Vidal, *op. cit.*, V, n. 666, note 34, VI.

[22] Wernz-Vidal, *Ius Canonicum*, V, n. 666, note 34, IV.

and obtain it, consent is presumed to be revoked, inasmuch as it is customary for persons to conform to a sentence favorable to themselves. But if a third party, e. g., a close relative, denounces the validity of the marriage while the parties themselves stand for its validity, consent can be presumed to persevere even if a declaration of nullity is given. In such a case radical sanation could be given and would very likely be granted.[23] On the other hand, if the parties seek a declaration of nullity and the court rules that their marriage is valid, consent is presumed to persevere. If at a later date an invalidating, but hitherto unknown impediment is discovered, radical sanation could be granted. However, in such a case the sanation would be granted conditionally, that is, on condition that only one party knew of the impediment. This would prevent any difficulties arising from a revocation of consent by the party that had once sought to obtain a declaration of nullity. It was just such a case as this that led some authors to declare that Benedict XIV had granted radical sanation when one of the parties to the marriage was suing for a declaration of nullity.[24]

The case in question concerned a petition for the radical sanation of a marriage which was known to be invalid because of an impediment that was discovered only after two petitions for a declaration of nullity had been rejected by the courts. Benedict XIV granted a radical sanation of the marriage at the petition of the husband. But his concession was a conditional one, that is, it was granted on condition that the wife did not know of the newly discovered impediment. This same Pontiff later declared that the sanation had not been effective because the condition he had added to the concession had not been verified. He further testified that by reason of his conditional concession of the sanation the woman had not lost her right to attack the marriage if she actually knew of the impediment at the time the sanation was granted.[25]

A sixth circumstance that must be considered in relation to the

[23] Wernz-Vidal, *op. cit.*, V, n. 666, note 34, VII.

[24] Cf. Wernz-Vidal, *op. cit.*, V, n. 666, note 34, V.

[25] Benedict XIV, instr. *"Cum Super,"* 27 Sept. 1755—*Bull. Rom. Cont.*, IV, 291.

perseverance of consent and the possibility of granting radical sanation is the presence of insanity in one or both of the parties.[26] In this connection there are two possible cases. The first is a case in which one of the parties is perpetually insane and has no lucid intervals. The other is a case in which the insane party does have lucid intervals. In the first case radical sanation properly so called could not be granted. The reason for this is that this type of sanation produces the convalidation of marriage as one of its effects. But there can be no convalidation of marriage without the virtual perseverance of marital consent in both parties, and a person who is no longer capable of human acts cannot be said virtually to persevere in this consent. For a case such as this radical sanation improperly so called could be granted for the purpose of procuring the legitimation of the offspring. In the second case proposed, namely, where the insane party enjoys lucid intervals, radical sanation properly so called can be granted during the lucid intervals, provided that during these intervals the use of reason is sufficiently restored and that consent is not actually revoked. However, in view of the fact that civil divorce is quite easily obtained because of the insanity of one of the parties, it is questionable whether the Church would be willing to grant radical sanation in such cases as these.

A seventh circumstance which would destroy the presumption in favor of the perseverance of consent is the act of the parties—even if placed some years after they exchanged true marital consent—by means of which they superimpose a condition which is capable of nullifying their original consent. This would happen, for instance, when the parties who already have a numerous family of children would interpose their will and intention to disown their mutual rights for the future procreation of children. Of course any agreement to exclude the future burden of children would have to amount to the placing of this condition as something contrary to the essential object of marital life, that is, as something which implies the denial of a right substantially and essentially inherent in the exchange of a matrimonial consent, before it would vitiate the previously valid matrimonial consent.

[26] Gasparri, *De Matrimonio,* n. 1222; Payen, *De Matrimonio,* n. 2615.

In a word, the agreement would have to be equivalent to a refusal by at least one of the parties to the other of the possession of the right which can eventuate in the procreation of children.[27] For if this were the nature of the agreement, it would amount to a revocation of the marital consent by which these rights were originally exchanged. But if, on the other hand, this agreement did not revoke the rights of either and only amounted to an intention of not using these rights, or of abusing them in order to prevent as far as possible the procreation of any more children, it would seem that the perseverance of consent could be presumed. In the prior case it is clear that radical sanation could not be granted. In the latter case it could be granted as long as it is certain that the simple intention of the party is to engage in the abuse of marriage and not an intention to revoke the rights of marriage. Each individual case would have to be judged according to its peculiar circumstances. But, when two people have been married for some years and are already parents of several children, it seems safe to presume that they are willing to persevere in their marital consent, even though one or both parties make a statement to the effect that there are to be no more children.

An eighth circumstance that clearly destroys the presumption in favor of the perseverance of consent is the occurrence of the impediment of perpetual impotency at some moment after the initial marital consent was exchanged but before an attempt was made to convalidate the marriage.[28] For in such a case the one in whom the impotency exists forfeits, whether willingly or not, the prerogatives of persevering in his former matrimonial consent, since it is impossible for anyone to give a valid and operative consent concerning something in relation to which he is permanently incapacitated.

Feije stated that it was not impossible to grant radical sana-

[27] Cf. Timlin, *Conditional Matrimonial Consent*, p. 307; Mahoney, Matrimonial Consent and the "safe period," *Clergy Review*, XIII (1937), 121-131.

[28] Wernz, *Ius Decretalium*, IV, n. 657, note 36; Payen, *De Matrimonio*, n. 2615.

tion in such a case in view of the fact that this mode of convalidation heals the consent given at the beginning of the marriage.[29] But the Holy Office stated that radical sanation could not be given when it was petitioned for this favor in just such a case.[30] The reason is clear. There can never be a convalidation of a marriage which is rendered impossible by the existence of a diriment impediment of the natural law, namely, the impediment of antecedent and perpetual impotency, therefore, in the face of such a circumstance the parties should be separated, if that is possible. If it is not possible, the pastor or confessor should proceed in accordance with the principles of Moral Theology, which govern the direction of such cases.

In respect to this one condition, namely, the perseverance of consent, it can be said in conclusion that the radical sanation will be valid, if both parties are persevering in their consent at the moment concession is made. For it is at the very moment of concession that convalidation occurs. Just when the moment of concession occurs will depend on the manner in which this favor is granted. If it is granted in *forma gratiosa,* it takes effect at the very moment when the superior effectively accedes to the request, which is usually the moment when he signs the rescript. If it is granted in *forma commissoria,* the moment of concession is that moment when it is executed. With these points in mind, attention can now be given to the third condition governing the nullifying obstacle.

ARTICLE II. CONDITION GOVERNING THE NULLIFYING OBSTACLE

The third condition required for the granting of radical sanation concerns the impediment which rendered the original marital consent juridically ineffective. It is one of the conditions enumerated in Canon 1139, §1 and consists in this that it must be an impediment of the ecclesiastical law or a lack of the canonical

[29] *De Impedimentis et Dispensationibus Matrimonialibus,* n. 769.

[30] *S. C. S. Officii (ad Episc. S. Alberti),* 8 Mart. 1900—*Fontes,* n. 1236.

form. Two facts are at once evident in relation to this condition. In the first place, impediments of the divine positive and the natural law are excluded. In the second place, not all impediments of ecclesiastical law are directly referred to at this point, but only those which render the marriage invalid, namely, the diriment impediments and the defect of canonical form. This does not mean that, if there are any prohibitive impediments also present, they will not be dispensed when radical sanation is granted. But this canon is concerned only with the nullifying obstacle that renders the original marital consent juridically ineffective and this the prohibitive impediments cannot do. However, if, together with a diriment impediment or defect of canonical form, there is also present a prohibitive impediment it will have to be dispensed from when radical sanation is granted. For the sake of clarity the question of impediments of the divine positive or natural law will be considered first. Thereupon a consideration of the impediments of ecclesiastical law for which sanation can be granted will follow.

A. Regarding Impediments of the Divine and Natural Law

In establishing the conditions for radical sanation, the canon first states that it can be granted for any marriage that was entered with a naturally sufficient consent which is juridically ineffective because of an impediment of the ecclesiastical law or a defect of canonical form. In relation to marriages which are invalid because of an impediment of the divine positive or natural law which is still existing the Code makes no mention in the canons on sanation. The reason for this exclusion is the lack of jurisdiction on the part of the Church over such impediments. For these impediments have their source in divine authority and can not be revoked by any human power, either by way of a complete abrogation or by way of a dispensation in a particular case. Therefore, there is and there can be no difficulty on this point when any given marriage is invalidated by an impediment that is undoubtedly an impediment of the divine positive or natural law. But what if there is a doubt about whether or not an impediment is of the divine positive or natural law? Sanchez stated very definitely that in the face of such a doubt the Roman Pontiff must not be despoiled of his power to dispense.[31] Gasparri, however, says that the power of the Roman Pontiff to dispense in such a case is doubtful and that it ought never to be used.[32] The Church does have the power to determine whether an impediment of the divine law is a diriment impediment or a prohibitive impediment.[33] But that is a different question than the one which concerns the power of the Church to dispense from a doubtful impediment of the divine law. If the question concerns an impediment or obligation of the divne law which is conditioned, that is, one which is depending on the human will, as for instance in the case of a vow, the Roman Pontiff can dispense.[34] However in this case, it is not from the observance of the law itself that a dispensation is given but it is rather the matter of the law which is taken away or changed in such a way that the obligation ceases. In other words, the material basis for the law is either removed or so altered by the dispensation that the obligation which once arose from that basis has become extinguished in consequence of the change brought about by the dispensation.[35]

Although the Church cannot dispense from an impediment of the divine law, it is possible for some of these impediments to cease and thus leave the party who was previously bound by it, free to contract a valid marriage. A practical instance of the cessation of an impediment of the divine law is found in the impediment of *ligamen* which ceases when one of the partics to the prior marriage dies or when the marriage has been legitimately dissolved. The question now arises whether or not a marriage, attempted while one of the two parties was laboring under the impediment of *ligamen*, can be convalidated by radical sanation after the impediment of *ligamen* has ceased. In relation

[31] *De Sancto Matrimonii Sacramento*, tom. III, disp. VII, lib. VIII, n. 10.

[32] *De Matrimonio*, n. 263.

[33] Canon 1038, § 1.

[34] Canons 1311 and 1313.

[35] Gasparri, *op. cit.*, n. 263.

to such a marriage two distinct points must be considered. The first point is concerned with the possibility of a perfect radical sanation for such a marriage. The second point refers to the possibility of an imperfect sanation of such a marriage.

Relative to the possibility of a perfect radical sanation for such a marriage it must be remembered that such a sanation would mean that the retrotractive force would extend back to the first celebration of the invalid marriage. It is evident, from the very nature of a perfect radical sanation, that for such a marriage the Church can not grant a perfect radical sanation. For in conceding such a sanation the Church not only dispenses from the law requiring a renewal of consent and thus accepts the consent given at the time the invalid marriage began, but also through a fiction of law it would draw the dispensation back to the beginning of the marriage and thus consider the marriage as if it had begun without any impediment and therefore as if it had been valid. But the Church cannot, even through a fiction of the law, consider a marriage to be valid which is forbidden by a diriment impediment of the divine law.[35a]

This fact being established consideration must now be given to the second point of this discussion, namely, the possibility of an imperfect sanation for such a marriage. This would mean that the retrotractive force of radical sanation would reach back only to that moment of the invalid marriage in which the impediment of *ligamen* ceased. It would also mean that only those children who were born (of the invalid marriage) after the impediment ceased would be legitimated by means of the radical sanation. This question, as it has been pointed out in an earlier part of this work, is not without an historical background.[36] There is on the one hand the example of the Sacred Penitentiary, which actually did grant such a sanation, and there is, on the other hand, a decree of the Holy Office, which declares that for such marriages radical sanation could not be granted. However, the answer to the question at hand is the one given by the Code which states

[35a] Gasparri, *op. cit.*, n. 1216.

[36] Cf. Supra, pp. 36-38.

that the Church *does* not grant sanation, perfect or imperfect, for such marriages.

When one considers the declaration of the Code that the Church does not grant radical sanation for marriages involving an impediment of the divine or natural law and at the same time realizes that cases will arise in which one or both parties may refuse to renew consent when it is required in a public manner, it would appear that every avenue of convalidation has been blocked. It appears to be the opinion of Gasparri, however, that, notwithstanding the wording of Canon 1139, §2 and the reply of the Holy Office in this matter, the same Holy Office and the other Sacred Congregations as well as the Sacred Penitentiary do grant the necessary imperfect radical sanation for some cases.[37] The action of the Holy See will depend on the circumstances surrounding the particular case. But in view of the gravity of the matter in such instances, there would seem to be little or no excuse for not making the petition for this favor to the proper congregation or to the Sacred Penitentiary, when every other effort to bring about the simple convalidation of the marriage has failed.

B. *Regarding Impediments of Ecclesiastical Law and the Lack of Form*

In the very strictest sense of the word, a marriage is *null* only when there is a lack of marital consent; for without consent there is literally *no* marriage. But, for Catholics, marriage is *invalid* only when the naturally sufficient consent of the parties is rendered juridically ineffective by an invalidating impediment of the divine or ecclesiastical law or when the juridical form of marriage prescribed by the Church has not been observed by those whom it binds. It is true that the terms *"null"* and *"invalid"* are used interchangeably and that for practical purposes it is of little importance. On the other hand, although marital unions in which the needed dispensation from an impediment

[37] *De Matrimonio,* n. 1219.

was not obtained or in the contracting of which the prescribed form was not observed, are not regarded as marriages in the eyes of the Church (and therefore are null in the broad sense), it would seem more appropriate to use the term "invalid marriage" in referring to such unions. For there is present a naturally sufficient but juridically ineffective consent in view of an extant diriment impediment or by reason of non-observance of the prescribed form. Whereas the word "null" implies non-existence the word "invalid" simply indicates that although something exists it is lacking in legal force. To a non-existent thing the law cannot accord any legal force; but to an existent thing which is minus its legal force the law can supply this lack of legal force.

It is precisely the supplying of this lack that accompanies the simple convalidation or radical sanation of an invalid marriage. Through the processes of law or through an act of the legislator legal force is given to a marriage which was hitherto lacking it. It is evident, however, that the processes of law by which an invalid act obtains legal force must have been established by the same law-giver who established the invalidating law. The divine law established no such process for marriages which are invalid because of an impediment of that law that is still extant. But if the impediment of divine law has ceased the marriage could obtain legal force of itself, as far as the divine law is concerned, without the necessity of any further formality. Actually such marriages (of Catholics) do not validate themselves upon the cessation of the impediment of the divine law because the ecclesiastical law has interposed the necessity of renewing the marital consent. The ecclesiastical law has established several processes by which legal force can be supplied to marriages lacking it because of the non-observance of the canonical form of marriage. Having the power to establish invalidating laws, the Church also has the power to give legal force to acts performed contrary to those laws. It is for this reason that in the enumeration of the conditions necessary for radical sanation, Canon 1139, §1 mentions only the diriment impediments of the ecclesiastical law and the defect of form. It is true that marriages which are invalid because of an impediment of the divine law are subject to the laws of convalidation when the impediment of the divine law has ceased, but in paragraph 2 of the same canon, the Code states that the Church does not grant sanation for such marriages.

It is clear that any marriage whatsoever that is invalid because of an impediment of ecclesiastical law or by reason of defect of form can, strictly within the possibilities of the law, be granted the favor of radical sanation. This means that no impediment of ecclesiastical law is beyond the sanative power of the Church whether the impediments be ones that have been abrogated or ones that are still binding. This is of particular importance in view of the fact that marriages which were invalid because of an impediment which has been abrogated by the Code are still invalid after the Code and obtain validity or legal force only by means of simple convalidation or radical sanation.[38]

Although every marriage that is invalid because of an impediment of ecclesiastical law can be granted the favor of radical sanation, since the jurisdiction of the Church over its own laws is not limited, nevertheless there are some impediments from which the Church is accustomed not to dispense and there are others from which the Church only rarely dispenses. Consequently the declaration of Canon 1139, §1, to the effect that "any marriage entered into with a naturally sufficient consent which is juridically ineffective because of an impediment of the ecclesiastical law can be sanated" is not to be interpreted to mean that all such marriages will be granted this favor. For, in respect to the impediments from which the Church is accustomed not to dispense or from which the Church practically never dispenses, namely, the episcopate, the priesthood and affinity in the direct line once the valid marriage which gives rise to it has been consummated, it can be safely stated that radical sanation will never be granted. This is evident from the constant practice of the Church and from the fact that these impediments are expressly excluded from the extraordinary faculties granted by law in Canons 1043-1045 and from the quinquennial faculties of local Ordinaries.

Besides these two impediments, namely, priestly orders and affinity as here qualified, from which the Church regularly does

[38] Pont. Com. Interpr., June 3, 1918—AAS, X (1918), 346.

not dispense, there are other impediments from which the Church ordinarily does not dispense for the purpose of allowing persons to contract marriage. Among these might be mentioned the impediments of age and abduction. But once a marriage has been contracted invalidly because of these and other merely ecclesiastical impediments, excepting (regularly) priesthood and affinity in the direct line, the Church dispenses from these impediments more readily in order to procure the convalidation of the marriage. Therefore, it may be said that in respect to these impediments, the favor of radical sanation will be granted if the circumstances and reasons attending the petition warrant the use of this extraordinary mode of convalidation. This would seem to be especially true of marriages that are invalid because of impediments abrogated by the Code. For there will often be an urgent reason for granting radical sanation in view of the difficulty of obtaining a renewal of consent in the prescribed form from persons who have been living together as man and wife for at least twenty years. At the same time it is to be noted that if the abrogated impediment which invalidated the marriage was not of public character, a private renewal of consent will suffice for convalidation, providing the marriage had been contracted with due form and recourse to radical sanation should seldom be necessary.

A third group of impediments of ecclesiastical law which come within the scope of this condition for radical sanation are those which are in force among the various Oriental Rites. For the most part they are almost identical with the diriment impediments of the Latin Church prior to the promulgation of the Code. In general it may be said that Latin Bishops do not possess any power to dispense from the impediments binding in the Oriental Rites.[39] Therefore, petitions for radical sanation of these marriages must be sent to the Sacred Congregation for the Oriental Church or to the Holy Office. On the other hand, Duskie states that Latin Ordinaries, Pastors and Confessors may use the

[39] Duskie, *The Canonical Status of the Orientals in the United States*, p. 178-179.

faculties of Canons 1043-1045 for their Oriental subjects.[40] Attention is called to this fact because the use of these faculties may sometimes obviate the necessity of petitioning for radical sanation in cases in which it would otherwise be necessary. It is to be noted that these canons do not grant power for radical sanation.

Up to this point the discussion of this present article has been limited to diriment impediments in the strict sense of that term. But now it is necessary to consider marriages that are invalid because of defect of form. For such marriages are not excluded from the benefit of a radical sanation. But for such marriages, as for marriages which are invalid because of a diriment impediment, radical sanation is the extraordinary mode of convalidation and should be resorted to only when urgent reasons warrant such a recourse. In the event of a marriage being invalid because of defect of form it should be convalidated according to the norm of Canon 1137, which prescribes a renewal of consent in the form prescribed by the Code. This is the rule whether the marriage is invalid because of the non-observance of the law of the Code or of the decrees *"Tametsi" or "Ne temere"*.

Under the law as it exists in the Code, the marriage of two Catholics, or of a Catholic and non-Catholic will be invalid if it is contracted in the presence of a duly authorized priest but without the necessary two witnesses. It will also lack the proper canonical form if the priest performing the marriage rite lacks the proper authorization to assist at the marriage. Finally, it will be invalid for the lack of form if it is attempted before a civil officer, or if it is enterted into before a non-Catholic minister prior to a Catholic marriage ceremony. In any of the foregoing instances the marriage will remain invalid until the prescribed canonical form has been observed or until a radical sanation has been obtained for the marriage. The possibility of obtaining radical sanation for such marriages will be accorded further treatment in the articles of this work which deal with the faculties of the Apostolic Delegate and the local Ordinaries.

[40] *Op. cit.*, p. 178.

In the case of Oriental Catholics, whose marriages are invalid because of defect of form, the norm of Canon 1137 must also be followed, that is, the parties must renew their consent according to the prescribed form. But since Oriental Catholics, with the exception of those who are members of the Greek Ruthenian Rite, when they marry among themselves, are not bound to observe the juridical form prescribed by the Code, they will observe the form that is prescribed for them by the laws proper to the Rite to which they belong.[41] Members of the Greek Ruthenian Rite, when they contract among themselves or with others, are bound to observe the form prescribed by decree *Ne temere*,[42] and not by the form prescribed by the Code as it has been mistakenly declared.[43] But if there be a question of a marriage between a member of any Oriental Rite except the Greek Ruthenian and a member of the Latin Rite, it must be convalidated according to the form prescribed by the Code. For in this instance, the Oriental Catholic is bound to the Latin form of marriage.[44]

Article III. Condition Governing the Cause

In the various writings of the canonist Pope, Benedict XIV, it is constantly stated that radical sanation cannot be granted without a grave and urgent cause.[45] In view of this it may at first seem strange that this condition was not specifically enumerated together with the others menioned in Canon 1139, § 1, But this would have been a needless repetition of a principle of law already set forth in the general norms of the Code in Canon 84, § 1. A summary exposition of that canon will be sufficient to demon-

[41] Vide Canon 1.

[42] S. C. pro Eccl. Orient., decr., March 1, 1929, art. 39—AAS, XXI (1929), 159.

[43] Brennan, *The Simple Convalidation of Marriage* (Washington, 1937), p. 88.

[44] Canon 1099, § 1, 3°.

[45] Epist. *"Redditae Nobis,"* 5 Dec. 1744—*Fontes,* n. 350; instr. *"Cum Super,"* 27 Sept. 1755—*Bull. Rom. Cont.*, IV, 291; *De Synodo Dioec.*, lib. XIII, cap. XXI, n. 7.

strate the necessity of a grave cause for the granting of radical sanation. At the same time special note will be taken of the circumstances and reasons which are considered sufficient to constitute a grave and urgent cause for this favor.

A. Necessity of a Grave Cause for Radical Sanation

Canon 84, § 1.—A lege ecclesiastica ne dispensetur sine justa et rationabili causa, habita ratione gravitatis legis a qua dispensatur; alias dispensatio ab inferiore data illicita et invalida est.

This declaration that a dispensation cannot be given without a just and reasonable cause, serves as a complement to the principle embodied in Canon 81, namely, that before one can grant a dispensation he must possess the lawful power to do so. The two principles go hand in hand and cannot be separated, for just as one lacking dispensatory power cannot dispense, even if there be present a just and reasonable cause, so neither should one possessing that dispensatory power act without a just and reasonable cause for doing so. But it is to be noted immediately that the justness and reasonableness of the cause are not to be decided in some indefinite and uncertain way, but are to be measured by the gravity of the law from which the dispensation is given. Thus, in respect to some laws a relatively slight circumstance will prove to be a just and reasonable cause, whereas in respect to other laws only a grave or a very grave reason will be a sufficiently just and reasonable cause for granting a dispensation. This, of course, means that in deciding what constitutes a just and reasonable cause for a dispensation one must take into account the hierarchy of importance that exists in the entire body of laws. The Code itself indicates the existence of such a hierarchy among the laws in its application of the principle of Canon 84, § 1, to specific questions.

The principle established in this canon is not merely a theoretical one. It has a very practical value of great importance inasmuch as it circumscribes the dispensatory power. This is evidenced by the fact that the concluding sentence in the first paragraph of Canon 84 makes it clear that unless there is present a just and reasonable cause, a dispensation granted by an inferior is illicit and invalid. The "inferior" referred to is anyone (capable of possessing dispensatory power) of lesser rank and authority than the legislator who enacted the law from which a dispensation is given. Thus, in relation to the general marriage legislation of the Church, a local Ordinary is an "inferior" of the Roman Pontiff who enacted these laws. Therefore, a dispensation from these laws will be illicit and invalid if it is given by a local Ordinary without a just and reasonable cause. In respect to the legislator himself it is to be stated that the dispensation can be valid if he grants it without a just and reasonable cause. In other words, it is the most common opinion among canonists that the Pope can grant a valid dispensation from an ecclesiastical law without a just and reasonable cause.[46] In practice, however, the Roman Pontiff is accustomed to require that a just and reasonable cause be present before he will grant a dispensation. This requirement is for the validity of the dispensation and not merely for its licitness.[47]

An application of the principle under discussion can easily be made to the question of granting radical sanation. For radical sanation implies at least one dispensation from a general marriage law of the Church. But it frequently happens that local Ordinaries are empowered to grant radical sanation in virtue of their quinquennial faculties. Any radical sanation granted by them for a marriage invalid because of a diriment impediment of major degree of ecclesiastical law will be illicit and invalid if they grant it without a just and reasonable cause. But, in virtue of the prescripts of Canon 1054, if the sanation is granted for a marriage invalid because of a diriment impediment of minor degree of the ecclesiastical law it will be valid even if the final cause is false. In relation to a sanation granted by the Roman Pontiff it must be stated that, although it is the accepted doctrine that he could

[46] O'Mara, *Canonical Causes for Matrimonial Dispensations* (Washington, 1935), p. 41.

[47] Cf. Canon 42, § 2.

grant a sanation validly without a just and reasonable cause, nevertheless it is not his will or intention to do so. Therefore, in view of the precept of Canon 42, § 2, the sanation will be invalid unless a just and reasonable cause is present. Needless to say, the limitation on this principle that is established by Canon 1054 would seem to be applicable to the sanations granted by the Roman Pontiff. It now remains to be seen what causes are considered sufficient for this favor.

B. *Causes Sufficient for the Granting of Radical Sanation*

It is to be remarked in relation to the causes which are sufficient for radical sanation that these causes are not to be confused with the causes necessary for a dispensation from an impediment. In other words, the causes which are usually advanced for obtaining a dispensation from a matrimonial impediment are not of themselves sufficient for the concession of radical sanation. Thus, the convalidation of a marriage is considered to be a grave and urgent cause for the granting of a dispensation from most matrimonial impediments. But, of itself the convalidation of marriage is not a sufficient cause for the concession of radical sanation, which is more than a dispensation from an impediment, inasmuch as it also includes a dispensation from the renewal of consent. It is true that the convalidation of marriage is the occasion for the concession of radical sanation, but only when every effort to convalidate the marriage according to the norms of simple convalidation has proved impossible. In brief, then, it may be said that the basic cause for the concession of radical sanation is the impossibility of adhering to the norms of simple convalidation.[48]

Simple convalidation consists essentially of two elements. One of these elements is the removal of the nullifying obstacle to the marriage, whether that be a diriment impediment, a defect of form or a defect of consent. The second element is the renewal of consent. This renewal of consent is required no matter from what source the invalidity of the marriage arose. But, as it has

[48] Payen, *De Matrimonio,* n. 2616.

been seen, it is sometimes made by one or both parties privately and secretly, while at other times the law requires that it be made in the juridical form. Now, if the basic cause for the concession of radical sanation is the impossibility of adhering to the norms of simple convalidation, the impossibility must be in respect to one or other of these two elements of simple convalidation. But it cannot be in respect to the first of these elements, namely, the removal of the nullifying obstacle. For it is impossible to convalidate the marriage at all if it is impossible to remove the nullifying obstacle, since the removal of that obstacle is equally necessary for simple convalidation and radical sanation. Consequently the impossibility of adhering to the norms of simple convalidation must necessarily refer to the second element, namely, the necessity of renewing consent. This impossibility may be the impossibility of warning one or both parties that a renewal of consent is necessary; or it may be the impossibility of getting one or both parties to agree to renew their consent; or it may be a combination of both of these items.[49]

It sometimes happens that after assisting at a marriage a priest discovers that it is invalid, either because he did not have the proper jurisdiction, or because the dispensation he had obtained was insufficient owing to some substantial defect. This defect may arise from the fact that the one requesting the dispensation did not ask for the proper and necessary dispensation. It may also result from the fact that the one who granted the request did not have the proper faculties for such a dispensation. If the parties (who supposedly are unaware of the invalidity of their marriage) have left the place where the marriage took place and could be located only at great expense and after considerable delay (either of which facts would constitute a grave inconvenience) there is certainly present a grave, urgent and sufficiently just cause for granting radical sanation. If, on the other hand, the parties could be located but could not be warned of the invalidity of their marriage without danger of scandal, radical sanation can validly be granted. A sufficient cause is likewise present when

[49] Feije, *De Impedimentis et Dispensationibus Matrimonialibus,* n. 770; Giovine, *De Dispensationibus Matrimonialibus,* I, consult. XXIII, sect. 330.

one party, discovering a public impediment that is still unknown to the other party, does not wish to inform that party of the necessity of renewing consent, because of a justified fear that if the other party learned of the invalidity of the marriage he would refuse to renew consent and would take advantage of the situation to break up the union, although otherwise he will be willing to continue in the marriage as long as he believes it to be valid.[50] In such a case as this, however, if it is foreseen that a divorce is almost inevitable because of the strained domestic relations of the parties, radical sanation could indeed be granted, if only for sake of legitimating the children, but it is the mind and the constant practice of the Church not to grant this favor in such circumstances.[51] Finally, the fear of infamy sometimes renders it impossible for one party to inform the other party of the invalidity of their marriage because of some impediment known only to the first party. A conceivable instance of this would be found in the case where one party, unknown to the other, was laboring under the impediment of sacred orders resulting from the diaconate or subdiaconate, or under the impediment resulting from solemn profession. In summing up these points it may be said that there is a grave and urgent cause to grant radical sanation if it is impossible to warn one or both parties of the necessity of renewing their consent. It is the commonly accepted opinion that it is impossible to give this warning if there is danger of scandal, infamy or the dissolution of the marriage.[52]

The second point to be considered is the impossibility of getting one or both parties to agree to renew their consent in the prescribed form. For in certain circumstances this impossibility can prove to be a sufficient cause for having recourse to radical sanation, especially when this recourse is necessary for the easing of a conscience and the legitimation of offspring. This can easily

[50] Gasparri, *De Matrimonio,* n. 1229.

[51] *Secret. Status instruct.,* 27 Mart. 1830—*Collect. S. C. de Prop. Fide,* n. 1426.

[52] Payen, *op. cit.,* n. 2616; Gasparri, *op. cit.,* n. 1229; Wernz-Vidal, *Ius Canonicum,* V, n. 667; Cappello, *De Sacramentis,* III, n. 853; Cerato, *Matrimonium,* n. 144; Farrugia, *De Matrimonio,* n. 359.

be the case when two Catholics have contracted marriage outside the Church and afterwards one of the parties, being troubled in conscience, wishes to convalidate the marriage, but the other refuses to go through the form of marriage in the Church.[53] But it is more generally the case when a Catholic has married a non-Catholic outside the Church and later, wishing to rectify the wrong and to make amends, discovers that the non-Catholic, because of his attitude towards the Church, refuses to renew his consent in the presence of a priest. If both parties are so ill disposed that it is forseen that they would refuse to renew consent in the prescribed form if warned of the necessity of doing so, radical sanation could be granted especially when it is in the interests of their offspring.[54] But if two people, on being informed of the obligation of renewing consent in the prescribed form, persistently refuse to do so, they must be regarded as contumacious and unworthy of this favor from the Church and for them radical sanation should not be granted.[55] Finally, if two people, otherwise well disposed and willing to renew their consent, refuse to do so in the prescribed form because of the publicity attending that act, it will generally not be necessary to have immediate recourse to radical sanation. There are other possible remedies for such cases. The first of these would be to obtain a dispensation from the form.[56] If the parties, one or both, are in danger of death this dispensation can be given in virtue of the faculties conceded in Canon 1043. The second remedy would be to renew consent in the presence of a priest and two witnesses, but to do so in a manner that would insure the parties of as little publicity as possible. Thus, for instance, the permission of the Ordinary could be obtained for the marriage to take place in a private home, since there is a just cause for him to grant this permission. A third possibility in the handling of such cases is the marriage of con-

[53] Gasparri, *op. cit.*, n. 1229; Ayrhinac-Lydon, *Marriage Legislation in the New Code of Canon Law*, n. 316.

[54] Petrovits, *Church Law on Matrimony*, n. 600; Payen, *op. cit.*, n. 2617; Vermeersch-Creusen, *Epitome Iuris Canonici*, II, n. 454.

[55] Payen, *op. cit.*, n. 2617.

[56] Payen, *op. cit.*, n. 2617.

science as it is outlined in Canons 1104 to 1107 inclusively. But in the event of these possible remedies proving inadequate, radical sanation would seem to be the only solution and in the proposed case there would be a grave reason for granting this favor.

The third point to be considered is the combination of the two preceding points, that is, both the impossibility of warning the parties of the necessity of renewing consent in the prescribed form and the impossibility of getting them to make such a renewal of consent. This combination of circumstances can easily arise when several or one or more marriages are invalid for the same reason or for different reasons. This might happen through the lack of jurisdiction on the part of the priest performing the marriage or through the granting of an invalid dispensation. In such instances the Holy See has been known to grant a general sanation for the invalid marriages.[57] In other cases it may be the mind of the Holy See not to grant a general sanation for these marriages, but to leave the parties in good faith until such time as one circumstance or another might make it possible to handle each case individually. However, the mind of the Holy See in this matter can be determined only by a petition made to the proper Congregation, which will be moved to grant or to refuse the favor according to the peculiar circumstances attending each petition for a general sanation.

There is yet one possible circumstance which may give rise to a grave cause for granting radical sanation. This would be the refusal of the non-Catholic party to give the formal guarantees (*cautiones*) required by the law before a dispensation for mixed marriage can be granted. But it seems advisable to postpone discussion of such a circumstance until the present formulas of the quinquennial faculties are given detailed consideration. For, this being a question of very practical moment, it seems better to view it in the light of the present practice of the Church as it is demonstrated in the faculties which the Holy See extends to Apostolic Delegates and local Ordinaries.

[57] Payen, *op. cit.*, n. 2617; Wernz-Vidal, *op. cit.*, V, n. 667; Cappello, *op. cit.*, III, n. 853.

CHAPTER VI

THE POWER TO GRANT RADICAL SANATION

The subject matter of this chapter will not be confined to the power to grant radical sanation that is possessed by the Holy See, but will also embrace the subject of delegated power in this same matter. This latter consideration will entail a study of the various faculties enjoyed by the Legates of the Holy See and by the local Ordinaries. Finally, it will embrace an inquiry into the scope of the power conceded by the law in relation to matrimonial dispensations. The division of the chapter will be as follows. Article 1. Ordinary power to grant radical sanation; Article 2. Delegated power to grant radical sanation; Article 3. Power to grant radical sanation in extraordinary cases.

Article I. Ordinary Power to Grant Radical Sanation

The source of the power to grant radical sanation is found in the person of the Roman Pontiff as the supreme legislator for the universal Church. But the exercise of that power in the normal course of events rests with the various Roman Congregations to which the Holy Father has given jurisdiction in this matter. In order to obtain a complete view of this question, it will be well to consider it under two aspects, as follows: A. The power of the Roman Pontiff; B. The jurisdiction of the Roman Congregations.

A. The Power of the Roman Pontiff

In all matters concerning faith, morals and ecclesiastical discipline the Roman Pontiff holds a primacy not only of honor but also of jurisdiction.[1] He is the supreme legislator for the entire

[1] Canon 218, § 1.

Church and upon his will depends the force of all the laws enacted by himself and by his predecessors. Consequently, being the very source and origin of all general Church laws, his jurisdiction over these laws is not and cannot be limited by any human power. He is, in a sense, above all his laws, inasmuch as he cannot be coerced into observing them and at the same time he has it within his power to change, abrogate or relax any and all ecclesiastical ordinances. Moreover, he not only has the power to relax the law through his dispensation, but he can also erase the effects which have followed from the non-observance of ecclesiastical laws.[2] This, in fact, is exactly what he does when he grants the favor of radical sanation for a marriage that has been invalidly contracted. Such an act is in complete accord with the fullness of power and jurisdiction possessed by the Sovereign Pontiff in respect to those matters which make up the body of ecclesiastical laws. It represents no arrogation of power that is not fundamentally his by reason of his office, nor does it involve any contradiction or absurdity. Yet, it does at the same time represent such an exercise of the plenitude of the papal power that no one other than the Roman Pontiff could dare to claim the right to grant radical sanation solely of his own right.

In the present day there is little need of defending this right of the Roman Pontiff to grant radical sanation. Yet, in an earlier day this right was entirely denied by some and strangely limited to a few impediments by others.[3] However, it is more than likely that if these objectors had had a true concept of the nature of radical sanation, they would not have fallen into the error which they defended. In fact, they were altogether right in denying to the Roman Pontiff as to anyone else the right to grant radical sanation as they understood it. For, as they saw it and believed it to be, radical sanation involved a metaphysical impossibility, and would have meant that the Roman Pontiff claimed the right to convalidate a marriage from its very beginning and in such a way that through some mysterious means it was saved from being invalid at the start. Such an opinion could not and did not long

[2] C. un., *de immunitate ecclesiarum*, III, 17, in Clem.

[3] Giovine, *De Dispensationibus Matrimonialibus*, I, consult. XXIII, sect. 323.

prevail against the common teaching of able canonists and the constant usage of the Holy See.[4]

The power of the Roman Pontiff to grant radical sanation may be better understood if one considers his power relative to each of the elements of this mode of convalidation. The first of these elements is the dispensation or cessation of the invalidating impediment. If this impediment is an extant impediment of the divine positive or natural law it is clear that the Roman Pontiff cannot dispense. But if it is an impediment of the divine law which has ceased the Pope could, according to some, grant sanation but the Code says that the Church does not sanate marriages in such cases. If the nullifying impediment is a lack of or defect of consent, it is also clear that he cannot grant the favor, for consent cannot be supplied by any human power.[5] But if it is of the ecclesiastical law, his right to dispense is clearly set forth in Canon 1040. The second element of radical sanation is the dispensation from the renewal of consent. If the renewal of consent refers to the actual giving of consent by one in whom there has been no prior consent or in whom the prior consent was defective, it is clear that the Roman Pontiff cannot dispense, because in this instance the placing of consent is required by the natural law. But if the renewal of consent refers only to a repetition of consent by those who have already exchanged a naturally sufficient consent, it is undoubted that the Roman Pontiff can dispense, for Canon 1133, § 2, clearly states that this renewal of consent is required by ecclesiastical law for the validity of convalidation. But, inasmuch as it is required by a general law of the Church, it requires one who has supreme power to relax that law and to say, in effect, that the Church will be satisfied with the prior consent of the parties, since it at least fulfills the requirements of the natural law. The third element of radical sanation is its retrotractive force. As a consequence of this retrotractivity the effects of the invalid marriage are completely erased and the children of that marriage are legitimated in so complete a manner that they

[4] Wernz, *Ius Decretalium,* IV, n. 652, note 11.

[5] Canon 1081, § 1.

are considered as if they had been born of a valid marriage.[6] But to annex such an extraordinary force to a dispensation requires the very plenitude of power, for the effects of a law as well as the law itself are subject to the will of the law-giver. It is to be noted again that this power of the Roman Pontiff to annex to his dispensations a retrotractive force, whereby the detrimental effects of the violated law are erased, is not confined to matrimonial dispensations, but extends to every matter over which he has jurisdiction.

In theory no doubt or question is possible concerning the power of the Roman Pontiff to grant radical sanation. In practice, however, most probably the Roman Pontiff seldom exercises this power personally for individual cases. For it would be a human impossibility for any single person to attend to the multitude of affairs that are constantly calling for attention on the part of the Holy See. Therefore, it is only through various Congregations, Tribunals and Offices that the Holy Father is able to expedite the matters requiring his supreme power. It is to the several Congregations through which the Roman Pontiff is accustomed to grant radical sanation that attention must now be given.

B. Jurisdiction of the Roman Congregations

There are four Congregations, besides the Sacred Penitentiary, which have competence in relation to the concession of radical sanation. They are the Sacred Congregation of the Holy Office, the Sacred Congregation of the Sacraments, the Sacred Congregation of the Propagation of the Faith and the Sacred Congregation for the Oriental Church. But they do not possess identical competence in this matter, except inasmuch as all four are competent in the external forum, whereas the Sacred Penitentiary is competent only for the internal forum. In other respects the competency of the several Congregations is distinguished either by the territory over which they have jurisdiction or by the matters which have been committed to them by the Roman Pontiff.

[6] Cf. supra, p. 9-10.

Thus, the Sacred Congregation of the Propagation of the Faith has jurisdiction only in those regions where the episcopal hierarchy has not yet been established and in those countries where, although the hierarchy has been constituted, it is not yet well established.[7] Again, the Sacred Congregation of the Holy Office alone is competent in matters pertaining to the impediments of Mixed Religion and Disparity of Worship and therefore it alone can grant radical sanation for marriages invalid because of the latter impediment.[8] The relative competency of each will be more easily understood if each is considered individually.

Before considering the Congregations individually it will be expedient to note several facts. In the first place there is an important rule established by Canon 43, which applies to petitions for radical sanation as well as to other matters. On its observance will depend the validity of certain petitions. It seems useful for the present purpose to give it as it is found in the Code:

> **Canon 43.—Gratia ab una Sacra Congregatione vel Officio Romanae Curiae denegata, invalide ab alia Sacra Congregatione vel Officio aut a loci Ordinario, etsi potestatem habente, conceditur sine assensu Sacrae Congregationis vel Officii quocum vel quibuscum agi coeptum fuit, salvo iure S. Poenitentiariae pro foro interno.**

From this canon it is clear that the permission of the Congregation or Office which first denied the favor must be obtained before that favor can be validly given by another having power in the same matter. If, however, a favor has been refused in the external forum by a Sacred Congregation or Office, the permission of that Congregation or Office is not necessary in order that this favor be validly obtained from the Sacred Penitentiary for the internal forum.[9] This does not work conversely, however, because a favor that has been denied by the Sacred Penitentiary cannot be granted for the external forum without the permission

[7] Canon 252.

[8] Canon 247.

[9] O'Neill, *Papal Rescripts of Favor* (Washington, 1930), p. 142.

of the same Sacred Penitentiary.[10] This is more a theoretical than a practical possibility, nevertheless the reason is clear. For a favor granted by the Sacred Penitentiary is generally effective only in the internal forum, whereas a favor granted by a Congregation is effective for both forums. It is to be noted also that a favor denied by an Ordinary having the power to concede it, can still be granted by a Congregation, an Office or the Sacred Penitentiary. The consent of the Ordinary is not required for the validity of the rescript. In practice it would avail little to go to a higher authority, unless the Ordinary who first refused the favor would be willing to recommend the granting of the favor, for without his recommendation the matter in all probability would be referred back to him.[11] Finally, it is to be remarked that the canon speaks of a favor that has been denied. Therefore, if a petition has been sent to a Congregation but has not been formally denied, the local Ordinary could in an urgent case use his faculties and validly grant the favor.[12]

Another point useful to recall in relation to petitioning the Holy See for favors is the rule of conduct to be observed by those having faculties in the same matter. The Code states in Canon 1048 that, once a petition has been sent to the Holy See, local Ordinaries cannot any longer use their corresponding faculties excerpt according to the norm of Canon 204, § 2. This canon prescribes that if an inferior in a grave and urgent case enters into an affair that has been submitted to a superior, he must notify the superior of that fact at once. A further norm of action is established in Canon 1050 and is especially pertinent in the matter of radical sanation. It decrees that if, together with an impediment from which he can dispense, a bishop discovers an impediment from which he cannot dispense, he is to refer the entire matter to the Holy See and refrain from using his faculties even in respect to the impediment from which he can dispense. But if, after petitioning the Holy See for a dispensation from an

[10] O'Neill, *op. cit.*, pp. 142-143.

[11] O'Neill, *op. cit.*, p. 145.

[12] O'Neill, *op. cit.*, p. 142.

impediment for which he has no faculties, a bishop discovers an impediment for which he does have faculties, he may use his faculties without further recourse to the Holy See. With these things in mind it will be of some practical value to consider the various Congregations from which the favor of radical sanation can be obtained.

There are certain general principles governing the discipline and business of the various Congregations which serve to explain their respective policies in reference to the affairs committed to them by the Roman Pontiff. It is to be remarked first of all that the chapter of the Code which treats of the Roman Curia indicates only in broad outlines the work of the various departments of the Curia. Canon 243 §1, prescribes that each Congregation, Tribunal and Office of the Roman Curia is to follow the disciplinary regulations and is to conduct its business according to the general and particular norms which have been established by the Roman Pontiff. For the Sacred Congregations of the Holy office, of the Sacraments and of the Propagation of the Faith the general norms are those which accompanied the celebrated constitution *"Sapienti consilio"* issued by Pope Pius X on June 29, 1908.[13] The special norms to be followed by these same Congregations are those which are established in the *Ordo Servandus*: *Pars Altera* that was published by the Secretariate of State on September 29, 1908.[14] On March 25, 1935, the present Pontiff, Pope Pius XI, in his Apostolic constitution *"Quae Divinitus"* dealt extensively with the organization, powers and procedure of the Sacred Penitentiary, but apart from confirming the regulations issued by his predecessors for the most part and introducing changes required by the exigencies of the present time, this decree has altered nothing concerning the powers of the Sacred Penitentiary over radical sanation that would be of practical value in this work.[15] Therefore, it is to the norms established by the constitution *"Sapienti Consilio"* and the *"Ordo servandus"*

[13] *Fontes,* n. 682.

[14] AAS, I (1909), 59-108.

[15] AAS, XXVII (1935), 97-113.

that reference will be made. The Sacred Congregation for the Oriental Church was not constituted as a distinct Congregation until May 1, 1917, on which date, in a *Motu Proprio* entitled *"Dei Providentis"*, Pope Benedict XV separated it from the Sacred Congregation of the Propagation of the Faith.[16] It is to this constitution of Benedict XV that reference will be made when considering this latter Congregation.[16a]

A second point to be noted here is that petitions for favors in the external forum should be sent to the proper Congregation through the office of one's local Ordinary. Two reasons favor such a course of procedure. First of all, in thus bringing the matter in question to the attention of the local Ordinary, it may be possible to take advantage of whatever faculties he may have in relation to that matter. In the second place the various Congregations generally require a letter of approval from the Ordinary of the one submitting the petition *pro foro externo*. Needless to say, there is nothing to prevent an individual pastor or other priest from attending to the mailing of the petition, provided he has obtained the letter of approval from his Ordinary. It is quite likely, however, that the general practice in most episcopal curias is to expedite such matters at the diocesan chancery. Another item to be recalled is that petitions are to be sent to the Congregations having competency in this matter, unless the Ordinary submits it through the Sacred Consistorial Congregation. In this country

[16] *Fontes,* n. 710*.

[16a] In the year 1925, His Holiness, Pope Pius XI instituted the Commission for Russia and joined it to the Sacred Congregation for the Oriental Church, giving it charge of everything pertaining to Russians, whether they were in or out of Russia.—AAS, XVIII (1926), 62. On April 6, 1930, by a *motu proprio,* the Holy Father separated this Commission from the Sacred Congregation for the Oriental Church and made it *sui iuris.*—AAS, XXII (1930), 154-183. On December 21, 1934, the Holy Father issued a new *motu proprio* in which he restricted the competency of this Commission to the affairs of Russians dwelling in Russia. In order to determine the nature and the extent of the competency of this Commission it is necessary to consider the following excerpt of this latest *motu proprio.* *"Itaque . . . statuimus ac decernimus ea tantummodo negotia et causas, quae ad Russos pertinent, qui in patrio solo degunt, 'Commissioni pro Russia' reservare ac*

the Ordinaries obtain their quinquennial faculties through the Sacred Consistorial Congregation and not directly from the Congregations which have competency over the matters for which they have faculties. But in this matter the Consistorial Congregation is acting as the agent of the other Sacred Congregations by special permission of the Roman Pontiff in acquiescence to a request made by many Bishops who felt that this procedure would be more expedient for all concerned.[17]

In the following treatment of the Sacred Penitentiary and of the various Congregations a full report will be made of whatever portions of the law seem useful or necessary for the understanding of the competency of these departments.

1. *Sacred Congregation of the Holy Office*

Canon 247, § 1.—Congregatio S. Officii, cui ipse Summus Pontifex praest, tutatur doctrinam fidei et morum.

3.—Ipsa sola cognoscit ea quae, sive directe sive indirecte, in iure aut in facto, circa privilegium, uti aiunt, Paulinum, et matrimonii impedimenta disparitatis cultus et mixtae religionis versantur; itemque ad eam spectat facultas dispensandi in hisce impedimentis. Quare quaelibet huiusmodi quaestio ad hanc Congregationem est deferenda, quae tamen potest, si ita censeat et casus ferat, quaestionem remittere ad aliam Congregationem vel ad Tribunal Sacrae Romanae Rotae.

concedere, incolumi tamen Sacrae Congregationis pro Ecclesia Orientali auctoritate ac iure ad normam canonis 257."—AAS, XXVII (1935), 66. From these words it might appear that the Commission for Russia has complete jurisdiction over all Russians actually living in Russia even in respect to such a matter as radical sanation. However such an opinion does not now seem tenable in view of an Apostolic Letter of Pope Pius XI, issued on March 25, 1938.—AAS, XXX (1938), 154-159. From the wording of this latest document it seems very evident that the Sacred Congregation for the Oriental Church has the sole competence in the matter of radical sanation even for Russians living in Russia and that the Commission for Russia has the character of a business agency alone.

[17] Pius XI, *Motu Proprio, "Post datam instructionem."* 20 April, 1923—AAS. XV (1923), 193.

Normae Peculiares:—Congregationi Sancti Officii, in suae competentiae rebus, territorii limites nulli sunt. —(18).

From the foregoing excerpts of the law, it is readily discerned that the Congregation of the Holy Office is the supreme congregation and is not limited in its competency by geographical lines. But of all the matters over which it has competency the one that pertains to the present work is its power to grant radical sanation for marriages which are invalid because of disparity of worship or which involve the impediment of mixed religion. It has obtained sole competence over these impediments because it involves a question intimately related to the faith of the parties concerned. It is this congregation that gives faculties to the bishops and determines how they are to use them. In this country the Apostolic Delegate and the local Ordinaries have received faculties for the concession of radical sanation for invalid marriages involving the impediments of mixed religion or disparity of worship. Consequently there should seldom be any necessity for applying directly to this Congregation in this matter. But when the faculties of the local Ordinaries do not suffice, application must be made.

2. *Sacred Congregation of the Sacraments*

Canon 249, § 1.—Congregationi de disciplina Sacramentorum proposita est universa legislatio circa disciplinam septem Sacramentorum, incolumi iure Congregationis S. Officii circa ea quae in Can. 247 statuta sunt, et Sacrorum Rituum Congregationis circa ritus et caeremonias quae in Sacramentis conficiendis, ministrandis et recipiendis servari debent.

2.—Ad illam itaque spectant ea omnia, quae decerni concedique solent tum in disciplina matrimonii, etc. . . , iis tantum exceptis quae aliis Congregationibus reservata sunt.

"Sapienti Consilio":—Itaque eidem Congregationi

[18] Caput I, n. 1, a.—AAS, I (1909), 59.

> **tribuuntur ea omnia, quae huc usque ab aliis Congregationibus, Tribunalibus aut Officiis Romanae Curiae decerni concedique consueverant tum in disciplina matrimonii, uti dispensationes in foro externo tam pauperibus quam divitibus, sanationes in radice, etc.**[19]
>
> **Normae Peculiares:—Congregationi de disciplina Sacramentorum in iis, quae matrimonium spectant, competunt quoque loca Congregationi de Propaganda Fide obnoxia, ad memoratae Constitutionis normam.**[20]
>
> **Ibidem:—Plenae Congregationis iudicio reservatur:—in re ad matrimonium pertinente, . . . sanationes in radice; . . .** [21]

In general it may be said that the Sacred Congregation of the Sacraments has the most extensive competency in matters concerning the discipline of the Sacraments, for ultimately questions concerning this aspect of the Sacraments will be referred to this congregation. In particular, however, it is to be noted that the competency of this Congregation does not in any way overlap or interfere with the competency of other Congregations. For, in the first place, it is specifically provided in the Code that it has no competency in those matters which have been committed to the Holy Office, e.g., the impediments of mixed religion and disparity of worship. In the second place, it is also provided that the competency of this congregation does not extend to those matters which have been committed to other congregations, for example, those affairs that have been referred to the Sacred Congregation for the Oriental Church. On the other hand, it is to be remarked that in questions referring to the Sacrament of Matrimony other than requests for dispensations and sanations, the Congregation of the Sacraments has competence even in those territories which are subject to the Congregation of the Propagation of the Faith. But, for the granting of Matrimonial dispensations and sanations this latter Congregation of Propaganda has faculties of its own. For those who are required to submit their petitions to the Con-

[19] Sect. I, n. 3, 2.—AAS, I (1909), 10.

[20] Cap. I, n. 1, c.—AAS, I (1909), 59.

[21] Art. III, n. 11, a.—AAS, I (1909), 87.

gregation of the Sacraments directly, it seems sufficient to state that the faculties of this congregation embrace not only the juridical form of marriage but also all those impediments of ecclesiastical law from which it is accustomed to grant dispensations or sanations. In any event it will be to this congregation that recourse must be had for any dispensations or sanations of marriage, the invalidity of which is a matter of the external forum except for the impediments of mixed religion and disparity of worship. It would be to this congregation also that one would have recourse if an attempt were being made to secure radical sanation for a marriage that was invalid because of an impediment of the divine or natural law, after that impediment had ceased. This, of course, refers to any attempt to secure radical sanation in the external forum, for the internal forum the petition would have be be submitted to the Sacred Penitentiary.

3. *Sacred Congregation of the Propagation of the Faith*

Canon 252, § 1.—Congregatio de Propaganda Fide missionibus ad praedicandum Evangelium et Catholicam doctrinam praeest, ministros necessarios constituit et mutat, facultatemque habet tractandi, agendi et exsequendi omnia hac in re necessaria et opportuna.

§ 3.—Eius iurisdictio iis est circumscripta regionibus, ubi, sacra hierarchia nondum constituta, status missionis perseverat. Huic Congregationi sunt etiam subiectae regiones, quae etsi hierarchia inibi constituta sit, adhuc inchoatum aliquid praeseferunt. . . .

§ 4.—Haec autem Congregatio tenetur ad competentes Congregationes deferre negotia quae aut fidem attingunt, aut causas matrimoniales, aut generales normas circa sacrorum rituum disciplinam tradendas vel interpretandas.

"Sapienti Consilio."—Nihilominus, ut unitati regiminis consulatur, volumus ut Congregatio de Propaganda Fide ad peculiares alias Congregationes deferat quaecumque aut fidem attingunt, aut matrimonium aut sacrorum rituum disciplinam.[22]

[22] Sect. I, n. 6, 4.—AAS, I (1909), 12.

The paragraphs of Canon 252 which have been quoted here offer little difficulty. In the first place the territory over which this Congregation has jurisdiction is clearly established. Secondly, it is clearly stated that it has the obligation to attend to the spread of the Gospel and at the same time has the faculty to do all those things which are necessary and opportune for this work. It may appear, however, that from paragraph four of this canon as well as from the prescripts of the constitution *"Sapienti Consilio"* that it is not clear that this Congregation has faculties to grant dispensations for matrimonial impediments. In fact this very question was proposed to the Sacred Congregation of the Consistory in 1908 by the Cardinal Prefect of the Sacred Congregation of the Propagation of the Faith who asked if the Congregation of which he was prefect could grant formulas of faculties, including those pertaining to marriage, to the Ordinaries subject to it. The reply of the Consistorial Congregation was in the affirmative, adding, however, that the matter in question should be discussed with the Sacred Congregation of the Sacraments.[23] This means that the Congregation for the Propagation of the Faith will determine, after consultation with the Congregation of the Sacraments what faculties it will be advisable to extend to the Ordinaries of mission countries. Generally these faculties are very extensive and Payen rightly concludes that it will happen very rarely that a missioner will have to petition the Holy See for a dispensation.[24] However, if such a necessity should arise, the petition ought to be sent to the Sacred Congregation of the Propagation of the Faith and not to the Sacred Congregation of the Sacraments. It is Payen's opinion that, in such an event, the Congregation of the Propagation of the Faith will then send the petition to another Congregation in order to obtain the dispensation or sanation.[25]

But, if this were true, it would in effect be making the Congregation for the Propagation of the Faith merely an agent of the

[23] S. C. Consist., 12 Nov. 1908—*Fontes,* n. 2056, ad II.

[24] *De Matrimonio,* n. 2620.

[25] *De Matrimonio,* n. 2620.

other Congregations, just as the Consistorial Congregation is an agent in relation to the quinquennial faculties of the Ordinaries subject to it. This does not seem to be the case, however, for it is a more common and a more probable opinion that the Congregation for the Propagation of the Faith is competent to grant dispensations and sanations.[26] Wernz-Vidal seem to extend this competency to dispensations from the impediments of mixed religion and disparity of worship and declare that it would not be necessary for this Congregation to refer to the Holy Office in this matter.[27] Their opinion seems to be founded on the reply of the Consistorial Congregation to the Prefect of the Congregation for the Propagation of the Faith when the latter asked whether or not the Congregation for Oriental Affairs, which was then a section of the Congregation of the Propagation of the Faith, could grant dispensations for the impediments of mixed religion and disparity of worship.[28] The reply to this question was in the affirmative, but it does not seem possible to maintain that from this reply it can be asserted that at the present time the Congregation of the Propagation of the Faith has the power to grant these dispensations. For, in the first place, the reply referred to the granting of these dispensations only for Orientals who were then subject to the Congregation of the Propagation of the Faith. Secondly, this latter Congregation no longer has jurisdiction over Oriental affairs. Moreover, in view of the exclusive competency of the Holy Office in these affairs it seems safe to state that in any question pertaining to the radical sanation of marriages which entail either the impediment of mixed religion or disparity of worship, recourse will have to be made by the Sacred Congregation for the Propagation of the Faith to the Sacred Congregation of the Holy Office.

[26] Gasparri, *De Matrimonio,* n. 273; Cappello, *De Sacramentis,* III, n. 226, III; Wernz-Vidal, *Ius Canonicum,* II, n. 495, III, d.

[27] *Ius Canonicum,* II, n. 495, note 82.

[28] S. C. Consist., 12 Nov. 1908, ad VI—*Fontes,* n. 2056.

4. *Sacred Congregation for the Oriental Church*

Canon 257, § 1.—Congregationi pro Ecclesia Orientali praeest ipse Romanus Pontifex. Huic Congregationi reservantur omnia cuiusque generis negotia quae sive ad personas, sive ad disciplinam, sive ad ritus Ecclesiarum Orientalium referuntur, etiamsi sint mixta, quae scilicet sive rei sive personarum ratione latinos quoque attingant.

§ 2.—Quare pro Ecclesiis ritus Orientalis haec Congregatio omnibus facultatibus potitur, quas aliae Congregationes pro Ecclesiis ritus latini obtinent, incolumi tamen iure Congregationis S. Officii ad norman Can. 247.

The two sections of Canon 257 which are reported here are substantially the same in their wording as those sections of the *Motu Proprio "Dei Providentis"* which treat of the same matter.[29] Relative to the competency of this Congregation it is to be noted first of all that its jurisdiction embraces all Oriental Catholics, not only when they are living in their own countries, but wheresoever they may be. From the most recent *motu proprio* on the Commission for Russia, it appears that this Commission has no competency in those things which, according to Canon 257, pertain to the Sacred Oriental Congregation. It is to be understood that the term "Oriental Catholics" refers to those persons who belong to any of the various Oriental Rites. According to Canon 98, §1, a person belongs to the Rite in which he was baptized. But if a person were baptized through fraud by the minister of another Rite, or in view of some exigency he was baptized by a priest of another Rite when a priest of his own Rite could not be had, he would still belong to the Rite in which, by law, he was supposed to be baptized. So, also if by dispensation granted by the Holy See a person received Baptism in a certain specified rite without being thereby enrolled in the rite of his actual Baptism, he would still belong to that rite in which, except for the dispensation, he should have received his Bap-

[29] *Fontes*, n. 710*.

tism. If, on the other hand, a person were baptized in a strange rite in virtue of an Apostolic dispensation which is accompanied with the permission to effect a transfer to that rite, he would then belong to the rite in which by dispensation he received his Baptism. Thus, a child whose parents belong to the Latin Rite would itself belong to this same rite, even if it were baptized by a priest of another rite in any but the last of the circumstances just mentioned. The same rule obtains for a child born of parents who belong to an Oriental Rite. It is possible, however, for a person to transfer from one rite to another with proper authorization. He may do so when he has obtained the requisite permission of the Holy See, or that of the Apostolic Delegate of the country in which he lives for the latter is now empowered by the Holy See to grant this permission.[30] A wife may, of her own accord, transfer to the rite to which her husband belongs, either at the time of her marriage or at any time during the marriage. Unless there is some particular law to the contrary, she may return to her former rite upon the death of her husband.[31] During the time that she follows and belongs to the rite of her husband she will, of course, be subject to the laws which are proper to that rite.

The second point to be noted in reference to the competency of the Sacred Oriental Congregation is the extent of the affairs committed to it. To it are reserved all matters of business pertaining to persons, discipline or rites of the Oriental Church even when these affairs affect persons of the Latin Rite through the medium of an interdependent status created by personal relations or objective law. Thus, this Congregation enjoys competence for all marriages in which only one of the parties belongs to some Oriental Rite, as well as for the marriages in which both parties belong to an Oriental Rite. For the execution of the business commmitted to it, this Congregation has all those faculties which

[30] S. C. pro Eccl. Or., decr. *"Nemini licere,"* 6 Dec. 1928—AAS, XX (1928), 416-417. This decree empowers the Apostolic Delegate to grant the permission for such a change of rite to deacons and subdeacons as well as to subordinate clerics and lay people. But it does not empower him to grant such permission to priests.

[31] Canon 98, § 4.

the other Congregations have for the Churches of the Latin Rite. This immediately raises the question of the competency of this Congregation in the matter of dispensations or sanations for marriages which involve the impediments of mixed religion and disparity of worship. Wernz-Vidal,[32] Cappello,[33] Gasparri[34] and Payen[35], hold that for these impediments this Congregation is not of itself competent. Blat, on the other hand, says that it has competency and cites the reply of the Consistorial Congregation which has already been noted.[36] He seems to base his opinion on the fact that in constituting a separate Congregation for the Oriental Church· Benedict XV stated that this Congregation had all the faculties enjoyed by the other Congregations with due regard for the existing rights of the Holy Office. He then notes that in view of the response of the Consistorial Congregation the Holy Office did not enjoy any rights over these impediments as far as Orientals were concerned. Therefore, he concludes, the Oriental Congregation continued to enjoy this competency as the successor of the Congregation of the Propagation of the Faith in Oriental affairs. All of this was undoubtedly true for the period of time falling between the operative institution of the new Congregation for the Oriental Church on December 1, 1917[36a] and the subsequent application of the Code on May 19, 1918. But the wording of Canon 257, §2, while substantially repeating the wording of section IV of the *"Dei Providentis"*, contains the added prescript that the Congregation for the Oriental Church is to have due regard for the prerogative of the Congregation of the Holy Office whose rights are preserved intact, in accordance with the competency defined for it in Canon 247. Thus Canon 257, §2 places a restriction to the otherwise extensive competency of the Oriental Congregation. With Canon 247, §3 for its

[32] *Ius Canonicum,* II, n. 500; V, n. 408.

[33] *De Sacramentis,* III, n. 226, IV.

[34] *De Matrimonio,* n. 272.

[35] *De Matrimonio,* n. 639.

[36] *De Rebus,* III, pars I, n. 439 ad VI.

[36a] Cf. Benedictus XV, motu proprio, *"Dei Providentis,"* 1 maii, 1917—*Fontes,* n. 710*.

jurdic basis, Canon 257, §2 vindicates for the Holy Office sole and exclusive competency for granting dispensations and sanations for marriages of Orientals which involve the impediments of mixed religion or disparity of worship. In practice, however, it would seem advisable to refer any requests and petitions of this nature to the Sacred Congregation for the Oriental Church, which in turn will refer them to the Sacred Congregation of the Holy Office in as far as this procedure proves necessary. It is to be noted that the foregoing discussion has pertained to the question of whether or not the impediments of mixed religion or disparity of worship are among the matters committed to the competence of the Oriental Congregation. There has been no intention of excluding either the possibility or the probability of this Congregation having specially conceded faculties in this matter. For in fact it seems certain that this Congregation does possess such faculties by reason of a special concession made to it by Pope Pius XI.[37]

In countries such as the United States, where Oriental Catholics are apt to intermarry with members of the Latin Rite, it must be remembered that in this case the Oriental party is bound to the form of marriage prescribed by the Code for Latin Catholics.[38] In view of this prescript of the Code it would seem that if this form has not been observed and it proves impossible to get the parties to renew their consent in the juridical form as required by Canon 1137, a radical sanation should be sought from the Congregation for the Oriental Church, inasmuch as it has exclusive competency in all affairs concerning Orientals, even when these affairs affect Latins. For marriages between Orientals account must be taken of the fact that they are bound by the impediments established by the laws of their proper Rite and not by those established in the Code.[39] For the most part the impediments binding Orientals are the same as those which were in force in the Latin Church prior to the Code.[40] Concerning the form of mar-

[37] Cf. Gasparri, *De Matrimonio*, II, pp. 443-444, n. 18 and 19.

[38] Canon 1099, § 1, n. 3.

[39] Canon 1.

riage there is a wide divergence of practice among the various Rites of the Oriental Church. Some Rites do not prescribe a juridical form as it is understood in the Latin Church.[41] Other Rites prescribe that their members conform to the provisions of the decree *"Tametsi"* or the decree *"Ne temere."*[42]

5. *The Sacred Penitentiary*

Canon 258, § 1.—Sacrae Penitentiariae praeficitur Cardinalis Poenitentiarius Maior. Huius tribunalis iurisdictio coarctatur ad ea quae forum internum, etiam non sacramentale, respiciunt, quare hoc tribunal pro solo foro interno gratias largiatur, absolutiones, dispensationes, commutationes, sanationes, condonationes; excutit praeterea quaestiones conscientiae easque dirimit.

Normae Peculiares.—Iuxta memoratae Constitutionis (In Apostolicae, 13 apr. 1744) Benedicti XIV praescripta, omnia secreto et gratis in hoc sacro tribunali expedientur.[43]

Canon 1047.—Nisi aliud ferat S. Poenitentiariae rescriptum, dispensatio in foro interno non sacramentali concessa super impedimento occulto, adnotetur in libro diligenter in secreto Curiae archivo de quo in can. 379 asservando, nec alia dispensatio pro foro externo est necessaria, etsi postea occultum impedimentum publicum evaserit; sed est necessaria, si dispensatio concessa fuerit tantum in foro interno sacramentali.

The first thing to be noted about the jurisdiction of the Sacred Penitentiary is that is is not limited or circumscribed by places or persons. Therefore its competency extends over the Universal Church as to territory and over the people of both the Latin and

[40] Cappello, *De Sacramentis,* III, n. 902-921.

[41] Cappello, *op. cit.,* n. 924-928.

[42] Duskie, *The Canonical Status of Orientals in the United States,* pp. 149-174.

[43] Cap. VIII, art. I, n. 3.—AAS, I (1909), 102.

Oriental Church. Of all the affairs entrusted to this Tribunal, the one that pertains to this work is its competency in reference to sanations. For it not infrequently happens that for one reason or another it is impossible or inadvisable to have recourse to one of the Congregations for radical sanation, while at the same time it suffices to obtain this favor through the Sacred Penitentiary. Generally the impediments for which dispensations or sanations are sought from this tribunal must be occult impediments, for since the reorganization of the Roman Curia by Pope Pius X the Sacred Penitentiary has no powers in reference to public impediments. These are a matter of the external forum.[44] However, it is important to note that the practice of the Sacred Penitentiary admits of a somewhat different concept of an occult impediment than that which is found in Canon 1037, in which an occult impediment is defined as one which cannot be proved in the external forum, by means of some document or by two reliable witnesses. It is clear that the possibility of proof in the external forum is the deciding factor according to the norm of the Code. If this concept is borne in mind it will be easier to understand wherein the practice of the Sacred Penitentiary differs in some respects in this matter.

The jurisdiction of the Sacred Penitentiary is confined to the internal forum. But the internal forum may be either sacramental or non-sacramental.[45] In the internal sacramental forum the Sacred Penitentiary dispenses only from impediments that are by nature occult or that are occult in fact.[46] However, according to Gasparri, it sometimes obtains permission from the Sovereign Pontiff to dispense in both the internal and external forums and in this case it warns the parties to sign their names to the rescript, which is then kept either in the episcopal archives or in the archives of the Tribunal itself.[47] For the internal non-sacramental forum the Sacred Penitentiary dispenses from impediments which

[44] Gasparri, *De Matrimonio*, n. 289.

[45] Canon 202, § 2.

[46] Cappello, *De Sacramentis*, III, n. 227.

[47] *De Matrimonio*, n. 289.

are occult according to its own concept of occult impediments. Thus it dispenses from impediments which are by nature public, but which are occult in that they are not generally known or apt to be known.[48] Consequently it will dispense from an impediment that is by nature public, if it is known to only five or six persons in a city and if these persons are not likely to divulge their knowledge to others.[49] From this fact the following becomes evident: if the Sacred Penitentiary judges an impediment to be occult, it is not simply because the impediment cannot be proved in the external forum, but also because it can be prudently forecast that the secret knowledge of it among a very limited number of persons will not be further revealed. If the Sacred Penitentiary regards an impediment to be public, it is not at all because the impediment can be proved in the external forum, but solely because it can be discreetly anticipated that the knowledge of it, though still secret, will very readily become widely disclosed, or because it must be acknowledged that the notice of it is already extensively divulged. Gasparri says that on April 19, 1918, the Sacred Penitentiary obtained the faculty from the Holy Father to dispense from impediments which are actually occult but which may become public in the future.[50] In this case, however, this Tribunal dispenses in both the internal and external forum.

If the Penitentiary dispenses in the internal non-sacramental forum, it will usually order that the rescript be filed in the secret archives of the episcopal curia, although a case has been reported in which it was ordered that the rescript be filed in the secret archives of the parish church.[51] In either case the dispensation will avail for both the internal and the external forum, inasmuch as it can be produced in the event of a future marriage case in the ecclesiastical tribunal. Consequently, if the impediment for which the dispensation or sanation was granted was an occult impediment, but later became public, it would not be necessary to secure another dispensation in the external forum. But if the

[48] Gasparri, *op. cit.*, n. 210.

[49] Cappello, *op. cit.*, n. 227.

[50] *De Matrimonio*, n. 289.

[51] Bouscaren, *Canon Law Digest*, I, p. 403, report on Canon 1047.

rescript were granted for the internal sacramental forum, the rescript would have to be destroyed immediately after its execution. In the event of the impediment becoming public later on, another dispensation or sanation would have to be procured, which alone would be of value for the external forum.[52] It is to be remembered that in petitioning the Sacred Penitentiary for any favor, the names of the parties for whom this favor is granted by this Tribunal are not to be mentioned.[53] It is needless to add, however, that if the favor is granted by this Tribunal for the non-sacramental forum and it is ordered that the rescript be placed on file, the names of the parties will have to be noted by the executor of the rescript, otherwise the record would be useless. The Penitentiary never requests nor expects any fee for a rescript which it grants. Consequently, anyone acting in virtue of faculties granted by this same tribunal must observe the same rule.[54]

In reference to the question of radical sanation it is to be observed that before recourse is had to the Sacred Penitentiary, every effort should be made to procure the convalidation of the marriage according to the norms of simple convalidation. This is particularly to the point in reference to marriages which are invalid because of occult impediments, because in such cases it will suffice for the parties to renew their consent secretly and privately. In such cases recourse will seldom be necessary. But it must be understood that here the word "occult" is used in accordance with the norm of Canon 1037, that is, in reference to an impediment that cannot be proved in the external forum. On the other hand, there will occur cases in which the impediment is public by nature, but unknown to any but a few people, and in which radical sanation will be necessary because the parties

[52] Payen, *De Matrimonio*, n. 816; Cappello, *De Sacramentis*, III, n. 287, 7; Gasparri, *De Matrimonio*, n. 376.

[53] S. Poeniten., *Monitum*, 1 Feb. 1935—AAS, XXVII (1935), 62. A report of this *monitum* is to be found in Bouscaren, *Canon Law Digest*, II, p. 90—Canon 889.

[54] Gasparri, *op. cit.*, n. 289; Kubelbeck, *The Sacred Penitentiaria and Its Relations to Faculties of Ordinaries and Priests* (Washington, 1918), p. 92.

refuse to renew their consent in the prescribed form. The Sacred Penitentiary will be competent because it admits such impediments as occult under its practice for the internal non-sacramental forum. Finally it is to be noted that the Sacred Penitentiary considers an impediment occult which, though by nature public, has remained occult in fact during a period of ten years. If the parties to the marriage had contracted publicly and are thought by everyone to be validly married, the Sacred Penitentiary can dispense from such a factually occult impediment.[55]

In concluding this article on the Sacred Congregations and the Sacred Penitentiary it will be helpful to mention several points. In the first place, before a recourse is had to the Holy See for radical sanation, the matter should be submitted to the local Ordinary unless there be danger of violating the seal of confession or of revealing an occult impediment which is a matter of the internal forum. The advisability of first submitting to the local Ordinary matters which pertain to the external forum arises from the fact that he may have all the necessary faculties to grant the favor. In the second place, the norms governing the petition for and the execution of rescripts must be observed in order to insure the validity of the rescript and of the sanation. Thirdly, consideration ought to be given to the kind of dispensations or sanations the petitioners expect to obtain through the agency of the Sacred Congregations and the Sacred Penitentiary. It is obvious that these departments of the Curia will observe the same general principles that have formed the practice of the Holy See for centuries. Thus, there will be some impediments for which it will not grant radical sanation, e.g., the priesthood; and there will be some for which it may only rarely grant a dispensation or sanation, e.g., the diaconate. It is able, however, and in some cases it is ready and willing to grant radical sanation for marriages which are invalid because of impediments for the dispensation from which they do not ordinarily give faculties to local Ordinaries. Apart from the ecclesiastical impediments arising (1) from the valid reception of the sacred order of priesthood; (2) from affinity in the direct line when the marriage which gave rise

[55] Cappello, *De Sacramentis,* III, n. 227.

to it has been consummated; and, (3) from consanguinity in the first degree of the collateral line, all of which are impediments from which the Church never dispenses, there will be more probability and possibility of obtaining radical sanation for the other impediments of ecclesiastical law than there would be of obtaining a dispensation from them for the purpose of contracting a marriage. Because, where the Church will be unwilling to dispense *ad contrahendum matrimonium*, it will often more readily dispense *ad convalidandum* or even grant a radical sanation.

Article II. Delegated Power to Grant Radical Sanation

The delegated power to grant radical sanation is that power which is enjoyed by those to whom the Holy See has given special faculties for this purpose. This does not refer to the Sacred Congregations or the Sacred Penitentiary, for these departments of the Roman Curia exercise a power in this matter which is ordinary, although vicarious. Consequently it includes only those who do not have any ordinary power in this matter, namely, Legates of the Holy See and local Ordinaries and any that may be subdelegated by them. In order to get a complete view of this question, the subject matter of this present article will include a summary of the laws governing delegated power and the use of habitual faculties and then will embrace an examination of the specific faculties held by the Apostolic Delegate to the United States and Ordinaries in this country. This treatment of the question points to the following division: A. Notions of delegated power and habitual faculties; B. The Faculties of Legates and Ordinaries.

A. Notions of Delegated Power and Habitual Faculties

According to Canon 197, § 1, delegated power is that which is committed to a person. It is immediate delegation if it comes from one having ordinary power. If it comes from one having only delegated power it is called mediate delegation or, as it is more commonly known, subdelegation.[56] In either case the

[56] Kearney, *The Principles of Delegation* (Washington, 1929), p. 58.

medium through which this delegated power is transferred is called a faculty or set of faculties. In relation to matters over which the Holy See alone exercises ordinary power, the medium by which it delegates its power to others usually takes the form known as the quinquennial faculties. These are so named because of their being conceded for a period of five years, which will generally run from the time of one *ad limina* visit to the next. Thus the formula of faculties granted to the American Ordinaries in 1934 will be renewed in 1939. In this connection it is important to note that the latest formula of faculties is the only one of any avail and that it frequently happens that substantial changes are made in the formula at the time of its issuance. An instance of such a change will be noted later when the faculties of the local Ordinaries will be given specific consideration. The faculties of Apostolic Delegates of the Holy See do not necessarily follow the five year rule of the faculties of local Ordinaries, but are issued to them at the time of their appointment and may or may not be altered during their term of office. The faculties of Apostolic Delegates and Ordinaries are known as habitual faculties and follow the norms established for habitual faculties in Canon 66.

Canon 66, § 1.—Facultates habituales quae conceduntur vel in perpetuum vel ad praefinitum tempus aut certum numerum casuum, accensentur privilegiis praeter ius.

§ 2.—Nisi in earum concessione electa fuerit industria personae aut aliud expresse cautum sit, facultates habituales, Episcopo aliisve de quibus in can. 198, § 1 ab Apostolica Sede concessae, non evanescunt, resoluto iure Ordinarii cui concessae sunt, etiamsi ipse eas exsequi coeperit, sed transeunt ad Ordinarios qui ipsi in regimine succedunt; item concessae Episcopo competunt quoque Vicario Generali.

§ 3.—Concessa facultas secumfert alias quoque potestates quae ad illius usum sunt necessariae; quare in facultate dispensandi includitur etiam potestas absolvendi a poenis ecclesiasticis, si quae forte obstent, sed ad effectum dumtaxat dispensationis consequendae.

This canon suggests various points for consideration, all of which are important if one is to understand the nature and the exercise of the delegated power to grant radical sanation or other matrimonial dispensations. The first thing to be noted in this canon is that habitual faculties may be conceded either in perpetuity or only for a prescribed time or even for a certain number of cases without reference to time. As it has been noted, the quinquennial faculties are granted for a prescribed time, but it frequently happens that in reference to some specific matter these faculties will contain a provision that they are given for a certain number of cases. Thus, for radical sanation the quinquennial faculties usually designate the number of cases for which the Ordinary has delegated power. But, whether they are given for a certain time or for a certain number of cases, these faculties are termed habitual to distinguish them from a faculty which is limited to one act or a single case.

The second point to be noted in reference to habitual faculties is their continuance after the grantee has ceased to hold office. For it is prescribed that unless the person having the faculties was chosen *ex industria personae,* or unless it is otherwise expressly stated in the faculties themselves, habitual faculties granted by the Holy See to a bishop or to others mentioned in Canon 198, § 1, will pass to their successors in office. It is evident that this continuance of the faculties is conditioned. In the first place, they will not pass to others if the original grantee was chosen *ex industria personae,* nor will they, in the second place, if it is expressly provided that they are not to pass on to others. A person is considered to have been chosen *ex industria personae* if it is clear that he has been granted the faculties because of some special aptitude or experience in a certain matter. Roelker states that the personal fitness of the person must be emphasized and that the mere mention of the bishop's name or reference to the matter as being left to his prudence does not always signify that he has been chosen *ex industria personae* and that the presumption is in favor of the continuance of the faculties, which means that proof to the contrary must be brought forth if this restriction is claimed.[57] As to the second condition against the continuance of the faculties, namely, an express contrary provision, it is clear that this can be determined only by consulting the formula of faculties, wherein this restriction would be set forth.

Relative to this same question of the continuance of the faculties *resoluto iure Ordinarii* there are several facts that may well be noted at this point. In general it is stated that the faculties given to the bishop or to those mentioned in Canon 198, § 1, pass on to their successors. Now, it is to be remarked that the canon in question includes not only those who are called local Ordinaries but also the major superiors of exempt clerical religious. It is clear, however, that in matters of matrimonial dispensations the latter group of Ordinaries do not customarily receive habitual faculties. For this reason consideration will be given only to the local Ordinaries and their successors. The "local ordinaries" named in this canon include residential bishops, abbots and prelates *nullius* and their vicars general; the administrator apostolic, vicars and prefects apostolic and those who by law or by approved constitutions succeed them in their respective offices. Besides these there are two others who are not mentioned in this canon. The first of these is the ecclesiastical superior who governs a mission territory from the time it is first established until it is erected into a prefecture or vicariate apostolic. The second of those not mentioned in this canon is the vicar delegate, who is to the vicars and prefects apostolic what the vicar general is to Ordinaries in non-mission territories.[58] The reason for the lack of any mention of these two officials is not the same for each. In respect to the ecclesiastical superior of a mission territory it

[58] The following is an excerpt from a letter of the Sacred Congregation of Propaganda dated December 8, 1919 and addressed to Vicars Apostolic: ". . . II. Elargitus est Ordinariis Missionum potestatem nominandi Vicarium Delegatum si eo indigeant, cui practice concessa sit jurisdictio in spiritualibus et temporalibus, qua ex Codice I.C. uti potest Vicarius Generalis in diocesi. Ex hac concessione, omnibus Superioribus Missionum facta, nunc tu poteris Vicarium Delegatum nominare, qui gaudeat omnibus facultatibus Vicario Generali tributis ad normam can. 368, § 1, § 2. . . ."—AAS, XII (1920), 120.

[57] *Principles of Privilege* (Washington, 1926), p. 152.

would seem that no mention was made in the Code because of the temporary character of his office. For, if the mission over which he rules is successful it will be raised to the status of a prefecture or vicariate apostolic. But if it fails, it will be suppressed. In respect to the vicar delegate, the reason for the absence of any mention is found in the fact that provision for this particular office has been made since the promulgation of the Code. But during their terms of office, both the ecclesiastical superior and the vicar delegate will exercise ordinary power.[59]

The successors of the Ordinaries mentioned in Canon 198, § 1, are mentioned in various places in the Code. Residential bishops are succeeded by the vicar capitular or administrator appointed in accordance with the prescripts of Canon 432. Abbots and prelates *nullius* are succeeded by a vicar capitular appointed in accordance with the norms of Canons 327 and 432. Vicars and prefects apostolic are succeeded by their pro-vicar or pro-prefect or by the priest who is senior in point of service according to the prescriptions of Canon 309. But whoever the successors may be, it is clear from Canon 66 that the habitual faculties pass on to them, even if their predecessors had already begun to use them. But during the term of office of a bishop to whom these faculties are conceded, they also belong to his vicar general. Although in reference to this point of law the canon uses the word *"Episcopo"* instead of the more inclusive word *"Ordinario"* there can be no doubt that the law intends to include the vicars general of abbots and prelates *nullius* and the vicars delegate of vicars and prefects apostolic. Therefore, they also have the right to use the habitual faculties of their respective Ordinaries unless these faculties were given *ex industria personae* or unless it was expressly prohibited in the faculties themselves. Excepting these two conditions, the vicar General or vicar delegate cannot be restricted in the use of these faculties by the Ordinary to whom the faculties were conceded.[60] He should use them in accordance with the will of his Ordinary, especially bearing in mind the provisions of Canon 44.

[59] Winslow, *Vicars and Prefects Apostolic* (Washington, 1924), pp. 67-68.
[60] Roelker, *Principles of Privilege* (Washington, 1926), p. 155.

The third point to be noted concerning habitual faculties is the provision made in paragraph three of Canon 66. There it is provided that the faculties carry with them whatever powers are necessary for their use. It mentions in particular the power of absolving from ecclesiastical penalties, if any are present, which would otherwise prevent the valid reception of the dispensation. In general there is less need of this special power today than there was under the old law. However, account must be taken of Canons 2265, §2. 2275, n 3; 2283. According to these canons, once a declaratory or condemnatory sentence has been given, any person upon whom an excommunication, personal interdict or suspension has been inflicted, cannot validly receive a pontifical favor. In practice, then, anyone having habitual faculties to grant radical sanation will also have the faculties to absolve persons who may be laboring under the penalties which make him incapable of the valid reception of that favor. But, inasmuch as this condition will result only from a declaratory or condemnatory sentence, it is safe to say that the use of the faculties of Canon 66, § 3, will be the exception rather than the rule.

It has been noted that there is a mediate delegation, commonly called sub-delegation. A person is said to be subdelegated when he receives his power from one having only delegated power himself.[61] At least that is the general use of the term. But it is also possible for one having subdelegated power to subdelegate another if he has received specific permission to do so.[62] Relative to such important matters as matrimonial dispensations it will seldom happen that one having subdelegated power will receive permission to subdelegate further. But it is not uncommon for one having delegated power from the Holy See to be able to subdelegate that power, either for a single case or habitually.[63] Two conditions will prevent this subdelgation of power received from the Holy See. One condition will be the express prohibition to subdelegate. The second condition will obtain if the delegated

[61] Canon 199, § 3.

[62] Canon 199, § 4.

[63] Canon 199, § 2.

person were chosen *exindustria personae*. In the matter of radical sanation, the habitual faculties are sufficiently clear in the matter of subdelegation to render any further discussion of this point unnecessary. Another point to be noted concerning delegation is the exercise of this power. In the first place it can be exercised only over the subjects of the one possessing the power. This will include those having a domicile or quasi-domicile in his territory and also those who are known in the law as *vagi*.[64] But when the delegation comes from the Holy See it will also extend to those persons who are called *peregrini* and who are actually in the diocese. On the other hand the one who is delegated can exercise his power over his subjects who may be absent from the diocese.[65] Consequently the one who has delegated power to grant radical sanation can concede this favor to his own territorial subjects whether they are in or outside of his diocese, and he can likewise concede it to others who are not his territorial subjects as long as they are actually resident in his diocese. The same principle applies for the Legates of the Holy See throughout the territory over which their jurisdiction extends. These are general principles of the common law, but they are generally repeated in the formula of faculties obtained from the Holy See.

B. *The Faculties of Apostolic Delegate and Local Ordinaries*

With the foregoing points of law in mind, attention can now be given to the habitual faculties possessed by Apostolic Delegates and local Ordinaries. For this purpose the faculties of the Apostolic Delegate to the United States will be used. A division is necessary in reference to the faculties of local Ordinaries. In the first place the faculties of the Ordinaries of the United States naturally offer the most favorable opportunity to study the faculties which are generally conceded to local Ordinaries of non-mission territories. In the second place the faculties of local ordinaries in mission territories subject to the Sacred Congrega-

[64] Kearney, *Principles of Delegation*, p. 99.

[65] Canon 201, § 3.

tion of the Propagation of the Faith offer a more varied and a somewhat more complicated field for study. Consequently these will have to be considered separately. The manner of proceeding in this survey will be to give the faculties first and then to make whatever commentary seems warranted by the faculties themselves.

1. *Faculties of the Apostolic Delegate to the United States*

N. 34. Sanandi in radice pro centum vicibus matrimonia nulla ob aliquod ex impedimentis dirimentibus, quibus in numero praecedenti (. . . ab omnibus impedimentis dirimentibus matrimonium, iuris tamen ecclesiastici, sive publicis sive occultis, sive minoris sive maioris gradus, iis tamen exceptis quae ex affinitate in linea recta consummato matrimonio, ex ordine sacro et solemni professione proveniunt.

Quod vero ad impedimentum dirimens disparitatis cultus, fas non sit dispensationem concedere nisi servatis iis quae in canonibus 1060-1064 praescripta sunt, et quoad matrimonia cum hebraeis vel mahumedanis, dummodi constet de status libertate partis infidelis ad removendum periculum polygamiae, absit periculum circumcisionis prolis, et si civilis actus sit ineundus, sit tantum coerimonia civilis nullaque Mahumetis invocatio aut aliud superstitionis genus interveniat . . . N. 33), cum facultate prolem exinde susceptam legitimam decernendi et declarandi, excepta tamen sacrilega et adulterina, ad effectus tantum canonicos, dummodo exinde nullum tertii iuri legitime quaesito praeiudicium inferatur et nullum scandalum proveniat, quando moraliter impossibilis est renovatio consensus modo ordinario, dummodo tamen prior maritalis consensus in unoquoque casu perseveret et absit periculum divortii, monita parte impedimenti conscia de sanationis effectu et debita facta adnotatione in libro baptizatorum et matrimoniorum. Rescriptum vero huiusmodi sanationis in Curia Episcopali diligenter custodiantur, quo omni tempore et eventu de matrimonii validitate et de prolis legitimatione constare possit.

Sed si matrimonium fuerit nullum ob defectum formae, danda non erit sanatio nisi in casu quo altera pars

> renuat renovare consensum iuxta formam, aut, si id ab ea exigatur, grave immineat alteri parti malum vel periculum: constito tamen semper de perseverantia prioris maritalis consensus et dummodo absit periculum divortii.
>
> Quod si matrimonium fuerit nullum ob non servatam formam in casu mixtae religionis aut disparitatis cultus, (the Apostolic Delegate has the faculty) "sanandi in radice quando pars acatholica ad renovandum coram Ecclesia matrimonialem consensum aut ad cautiones praestandas ad praescriptum Codicis I. C., can 1061, §2 ullo modo induci nequeat, exceptis casibus: 1) in quo pars acatholica adversatur baptismo vel catholicae educationi prolis utriusque sexus natae vel nasciturae; 2) in quo ante attentatum matrimonium, sive privatim, sive publicum actum, partes se obstrinxerunt educationi non catholicae prolis, uti supra; dummodo aliud non obstet canonicum impedimentum dirimens, super quo ipse dispensandi aut sanandi facultate non polleat. Servatis quoad cetera de iure servandis". (This latter part is a direct quotation from the Holy Office).

The foregoing formula may be said to be divided into three parts. The first part treats of marriages which are invalid because of diriment impediments of the ecclesiastical law. But since the word "impediment" is used here in its strict sense, the first part of the formula does not pertain to the form of marriage. In the second part reference is made to marriages which are invalid solely because of defect of form. The third part is also concerned with marriages which are invalid because of defect of form, but only in so far as these marriages were simultaneously accompanied with the impediment of mixed religion or disparity of worship. This threefold division will be kept in mind in discussing the questions or points of law that offer themselves as subject matter for this commentary.

From the first part of the formula it is clear that only three impediments of ecclesiastical law are excluded. The first of these is the impediment arising from the reception of sacred orders. Inasmuch as the formula reads *"ex sacro ordine"* it is possible to interpret this to mean that the Apostolic Delegate cannot grant radical sanation for marriages which are invalid because of any of the three sacred orders, namely, priesthood, diaconate or subdiaconate. On the other hand, in view of the fact that faculties may be given a wide interpretation it is possible to maintain that the Apostolic Delegate is empowered to grant a radical sanation for marriages which are invalid because of diaconate or subdiaconate, but not because of the priesthood. This would then be in conformity with the restriction placed on local Ordinaries in the United States who are empowered to grant radical sanation for marriages which are invalid because of sacred orders excepting the order of priesthood. The second impediment excluded is that of affinity in the direct line once the marriage has been consummated. Concerning this impediment two things are to be noted. First, affinity in the collateral line is not excluded. Secondly, affinity in the direct line is not excluded provided that the marriage which gave rise to it has never been consummated. Therefore, it appears that the Apostolic Delegate is empowered to grant radical sanation for a marriage that is invalid because of affinity in the direct line, provided that the marriage which gave rise to the impediment of affinity was a *ratum non consummatum* marriage that has been legitimately dissolved by the Holy See. The third impediment excluded from the formula is that of solemn profession. But this must be understood in the full sense of Canon 1073, which means that in virtue of this formula radical sanation cannot be granted for the marriages of those who are bound by solemn vows or of those who are bound by simple vows to which an equally nullifying force has been added by a special privilege of the Holy See, e. g., by the vows taken in the Society of Jesus.

Apart from these three impediments the Apostolic Delegate has power to grant radical sanation for marriages which are invalid because of any of the remaining diriment impediments of ecclesiastical law. It matters not whether they are public or occult. Concerning this extensive delegation various points may be noted. Delegation that is granted for the external forum can also be used in the internal forum, both sacramental and non-sacramental.[66]

[66] Canon 202, § 2.

Furthermore, this delegation for radical sanation covers all cases where the impediment is multiple, e. g., in multiple consanguinity; and it also covers the cases in which there is a concurrence of impediments from which the Apostolic Delegate has faculties to dispense, e. g., mixed religion and consanguinity.[67]

The faculty for sanation granted in the first part of this formula also includes the faculty of declaring legitimate any offspring born of marriages which were invalid because of impediments for which sanation can be granted. The first thing to be noted concerning this legitimation is that it refers to the offspring born of the invalid marriage, that is, born after the parents exchanged marital consent. For, if the children had been born to the same parties prior to the time that the latter exchanged marital consent, these children would be considered as having been born not of an invalid marriage, but rather of a non-marital union, and for such unions radical sanation has no effect.[68] A second point to be noted concerning this legitimation is that it excludes adulterine and sacrilegious offspring.[69] Adulterine children are excluded because radical sanation cannot be given for marriages that are invalid because of the impediment of *ligamen*. The exclusion of sacrilegious children refers to the offspring born of marriages that were invalid because of sacred orders or solemn profession. Therefore, although radical sanation can be granted for the marriages of those who are bound by the impediment of the two sacred orders below that of the priesthood, nevertheless this sanation will not carry with it the legitimation of any offspring which may have been born of that invalid marriage. A third fact concerning this legitimation is that it refers only to the canonical effects and not to the civil effects of legitimacy. The faculty further states that the legitimation can be granted, provided that it does not prejudice the acquired rights of a third party. The rights here spoken of undoubtedly comprise any and all rights of inheritance or succession which may have been acquired by a third

[67] Canon 1049.

[68] Cf. supra, p. 60-61.

[69] Cf. Canon 1051.

party because the offspring of this marriage was born illegitimate. All the authors who formerly treated this particular question of prejudice to the acquired rights of a third party admitted the power of the Roman Pontiff to grant legitimation that would prejudice the acquired rights of a third party, if he had a just cause for doing so. However, all of them declared that it should not be presumed that this was the wish of the Roman Pontiff, unless he expressly declared that it was. In these faculties it is clearly implied that it is not his wish. Therefore, in those countries where this would be a practical question, the legitimation that is obtained through radical sanation must not prejudice the acquired rights of a third party.

In the exercise of the power conceded in these faculties, it seems that the Apostolic Delegate is able to grant radical sanation for a marriage whether one or both parties are aware of the invalidity of the marriage. For, even if both parties are aware of the invalidity of the marriage, it may happen that it is morally impossible to obtain a renewal of consent as prescribed by the law, if one or both parties refuse to conform to that law. In such a case, provided the prior marital consent is enduring in both parties and there is no danger of divorce, radical sanation could be granted for the purpose of easing the conscience of the party who is willing to renew consent and at the same time for the purpose of legitimating the offspring of the marriage. On the other hand, if both parties refuse to renew consent, it seems that they are to be considered as undeserving of this favor and that it is to be refused them.[70] If the impediment is an occult impediment that is known to both, it would seem that there is less reason for the necessity of radical sanation, inasmuch as the Code requires only a private renewal of consent from them. But if the marriage is invalid because of an occult impediment of which neither party is aware, e. g., the occult impediment of crime, and the confessor forsees that the parties will not renew consent if he should notify them of the invalidity of their marriage it will be necessary either to leave the parties in good faith or else to apply to the Holy See

[70] Cf. supra, p. 78.

for a radical sanation of the marriage. The Apostolic Delegate's faculties do not empower him to grant sanation if both parties are unaware of the invalidity of their marriage. In view of this fact it follows that each case of this kind will have to be cared for according to the circumstances governing it if the parties eventually become aware of the invalidity of the marriage, unless recourse is had at once to the Holy See for radical sanation at the time that the invalidity is first discovered by the pastor or confessor. In the case of a radical sanation granted for a public impediment, it is obligatory that the party or parties who are aware of the impediment be informed of the effect of the sanation, namely, that their marriage is now valid and indissoluble. Furthermore, notation of the sanation should be made in the marriage records of the parish and in the records of Baptism of the parties concerned. Finally, the actual rescript of sanation is to be kept on file in the archives of the episcopal curia so that it will be available in case any attempt is made to seek a declaration of nullity of the marriage. If the rescript of sanation is granted for the internal sacramental forum, no record is kept. But if it is granted for the internal non-sacramental forum, the rescript of sanation is to be kept in the secret marriage record of the episcopal curia.

The second part of this formula of faculties deals with marriages which are invalid because of a defect of form. Two possible cases may be considered. In the first case a marriage is invalid because of defect of form if it has not been contracted according to the juridical form prescribed by the law. This may mean that the marriage was contracted before a civil officer or a non-Catholic minister, or that it was entered into without any particular form or ceremony. In the second case a marriage would be invalid because of defect of form if the attending priest did not have the necessary authorization or if there were not sufficient witnesses. It seems useful to consider each of these possibilities in relation to the faculties of the Apostolic Delegate, especially since the faculty to grant radical sanation for marriages which are invalid solely because of defect of form is not given to the local Ordinaries in this country.

The first case supposes that two persons, who are free from

all impediments, are invalidly married because of defect of form. Whether they contracted marriage without any form or whether they contracted it before a civil officer or non-Catholic minister, radical sanation is possible, if one party refuses to renew his consent in the form prescribed by the Church or if it is impossible to ask him to do so because of a prudent fear that some grave harm will result to the other party. But if both parties refuse to renew their consent in the prescribed form, there seems to be no reason for granting them this favor, for their bad faith in the matter may easily indicate a possibility of a future divorce. In a case where one of the parties is unwilling to renew consent and the other party is willing, it appears that it will be necessary to inform the recalcitrant party of the effect of the radical sanation. For, inasmuch as the other party will also be a Catholic it is to be presumed that he is aware of the invalidity of the marriage. Therefore, even though he refuses to renew consent or even though he cannot be asked to renew consent, the principle of informing the party who is aware of the invalidity of the marriage which is set forth in the first part of the formula would seem to be equally applicable to this case. In the forms used for granting sanation by the Apostolic Delegate it is stated that the Ordinary, through whom the sanation is sought, is exhorted to inform the other party at an opportune time and if it can be done prudently of the effect of the sanation. If the parties contracted their marriage before a non-Catholic minister and have incurred the censure which the law inflicts for that crime, it will be necessary to absolve them from censure, or at least to absolve the well disposed party. Unless there has been a declaratory or condemnatory sentence given in the case—and this is most unlikely—radical sanation can be granted even if one of the parties remains unabsolved, for, without a prior sentence handed down by lawful authority, the censure, of itself, would not bar the parties from receiving such a favor as sanation. Faculties for the absolution of this censure are granted in this same formula.

The second case supposes a marriage that is invalid because one or both of the witnesses were lacking or because the priest in attendance did not have the necessary delegation or authorization. In such an event two possibilities may ensue. The first possibility is that the parties would refuse to express their consent a second time upon being notified of the invalidity of the marriage. This may happen when both parties are Catholics but it is more likely to happen when only one of the parties is a Catholic. The second possibility consists in the circumstance in which the renewal of consent cannot be asked from the parties, lest grave harm come to one of the parties if the invalidity of the marriage became known. In the event of the first possible case occurring, the Apostolic Delegate could grant radical sanation since both parties are aware of the invalidity of the marriage. However, it is not likely that he would grant this favor if both parties refused to renew consent. In respect to the second possibility proposed, a distinction seems to be necessary. The Apostolic Delegate could grant radical sanation provided at least one of the parties knew of the invalidity of the marriage. But if both parties were unaware of the invalidity of the marriage the Apostolic Delegate could not grant the sanation and for such a case recourse would have to be had to the Holy See or else the parties would have to be left in good faith.

The third part of the Apostolic Delegate's faculties deals with marriages which are invalid because of defect of form in cases in which the impediment of mixed religion or disparty of worship is present. Several possibilities can arise. The first of these would concern a case in which a Catholic married a baptized or an unbaptized non-Catholic outside the Church. The second would concern a case in which a Catholic married a baptized or an unbaptized non-Catholic after obtaining the necessary dispensation, but nevertheless married invalidly for lack of canonical form, either because the marriage took place outside of the Church, or because it was contracted in the presence of an unauthorized priest, or because it lacked the required witnesses. The third possibility would concern a case of a marriage between a Catholic and a person who is thought to be a Catholic but who is actually an unbaptized person, the marriage taking place according to the prescribed form. The first of these three possibilities is really the only one which demands closer consideration here, for the cases brought under the second possibility can be sanated in virtue of the faculties enjoyed for the sanation of marriages which are invalid solely because of defect of form, while the case connected with the third possibility can be sanated in virtue of the faculties contained in the first part of the formula.

If a Catholic married a baptized non-Catholic or an unbaptized person before a civil officer or in the presence of a non-Catholic minister, the Apostolic Delegate can grant radical sanation if the non-Catholic party refuses to renew consent according to the form prescribed by the Code or if he refuses to give the prenuptial promises (*cautiones*) in writing as prescribed by Canon 1061, §2. However, the Apostolic Delegate cannot grant radical sanation in such cases if the non-Catholic party is opposed to the Catholic baptism and Catholic education of some or all of the children of both sexes, born or yet to be born of the marriage. Neither can he grant this favor if the parties in any way bound themselves to the non-Catholic education of some or all of the children of both sexes, to be born of their marriage. Finally, the favor cannot be granted if there is also present another impediment over which the Apostolic Delegate has no faculties to dispense or sanate. If none of these latter restrictive circumstances are present and the sanation is to be given, all the prescripts of the law in respect to such marriages must be observed. Thus, it must be certain that both parties are free to marry; the Catholic must give the necessary promises concerning the Catholic Baptism and education of all the children born of the marriage and there must be moral certitude that the non-Catholic party will not interfere with the Catholic in the practice of the Catholic religion or prevent the Catholic education and baptism of the children.

The foregoing survey of the formula of faculties which is conceded to the Apostolic Delegate to the United States will also serve for the most part as a survey of the faculties of local Ordinaries. The differences between the various formulas will be noted but where they are alike reference will be made to this commentary on the Delegate's faculties.

2. *Faculties of the Local Ordinaries in the United States*

1. *Ex Suprema S. Congregatione S. Officii*

No. 4. Sanandi in radice matrimonia attentata coram officiali civili vel ministro acatholico, a suis subditis etiam extra territorium, aut non subditis, intra limites proprii territorii, cum impedimento mixtae religionis aut disparitatis cultus, dummodo consensus in utroque coniuge perseveret, isque legitime renovari non possit, sive quia pars acatholica de invaliditate matrimonii moneri nequeat sine periculo gravis damni aut incommodi a catholico coniuge subeundi; seve quia pars acatholica ad renovandum coram Ecclesia matrimonialem consensum aut ad cautiones praestandas, ad praescriptum Cod. I.C. can. 1061, §2, ullo modo induci nequeat; exceptis casibus: 1. in quo pars acatholica adversatur baptismo vel catholicae educationi prolis utriusque sexus natae vel nasciturae; 2. in quo ante attentatum matrimonium, sive privatim sive per publicum actum, partes se obstrinxerunt educationi non catholicae prolis, uti supra: dummodo aliud non obstet canonicum impedimentum dirimens, super quo Ipse dispensandi aut sanandi facultate non polleat.

Ipse autem R.P.D. Episcopus serio moneat partem catholicam de gravissimo patrato scelere, salutares ei poenitentias imponat et, si casus ferat, eam ab excommuicatione absolvat iuxta Co I.C. can. 2319 § 1, n. 1, simulque declaret ob sanationis gratiam a se acceptatum, matrimonium effectum esse validum, legitimum et indissolubile iure divino et prolem forte susceptam vel suscipiendam legitimam esse; eique insuper gravibus verbis in mentem revocet obligationem, qua semper unversae prolis utriusque sexus, tam forte natae quam forsitan nasciturae, in catholicae religionis sanctitate et prudenter curandi conversionem coniugis ad fidem catholicam.

Cum autem de matrimonii validitate et prolis legitimatione in foro externo constare debeat, R.P.D. Episcopus mandet ut singulis vicibus documentum sanationis cum attestatione peractae executionis diligenter custodiatur in Curia locali, nec non curet, nisi pro sua prudentia aliter indicaverit, ut in libro baptizatorum paroeciae, ubi pars catholica baptismum recepit, transcribatur notitia sanationis matrimonii, de quo actum est, cum adnotatione diei et anni.

Mens autem est S. Officii ut Episcopus hanc facultatem per se ipse personaliter exerceat, scilicet nemini sub-deleget.

ADNOTANDA. 1. In singulis praefatis sive sanationibus sive dispensationibus concedendis, Episcopus vel Ordinarus expressam faciat mentionem Apostolicae delegationis (Cod. I.C. can. 1057).

2. Ordinarius in fine cuiuslibet anni referat ad S. Congregationem S. Officii de numero et specie dispensationum vigore praesentis Indulti enlargitarum.

2. *Ex S. Congregatione de disciplina Sacramentorum*

No. 4. Sanandi in radice matrimonia nulliter contracta ob aliquod ex impedimentis iuris ecclesiastici maioris vel minoris gradus, exceptis iis provenientibus ex sacro presbyteratus ordine et affinitate in linea recta, matrimonio consummato, si magnum adsit incommodum requirendi a parte, ignara nullitatis matrimonii, renovationem consensus, dummodo tamen prior maritalis consensus perseveret et absit periculum divortii; monita tamen parte conscia impedimenti de effectu huius sanationis et debita facta adnotatione in libro baptizatorum et matrimoniorum.

ADNOTANDA. 1. Ordinarius recensitis facultatibus, sive per se sive per alias idoneas ecclesiasticas personas ad hoc specialiter deputandas, uti poterit in matrimoniis sontrahendis et nulliter contractis cum suis subditis ubique commorantibus et aliis omnibus in proprio territorio actu degentibus, facta in unoquoque casu expressa mentione huius Apostolicae delegationis ad normam canonis 1057.

2. In usu earundem facultatum prae oculis habeantur quae in can. 1048 ad 1054 statuta reperiuntur.

3. Ordinarius, in fine cuiuslibet anni, referat ad Sacram Congregationem Sacramentorum, per tramitem S. Congregationis Consistorialis, de numero et specie dispensationum quas vigore praesentis Indulti ipse fuerit elargitus.

The formula of faculties which has been reported here is that which was issued to the American Ordinaries at the time of their *ad limina* visit in 1934. It will be due for renewal and possibly for revision in 1939. Although the entire formula comes to the Ordinaries through the Sacred Consistorial Congregation, it is clearly indicated which Congregation is the actual grantor of the faculties. In view of this fact it will be proper to survey these faculties according to their sources, that is, by considering first the faculties granted by the Holy Office and then those granted by the Sacred Congregation of the Sacraments. Together with the faculties themselves will be considered the official notes appended to each group of faculties.

The faculties granted by the Holy Office concern the same matter as that which is dealt with in the third part of the Apostolic Delegate's faculties, namely, marriages performed outside the Church and involving either mixed religion or disparity of worship. It is evident from the wording of these faculties that Ordinaries are empowered to grant radical sanation in either case if the non-Catholic party cannot be informed of the invalidity of the marriage or if he cannot be induced to renew his consent in the prescribed form or to give the required promises. It is safe to consider it impossible to inform the non-Catholic party of the invalidity of the marriage, if from that notification the Catholic party will probably be subjected to insults, contempt and other grave inconveniences or if the Catholic party will apparently be confronted with the hazard of separation and divorce by the other party, once he becomes aware of the invalidity of the marriage. Of course, if it is at all indicated that divorce may be expected from their unsatisfactory domestic relations, it will not be prudent to grant radical sanation. But the refusal to renew consent in the prescribed form must not necessarily be construed as a certain proof of a future divorce.

In the formula of faculties which is reported here it is stated that the Ordinaries are empowered to grant radical sanation if the non-Catholic party refuses to give the promises. But, unlike former faculties, a new restriction has been placed on this condition. This restriction is twofold and pertains to the opposition of the non-Catholic to the Catholic education or baptism of his children and to any prenuptial agreement between the parties to educate the children as non-Catholics. If neither of these conditions exists, radical sanation can be granted. In some cases it may not be possible to approach the non-Catholic party in regard to the matter of the Catholic baptism and education of his children, but his attitude can be determined from the status of this question in reference to the children already born. In other words, if his children have been baptized as Catholics and are being reared as Catholics, it can be accepted in the absence of positive evidence to the contrary that he is not opposed to either fact. If no children have been born, the attitude of the non-Catholic may be determined from his conduct towards his wife in relation to her practice of the Catholic religion. It frequently happens that non-Catholics are not willing to renew their consent in the form prescribed by the Church, but are not unwilling to acquiesce to the Catholic baptism and education of any children born or to be born of the marriage. This is primarily a question of fact and will have to be determined by the circumstances attending each individual case. The one point to be stressed here is that it is not necessary that the Ordinaries have the promises in writing from the non-Catholic party before granting the sanation. In respect to the second exception to this faculty of the local Ordinary, namely, any pre-nuptial agreement to have the children born of the marriage educated in a non-Catholic sect, it seems safe to state that if both parties have receded from their original pact a radical sanation may be given for their marriage. For it is reasonable to suppose that the local Ordinary is bound by this restriction only for the time during which the original pact is in force.

One question may be raised concerning this faculty insofar as it pertains to the impediment of disparity of worship, namely, whether it extends also to cases in which one party is a Jew. It must be noted in the first place that there is no specific restriction concerning Jews in this particular faculty for sanation, whereas in the faculty for the granting of a dispensation from disparity of worship for the purpose of contracting marriage it is specifically stated that the faculty does not extend to a marriage with a Jew or a Mohammedan. From this fact alone it would seem safe to conclude that the faculty for sanation also includes cases in which one party is a Jew. Faculties must be interpreted according to the general principles laid down in the Code for privileges and rescripts, namely, the rules contained in Canons 67 and 68. An application of these norms to this question appears to make it safe to answer this question in the affirmative. For the first principle for the interpreting of a privilege is to judge the privilege according to its tenor and not to restrict or extend it. But the tenor of any privilege can be judged only by its wording and certainly the wording of these faculties is sufficiently clear to include any and all persons who could be included under the impediment of disparity of worship. This seems confirmed from the exception that is made to such a general wording in the faculties for granting a dispensation from disparity of worship *ad contrahendum matrimonium*. But if the restriction in the earlier section of this formula causes a doubt about the extent of this section, then the interpretation, according to Canon 68, is to be made according to the norm of Canon 50. From this latter canon the only interpretation possible is a wide interpretation and the wide interpretation of the impediment of disparity of worship would comprise the case of marriage between a Catholic and a Jew.

Apart from these questions or points there seems to be little else to be discussed in relation to the faculties granted by the Holy Office that cannot be discerned from the formula itself. In the formula it is definitely stated, however, that it is the mind of the Holy Office that the bishop exercise these faculties personally. This means that they are not to be delegated to anyone and it would seem if they were delegated to another that they would be exercised invalidly by the subdelegated party. This does not represent an *ex industria personae* selection of the bishop, but it does represent a specific prohibiton to subdelegate. Needless to say, the vicar general is empowered to grant this favor by reason of these faculties, for the faculties conceded to the bishop belong also to the vicar general. In like manner these faculties pass to the administrator during the vacancy of the See, since they have not been granted *ex industria personae* and since there is not any express provision to the contrary in the faculties.

The faculties granted by the Sacred Congregation of the Sacraments to Ordinaries for the sanation of marriages which are invalid because of a diriment impediment of ecclesiastical law are briefer than those of the Apostolic Delegate. Substantially they are the same, with one notable exception concerning the number of impediments excluded from the faculty. It is to be recalled that besides the sacred order of priesthood and affinity in the direct line resulting from a consummated marriage, the Delegate's faculties specifically exclude the impediment resulting from solemn profession. This latter impediment is not excluded specifically from the faculties which the local Ordinaries receive from the Sacred Congregation of Sacraments. But does this mean that these Ordinaries are empowered to grant radical sanation for marriages which are invalid because of an impediment resulting from solemn profession? To answer this question it seems necessary to make the following distinctions: 1. If the Sacred Congregation of the Sacraments is competent to grant this faculty, it is clear that the local Ordinaries have this power, since it is not specifically excluded in the formula granted by that congregation; 2. If the Sacred Congregation for Religious is the only one competent to grant this faculty, it is certain that the local Ordnaries do not have the power since it is not included in the faculties granted by that Congregation. The question is one of law as well as of fact.

A study of the various commentators seems to indicate that they distinguish between the competency of the Sacred Congregation for Religious to grant a dispensation from the impediment of solemn profession and the competency of the Sacred Congregation of the Sacraments to grant a sanation for marriages that are invalid because they have been contracted with this impediment.[71] In other words, in accordance with the competency conferred on it in Canon 251 the Sacred Congregation for Religious

[71] Wernz-Vidal, *Ius Canonicum,* II, n. 494; Cappello, *De Sacramentis,* III, n. 226; Payen, *De Matrimonio,* n. 638; Gasparri, *De Matrimonio,* n. 629.

can dispense religious from their vows and thus free them from the impediment resulting from their profession of vows. But, if a person bound by solemn vows attempts marriage without such a dispensation from the Congregation for Religious, it seems that the Congregation of the Sacraments alone is competent to grant the necessary sanation for marriage. In this way the respective jurisdiction of both Congregations is kept intact and free from any overlapping. In view of these considerations, it seems that the Ordinaries could receive their faculties for this particular sanation only from the Sacred Congregation of the Sacraments. Therefore, inasmuch as there is no specific exclusion of this impediment in the formula of faculties which they receive from this Congregation, it is to be concluded that the local Ordinaries of this country are empowered to grant sanation for such marriages.

The faculties from this Congregation empower Ordinaries to grant sanation only where there is question of great inconvenience to require the renewal of consent from the party who is ignorant of the impediment. For it appears that the local Ordinaries are empowered to grant sanation only when one party is ignorant of the invalidity of the marriage and the other party is aware of it. Therefore, if both parties are aware of the invalidity or if both parties are ignorant of the invalidity of the marriage, the local Ordinaries apparently cannot grant sanation. It is to be noted, however, that the faculties speak of the party being ignorant of the nullity of the marriage. It does not speak of the party being ignorant of the impediment. For it is not inconceivable for a person to know of the impediment without realizing that it has a diriment effect on the marriage. Therefore, even if both parties know of the impediment or know the fact that induced the impediment, e.g., solemn profession, but only one of them is conscious of its nullifying force, the ordinaries could use their faculties.

Several more points may be noted concerning the faculties of local Ordinaries. In the first place apart from the two impediments which are specifically excluded, the formula concedes power to grant sanation for all the other diriment impediments of ecclesiastical law. Consequently the same thing applies here that has been noted already concerning the faculties of the Apostolic Delegate. In the second place, it is to be particularly noted that the formula of faculties for the ordinaries restricts their power to cases involving diriment impediments in the strict sense of that term. Therefore, marriages that are invalid solely because of a defect of form do not come within the range of these faculties.[72]

In an official note appended to this formula granted by the Sacred Congregation of the Sacraments it is stated that the local ordinaries can either use the faculties personally or delegate them for use by other suitable ecclesiastical persons, e.g., the chancellor of the diocese or the vicars forane or any other priest. It is also stated that the faculties can be used for the bishop's own subjects wherever they may be or for others who are actually staying in his territory. The act of dwelling in a place, in the sense in which it is used here, does not necessarily imply a residence with the intention of acquiring a domicile or quasi-domicile. But it does mean that the parties must actually be in the territory of the bishop granting the favor at the very moment when the favor is granted. In every case it is required, for the licitness of the act, that specific mention be made of the fact that the favor is granted in virtue of the apostolic delegation granted in the faculties. When the Ordinaries or those subdelegated by them, use the faculties granted in this formula they are reminded to observe the norms prescribed in Canons 1048 to 1054, both inclusive. The prescriptions of these canons have already been treated in other parts of this work and call for no special consideration at this point. However it is to be noted that according to the norm of Canon 1051, which deals with legitimation, sacrilegious and adulterine children are excluded from its benefits. Applying this principle to the faculties for sanation it is clear that local ordinaries cannot grant legitimation to either of these classes of illegitimates. Therefore, if he should grant sanation for a marriage that is invalid because of the sacred orders of diaconate or subdiaconate, the local ordinary could not grant legitimation to the offspring of that marriage. The same would

[72] Cf. Apollinaris, X (1937), 331.

be true of offspring born of a marriage invalid because of solemn profession. These restrictions are specifically stated in the faculties of the Apostolic Delegate in such a manner that they leave no reason to doubt that their universal application represents the will of the Holy See.

3. *Faculties Granted to Ordinaries of Mission Territories*

The Sacred Congregation of the Propagation of the Faith issue four different formulas of faculties, a different formula being given to Ordinaries according to the places in which they are resident. *Formula Tertia,* for instance, is granted to the Ordinaries of such places as China, Japan, the Oceanic Islands and parts of India.[73] It is this latter formula which will be reported here. It is in two sections, the first being called *"formula maior"* and the second being known as *"formula minor." Formula maior* contains the faculties granted to those Ordinaries of mission territories who have the episcopal character. *Formula minor* contains the faculties granted to those Ordinaries who do not have episcopal consecration. However, in relation to the granting of radical sanation the faculties of both formulas are the same and are reported here as one. The faculties which are marked with an asterisk can be subdelegated.

Formula Tertia, Maior et Minor

> *N.21. Dispensandi, canonicis existentibus causis, super impedimentis matrimonialibus sive minoris sive maioris gradus Can. 1042, tam publicis quam occultis, etiam multiplicibus, iuris tamen ecclesiastici: exceptis impedimentis provenientibus ex sacro presbyteratus ordine, ex defectu praescriptae aetatis et ex affinitate in linea recta consummato matrimonio.
>
> *N.22. Sanandi in radice, iuxta regulas in Codice a Can. 1133 ad Can. 1141 statutas, matrimonia ob aliquod impedimentum, de quo supra n. 21, nulliter contracta.

[73] Winslow, *Vicars and Prefects Apostolic* (Washington, 1924), p. 76.

Quod vero attinet, ad prolis legitimationem, Ordinarius prae occulis habeat Can. 1051.
*N.23 Sanandi pariter in radice matrimonia mixta attentata coram magistratu civili vel ministro acatholico. Sanatio in radice ne concedatur, nisi moraliter certum sit partem acatholicam universae prolis tam natae quam nasciturae catholicam educationem non esse impedituram. Quod autem attinet ad prolis legitimationem, Ordinarius prae oculis habeat canonem 1051.

ANIMADVERSIONES

II. Ordinarius insuper supradictis omnibus facultatibus sive per se sive per alios uti tantum valeat intra fines suae iurisdictionis; easque gratis et sive ulla mercede exerceat, et facta mentione apostolicae delegationis.
III. Quod si forte ex oblivione vel inadvertentia ultra tempus supra praefinitum, seu ultra . . . hisce facultatibus Ordinarium uti contingat, absolutiones, dispensationes, concessiones omnes exinde impertitae uti ratae atque validae habeantur. Insuper datis precibus pro renovatione seu prorogatione earumdem facultatum, ipsae in suo robore perseverare censeantur, usque dum responsum S.C. ad eundem Ordinarium pervenerit.

The first thing to be noted about the faculties conceded by this formula to Ordinaries of mission territories is that they can be subdelegated to missionaries in that Ordinary's territory. But, since there is no specific permission allowing it, these missionaries cannot further subdelegate these faculties. This provision is made in the interest of souls and of the missionaries alike and is undoubtedly prompted by the unusual and difficult circumstances under which both Ordinaries and Missionaries labor in these territories. In No. 22 of this formula, mention is made by Canons 1133-1137 which concern simple convalidation. These are undoubtedly added as a reminder to consult these canons and their prescriptions in order that a clear concept will be had of both modes of convalidation.

In number 22 of this formula the faculty is given for granting sanation for any marriage which is invalid because of the impediments mentioned in number 21 of the same formula. That number has also been reported and from its contents it is clear that the Ordinaries of mission territories have no faculties for three impediments. These are the impediments resulting from the priesthood, from affinity in the direct line after the consummation of the marriage and from the defect of canonical age. It will be noted that the first two impediments are also excluded from the other faculties which have already been studied. The exclusion of the third impediment from the scope of these faculties represents a special restriction for Ordinaries in mission territories. In other respects, these Ordinaries are empowered to grant sanation for all the other impediments of ecclesiastical law. Consequently, what has been said in respect to the other faculties applies in large part to these also. However, since there is nothing to indicate the contrary, these Ordinaries can grant radical sanation whether both parties are aware of the invalidity of the marriage; or whether only one party is aware of the invalidity of the marriage. The faculties, however, are restricted to marriages which are invalid because of a diriment impediment of the ecclesiastical law. Furthermore, since the word "impediment" is here used in its strict sense, it follows that these faculties do not empower the Ordinaries in mission territories to grant sanation for marriages which are invalid solely because of defect of form. Payen asserts that, if a marriage is invalid because of a diriment impediment which is not excluded from the faculty for sanation and also because of a defect of form, the Ordinaries in mission territories can grant sanation for that marriage.[74] This seems to be a reasonable opinion in view of the fact that the marriage is invalid because of a diriment impediment for which he has faculties to sanate. Moreover, if one were to adopt the view that he could not sanate such a marriage simply because there was present a defect of form it would be necessary to place a restriction on the use of the faculty that is not clear from the faculty itself. For, although the faculty speaks of sanating marriages invalid because of a diriment impediment it does not speak of sanating marriages invalid *solely* because of a dirimiment im-

[74] *De Matrimonio*, n. 2619.

pediment. Furthermore such a limitation would seem to militate against the broad interpretation which the law permits in respect to habitual faculties.

The second faculty pertains to mixed marriages that have been contracted before a civil officer or in the presence of a non-Catholic minister. The term "mixed marriages" is here to be understood in its broad usage, namely, as including marriages entailing either the impediment of mixed religion or the impediment of disparity of worship. The main question to be considered in relation to this faculty is whether or not these Ordinaries are empowered by this faculty to grant radical sanation when the non-Catholic party refuses to give the guarantees (*cautiones*) as required by Canon 1061. The faculty says that sanation may not be conceded unless it is morally certain that the non-Catholic party will not impede the Catholic education of all the children already born or yet to be born of the marriage. This wording does not require the formal guarantees or promises, given orally or in writing, for it requires only that the Ordinary have moral certitude about the non-Catholic's attitude regarding the Catholic education of the children.

This fact is likewise clear from a statement issued to the Ordinaries of Mission territories by the Sacred Congregation of the Propagation of the Faith in which it was explicitly declared that these Ordinaries should not grant radical sanation unless they had moral certitude that the non-Catholic party would not impede the Catholic Baptism and education of the children already born or yet to be born of the marriage.[75]

This moral certitude can be obtained from the attitude of the non-Catholic party in relation to his wife's practice of her religion and to the education of the children already born. Consequently, if every sign points to the fact that he will not impede the Catholic education of all the children, although he gives no formal, verbal or written promises in this matter, there seems to be no reason why the Ordinaries cannot use their faculties and

[75] S. C. de Prop. Fide, 2 Iulii 1930—*Australasian Catholic Record*, VIII (1931), 10.

grant sanation for the marriage even if the non-Catholic refuses to renew consent or cannot be asked to renew consent in the prescribed form. On the other hand, if moral certitude cannot be obtained solely from such signs and circumstances which can be observed because, for instance, up to now the Catholic party has been deliberately careless about the practice of religion or because no children have as yet been born of the marriage, it would seem that this moral certitude must be obtained through some sort of a formal promise. But this can be given verbally and it will have the same effect as a formal written promise if it is impossible to get the party to give the promise in writing. Although the faculties speak of moral certitude only in reference to the attitude of the non-Catholic party, this does not mean that a like moral certitude is not required in reference to the attitude of the Catholic party in respect to the Catholic education of the children. In fact there seems to be no good reason for exempting the Catholic party from the obligation of making the promises in accordance with the prescripts of Canon 1061.

In their commentaries on these faculties, Vromant[76] and Winslow[77] assert that the faculty contained in number 22 is for marriages that have been contracted in the prescribed form but which are invalid because of any diriment impediment of ecclesiastical law expect those specifically excluded. Payen apparently holds a contrary opinion since he claims that in virtue of this faculty the Ordinaries in mission territories can grant sanation for marriages which are invalid because of a diriment impediment as well as a defect of form.[78] In reference to the faculty contained in number 23 it is the opinion of all three of the above named authors that power is granted for the sanation of mixed marriages which are invalid solely because of a defect of form, in other words for mixed marriages for which a dispensation has been granted but which have not been contracted according to the form prescribed by the Church.

In respect to number 22, the opinion of Payen seems more

[76] *Ius Missionariorum* (Louvain, 1931), V. *(De Matrimonio)*, n. 264.
[77] *Vicars and Prefects Apostolic*, p. 109.
[78] *De Matrimonio*, n. 2619.

acceptable than that of Vromant and Winslow. For if their opinion is adopted it would mean that in virtue of this faculty the Ordinaries in mission territories could not grant sanation for marriages which are invalid because of a diriment impediment if it is also invalid because of a defect of form. But this does not seem to be in accord with the faculties which have already been studied. Furthermore it appears that the only basis for holding the opinion of Vromant and Winslow is the fact that the faculty speaks of *"matrimonia nulliter contracta"*. In other words that word *"contracta"* is used in a restrictive sense as referring to marriages which have taken place *coram ecclesia*. But this restriction does not seem warranted if one considers the broader interpretation which this word admits.

In respect to the faculty contained in number 23 it may at first appear that this is merely a repetition of a faculty contained in number 22. For in virtue of number 22 faculties are granted for the sanation of marriages which are invalid because of the impediment of disparity of worship. Number 23, however, does not represent a repetition of the faculty contained in number 22. This is evident from the fact that the faculties in number 22 are given for the sanation of marriages invalid because of the diriment impediment whereas the faculty in number 23 is for mixed marriages that are invalid because of defect of form. In accordance with the wording of number 23 it is to be presumed that the faculty is given for the sanation of mixed marriages for which a dispensation from the impediment of mixed religion or disparity of worship has been granted. For if the dispensation had not been granted in the case of marriages of parties bound by the impediment of disparity of worship, the marriage would be invalid also because of the impediment as well as defect of form. The natural question in respect to this faculty would seem to be why were faculties given for the sanation of mixed marriages invalid because of defect of form when other marriages which might be invalid because of defect of form were excluded. A possible answer to this question might be found in the fact that if special faculties were not given for these cases marriages entailing the impediment of mixed religion might not otherwise be convalidated. Since mixed religion is only a prohibitive impediment, such marriages could not be sanated in virtue of number 22 even if they were invalid because of defect of form. On the other hand it is not easy to say that they should be compelled to conform to the same norms of convalidation as other marriages which are invalid solely because of a defect of form. For, apart from mixed marriages, the only marriages which could be invalid because of defect of form would be the marriages of two Catholics. But the circumstances would not be the same. Because in the case of two Catholics the law binds both parties directly and there would be less reason for relaxing the law and of granting a sanation for their marriage than there would be in a case in which one of the parties is a non-Catholic who is bound only indirectly by the law and from whom it would be more difficult to obtain an observance of the law.

The foregoing commentary may be summed up as follows: first, in virtue of the faculty contained in number 22, Ordinaries in mission territories can grant sanation for marriages which are invalid because of any diriment impediments except those specifically excluded. Furthermore, that they can grant this sanation whether the invalid marriage was contracted according to the prescribed form or not. Finally, in virtue of this same faculty these Ordinaries can grant sanation only when the marriages are invalid because of a diriment impediment in the strict sense and not when they are invalid solely because of defect of form. Secondly, in virtue of the faculty granted in number 23, Ordinaries in mission territories are empowered to grant sanation for mixed marriages that have been attempted before a civil officer or in the presence of a non-Catholic minister. Payen also includes marriages that have been attempted according to the customs of the country without the intervention of either a civil officer or non-Catholic minister.[79]. There seems to be no reason for rejecting this opinion, for the intent of the faculty is to include marriages that have not been contracted in the form prescribed by the Church.

[79] *De Matrimonio*, n. 2619.

Article III. Power to Grant Radical Sanation In Extraordinary Cases

In addition to the ordinary power that belongs to them by reason of their office and the delegated power that is conceded to them in their quinquennial faculties, Ordinaries also have certain dispensatory powers given to them by the common law. This power is conferred in Canons 81, 1043 and 1045. For the purposes of this work these canons are of interest in relation to the granting of radical sanation. Therefore this article will consider whether or not the Ordinaries can grant sanation in virtue of Canons 81, 1043 and 1045.

A. Power to Grant Sanation in Virtue of Canon 81

Canon 81.—A generalibus Ecclesiae legibus Ordinarii infra Romanum Pontificem dispensare nequeunt, ne in casu quidem peculiari, nisi haec potestas eisdem fuerit explicite vel implicite concessa, aut nisi difficilis sit recursus ad Sanctam Sedem et simul in mora sit periculum gravis damni, et de dispensatione agatur quae a Sede Apostolica concedi solet.

The purpose of this canon is to make provision for urgent cases in which a dispensation from a general law is necessary. In a sense it grants a very broad dispensatory power. It is broader, for instance, than the power granted in Canons 1043 and 1045, for it makes provision for any urgent case, whereas the two other canons provide only for specific circumstances. Thus, Canon 1043 grants power to dispense only in the urgent danger of death and Canons 1045 provides dispensatory power only for cases in which all things are ready for the wedding. Therefore, Cappello's opinion that Ordinaries can grant dispensations in virtue of Canon 81 in cases in which the faculties of Canon 1045 are not sufficient seems entirely correct and in accord with the tenor of Canon 81.[80] For there seems to be no more reason to deny them this right, as Wernz-Vidal do,[81] than to deny them the right to use Canon 81 to dispense from impediments for which their quinquennial faculties are not sufficient. But, if they could not grant such dispensations under these circumstances, Canon 81 would lose its force and its value in the very circumstances for which it is supposed to provide.

The canon states very definitely that Ordinaries below the Roman Pontiff cannot grant a dispensation from general laws of the Church except in two cases. First, they cannot do it unless this power has been conceded to them explicitly or implicitly. Power is conceded explicitly either by the law or by the law-giver when granting it in actual or habitual faculties. There is an implicit concession of power in Canons 66, §3 and 200, §2. Secondly, these Ordinaries cannot dispense from the general law except in cases in which recourse to the Holy See is difficult and at the same time there is danger of grave harm in delaying the dispensation and finally the law is one from which the Church is accustomed to dispense. Now, the question is whether or not in virtue of this canon Ordinaries are empowered to grant radical sanation.

It is certain that they can grant sanation only if this power has been conceded to them explicitly or implicitly. It has not been granted to them explicitly in the common law and neither has it been granted to them implicitly by the law. It has been granted explicitly through habitual faculties to Legates of the Holy See and to other Ordinaries. But even in these faculties there are found limitations. Cases will arise for which these faculties do not concede power to grant sanation. Thus the Ordinaries of the United States have no faculties to grant sanation for the marriage of two Catholics that is invalid solely because of a defect of form. Can they, in the circumstance contemplated in the second part of Canon 81, grant sanation for this marriage if one of the parties refuses to renew consent and the convalidation

[80] *De Sacramentis,* III, n. 234, 13.

[81] *Ius Canonicum,* V, n. 413, note 61.

of marriage is imperative for the easing of conscience and the legitimation of offspring?

It appears that this power is denied by the authors either explicitly or by implication . Thus, Bouuaert-Simenon deny it explicitly,[82] while Gasparri,[83] Vromant,[84] Lydon[85] and others give sufficient indication that they do not believe that Ordinaries can ever grant sanation in virtue of the last part of Canon 81. All of them cite the fact that according to Canon 1141 sanation can be granted only by the Apostolic See. It is evident that they do not consider this canon to be in any way a repetition of Canon 1040, which forbids Ordinaries to dispense from impediments, unless that power has been conceded by the law or by special indult. This conclusion appears to be the only tenable one in view of the difference in the subject matter of the two canons. For, in Canon 1040 it is a question of granting a simple dispensation that will look only to the future, whether it is granted for the purpose of contracting marriage or for the simple convalidation of a marriage. But Canon 1141 is concerned with radical sanation, which differs from a simple dispensation in this that it carries with it a retrotractive effect concerning the canonical effects of the marriage. If it were not for this one element, there would be no doubt or question concerning the power of Ordinaries to grant sanation in virtue of Canon 81.

In order to determine the force of Canon 81 still further, it will be well to consider it in regard to each of the three elements of radical sanation. The first of these is the dispensation of the nullifying obstacle, whether it be a diriment impediment or the defect of form. Now, inasmuch as these exist and obtain their force merely by ecclesiastical and not by divine law, there is certainly no doubt that local Ordinaries can dispense from either of them in virtue of Canon 81, if all the circumstances considered there are verified. Therefore, supposing a case in which the mar-

[82] *Manuale Iuris Canonici*, lib. III, n. 345.

[83] *De Matrimonio*, n. 396.

[84] *De Matrimonio*, n. 253.

[85] *Marriage Legislation in the New Code of Canon Law*, n. 317.

riage of two Catholics is invalid solely because of defect of form, it seems certain that local Ordinaries could dispense from the form if the parties were willing to renew consent privately but refused to adhere to the prescribed form. But this would be only a simple convalidation and not radical sanation. The second element of radical sanation is the dispensation from the renewal of consent. Renewal of consent is required only by ecclesiastical law when the parties have already exchanged a true marital consent which is naturally sufficient for marriage, but juridically ineffective because of an impediment or the defect of form. Now the question is whether or not, in virtue of Canon 81, local Ordinaries can dispense from this renewal of consent if, in the case proposed, one of the two parties not only refuses to adhere to the prescribed form, but also refuses to renew consent at all, although he is willing to persevere in his prior marital consent. If they can do this, they can also grant radical sanation in virtue of Canon 81. But if they cannot do this, then they cannot grant radical sanation in virtue of that canon.

At first sight it might appear that they can do it, since it is a requirement of ecclesiastical law alone. But it seems certain that they cannot grant a dispensation from the renewal of consent in virtue of Canon 81, for to do so would be to dispense from the norms of simple convalidation and thus to effect convalidation in a manner different from that provided in Canons 1133-1137. Now, besides simple convalidation, radical sanation seems to be the only mode of convalidation provided by law. But radical sanation entails something more than just a dispensation from the nullifying obstacle and a dispensation from the renewal of consent, namely, a retrotractive force, which by a fiction of law, draws the dispensation back to the beginning of the marriage and renders it valid *ex tunc* in respect to its canonical effects and valid *ex nunc* in respect to the bond of marriage. Without this retrotractive force there is no radical sanation and without radical sanation there seems to be only one means of convalidation, namely, the simple convalidation provided for in Canons 1133-1137. Nowhere in these canons is there any provision for a dispensation from the renewal of consent. This being the case, the question resolves itself into whether or not local Ordinaries are able to annex a retrotractive force to their dispensations, so that they can validly effect the radical sanation of a marriage.

The answer is undoubtedly in the negative. For retrotractivity is not rooted in the dispensation from a law, but rather consists in a force superadded to the dispensation or the abrogation of a law. But this superadded force does not follow automatically from the fact of the dispensation from or abrogation of a law, but is present only when it has been so determined expressly and specifically by the one on whose will the law depends. An excellent instance of this is found in the fact that no retroactive force was given to the abrogation of the diriment impediments existing before the Code. Consequently marriages which were invalid before the Code by reason of the impediments, now abrogated, are still invalid. Therefore, if this retrotractive force does not follow automatically from the fact of the dispensation from a law, there seems to be no sound basis for believing that any power is given to local Ordinaries to super-add this force to their dispensations. It is not given to them by any express provision of the law and its very nature seem to point out that it is not given to them by any implicit provision of the law. It is not given to them by the implicit concession of power contained in Canon 66, §3, for this concession refers to the use of habitual faculties. It is not granted by the implicit concession of power contained in Canon 200, §2, for that refers to the use of delegated power. Finally, to super-add a retrotractive force to their dispensations does not fall within the range of power conceded in the latter part of Canon 81. For the subject matter of that Canon is simply a question of granting a true dispensation. It does not seem possible to extend the scope of the canon in such a way that it could be said to include the power of giving retrotractive force to a dispensation. Therefore, it must be stated that in virtue of Canon 81, local Ordinaries cannot grant sanation. It now remains to be seen whether or not they can grant it in virtue of the power conceded to them in Canons 1043 and 1045.

B. Power to grant radical sanation in virtue of Canons 1043 *and* 1045

Canon 1043.—Urgente mortis periculo, locorum Ordinarii, ad consulendum conscientiae et, si casus ferat, legitimationi prolis, possunt tum super forma in matrimonii celebratione servanda, tum super omnibus et singulis impedimentis iuris ecclesiastici, sive publicis sive occultis, etiam multiplicibus, exceptis impedimentis provenientibus ex sacro presbyteratus ordine et ex affinitate in linea recta, consummato matrimonio, dispensare proprios subditos ubique commorantes et omnes in territorio actu degentes, remoto scandalo, et, si dispensatio concedatur super cultus disparitate aut mixta religione, praestitis consuetis cautionibus.

Canon 1045, § 1.—Possunt Ordinarii locorum, sub clausulis in fine can. 1043 statutis, dispensationem concedere super omnibus impedimentis de quibus in cit. can. 1043, quoties impedimentum detegatur, cum iam omnia parata sunt ad nuptias, nec matrimonium, sine probabili gravis mali periculo, differri possit usque dum a Sancta Sede dispensatio obtineatur.

2.—Haec facultas valeat quoque pro convalidatione matrimonii iam contracti, si idem periculum sit in mora nec tempus suppetat recurrendi ad Sanctam Sedem.

It is not within the scope of this work to give a complete commentary on these canons, but it is merely proposed to find out if these canons can be so interpreted that local Ordinaries can grant radical sanation in virtue of them. For it is certain that the powers granted in these canons are also conceded for use in the simple convalidation of marriages already invalidly contracted. But if these power pertain only to the simple convalidation of marriages, it can be readily seen that there will be some cases for which recourse to the Holy See for the sake of radical sanation will be the only solution, if the local Ordinaries do not have the necessary power in virtue of their quinquennial faculties. For, as it has been seen, they do not seem to possess the necessary power to grant sanation in virtue of Canon 81.

It would avail little to begin this consideration in any other way than to state definitely that no commentator holds the opinion that radical sanation can be granted in virtue of these canons. This statement is true not only in respect to those who have written since the Code, but it is likewise true for pre-Code authors who commented on these powers. It is noteworthy that none of the authors make an extensive statement on this question and substantially the same thing is said by all. Cappello,[86] Lydon,[87] and Wernz-Vidal[88] simply state that these canons do not include the power to grant radical sanation. Gasparri[89] and Vromant[90] state that it cannot be granted in virtue of these canons, because it can be granted by the Holy See alone. Motry,[91] O'Keefe[92] and Brennan[93] also deny that these canons confer the power to grant radical sanation but they furthermore call attention to the fact that neither of these canons confers the power to grant a dispensation from the renewal of constant or makes any mention of a retrotractive force in respect to the canonical effects of the marriage.

In order to arrive at an answer to the question under consideration, it does not seem sufficient to deny that these canons confer the power to grant radical sanation and to base that denial on the fact that the Holy See alone can grant this favor. For, if the wording of Canon 1141 is the only reason for maintaining that Canons 1043 and 1045 do not grant the faculty to concede radical sanation, it would seem that this is equivalent to saying that the Holy See could not delegate this power. But the fact is that this power is frequently delegated to Legates and Ordinaries. It is true, of course, as Vromant states, that it is necessary for the one who

[86] *De Sacramentis*, III, n. 231, L.

[87] *Marriage Legislation in the New Code of Canon Law*, n. 72.

[88] *Ius Canonicum*, V, n. 413.

[89] *De Matrimonio*, n. 396.

[90] *De Matrimonio*, vol. 5, n. 98.

[91] *Diocesan Faculties According to the Code of Canon Law* (Washington, 1922), p. 134.

[92] *Matrimonial Dispensations, Powers of Bishops, Priests and Confessors* (Washington, 1927), p. 92.

[93] *Simple Convalidation of Marriage* (Washington, 1937), p. 101.

[94] *De Matrimonio*, Vol. 5, n. 25.

grants radical sanation to be placed above the law.[94] But the same is true of any dispensation, yet the very nature of these canons is to concede power to grant dispensations and thus place the one who will use them above the law in certain circumstances. It appears, then, that the only adequate reason for affirming or denying that radical sanation can be granted in virtue of Canons 1043 and 1045 must be sought in the canons themselves. For, in spite of the fact that Canon 1141 definitely states that radical sanation can be granted only by the Apostolic See, it would be absurd to deny that the Holy See could, if it wished, concede in the common law the power to grant this favor in certain circumstances just as it actually does concede other very broad and unusual powers in the very canons under consideration. Consequently, the question is whether or not the Holy See has actually conceded the power to grant radical sanation in these two canons. If it has, the fact will be evident from an examination of the powers conferred there. If it has not, it will not be simply because Canon 1141 states that only the Holy See can grant this favor, but rather because the Holy See did not wish to delegate its power over radical sanation in this manner.

In Canon 1043 local Ordinaries are empowered to dispense from all diriment impediments of the ecclesiastical law except two. Likewise they are empowered to dispense from the form that must be observed in the celebration of marriage. This means that the local Ordinary is able to permit the parties to exchange their consent without the presence of two witnesses. It does not appear, however, that the power to dispense from the form can be construed to include the power to dispense from the renewal of consent. For the canon speaks only of the form to be observed in the celebration of marriage and this, according to Canon 1094, means the exchange of marital consent in the presence of a priest and at least two witnesses. Therefore, to dispense in an urgent danger of death, from the form in the contracting of a marriage, means to dispense from the necessity of two witnesses. But this canon also confers power to dispense from the juridical form and the ecclesiastical impediments to marriage in cases of convalidation. All authors agree that, in effecting this convalidation, the norms of simple convalidation must be followed. Now, according to these norms, if a marriage is invalid in view solely of an occult impediment, the form having been observed, it can be convalidated by a merely private renewal of consent made by both parties, if both knew of the impediment, or by one party, if only one knew of the impediment. It would not be necessary for them to observe the form requiring a priest and two witnesses. Therefore, in this case the private renewal of consent may be regarded as the form of marriage. This being true, does the power granted to local Ordinaries to dispense from the form of marriage also include the power to dispense from the renewal of consent, when this is the only form that has to be observed according to the norms of simple convalidation? If it does, it means that power is granted in this canon for radical sanation. If it does not, then sanation cannot be granted in virtue of this canon.

Calling attention once again to the fact that the canon confers power only to dispense from the form to be used in the celebration of marriage, it appears clear that the form referred to is that prescribed by Canon 1094. In other words, it is that form which is commonly called the juridical form. For this reason it could scarcely be interpreted to include the private renewal of consent when that constitutes the only form required for convalidation. For, even if one could grant that this can be called a form of marriage in the wide sense of that term, there would be less reason for dispensing from the private renewal of consent than there would be to dispense from the form of Canon 1094. Moreover, from the very wording of the canon, it appears that the Church intends to grant dispensatory power only for cases in which the form of Canon 1094 is required and does not intend to extend it to cases in which the private renewal of consent is the only form required. The entire phrase points to this fact, since its wording is in accord with the other canons which deal in any way with the juridical form of marriage. Furthermore, from the canons on simple convalidation and radical sanation it is easy to see that the Code constantly distinguishes between the form of Canon 1094 and the simple renewal of consent alone. In view of these things, there seems to be no sound basis for interpreting this canon in such a way that it would appear to concede power for radical sanation. Over and above these considerations the even more evident observation may be made that nowhere in this canon is there any mention of a retrotractive force, which, as it has been pointed out before, is a very essential element of radical sanation.

In Canon 1045 local Ordinaries are empowered to dispense from all the impediments mentioned in Canon 1043. There has been considerable discussion as to whether or not the word "impediment," as it is used in this canon, is to be taken in a restricted or in a broad sense. If it is used in its restricted sense it will include only those impediments which are known as nullifying or prohibiting impediments. If it is used in its broad sense, it will include the form of marriage also. But the more acceptable opinion is that the word "impediment," as it is here used, does not include the juridical form of marriage. Every evidence seems to point to the fact that it is presupposed that the form of marriage will be observed. For the canon is conferring power to dispense from impediments only in one definite set of circumstances, namely, when all things are ready for the marriage. This situation is most commonly interpreted as occurring when the wedding date has been set, when the invitations have been issued and when the other usual formalities have been attended to which could not be altered or changed without danger of great harm. But, in reference to convalidating a marriage, all things are considered to be ready for the marriage, if the parties have been informed of the invalidity of the marriage and a time has been set for its convalidation. For in such case there well may be a special danger of harm in delaying the convalidation until such a time as a dispensation can be obtained. In either case, however, the canon is contemplating a situation in which the form of Canon 1094 is to be observed and for the observance of which all things have been prepared. For, if it was not contemplating such a situation, the phrase *"omnia parata ad nuptias"* would be rather meaningless. In view of the very evident fact that this canon presupposes that the form is to be observed and that it makes absolutely no provision for a dispensation therefrom, it must necessarily be concluded that in virtue of Canon 1045 local Ordinaries have no power to grant radical sanation. For, if the form cannot be dispensed from, by a much stronger argument neither can the renewal of consent be dispensed from. Because the form exists for the exchange or renewal of consent and not the renewal of consent for the form. Consequently, if it is clear that the form must be observed, it would be absurd to suggest a dispensation from the renewal of consent, inasmuch as such a dispensation would eliminate the very necessity of observing the form.

In view of these things it seems to be an incontrovertible fact that sanation cannot be granted in virtue of either of these two canons. It may be asked, however, why this power was not conceded in these canons which otherwise confer such extraordinary powers. These canons give ample evidence of the willingness of the Holy See to come to the aid of her children at moments of great stress and need. Viewed in this light it would seem logical that the Holy See would wish to provide for every possible contingency, especially when it is a question of the danger of death. Yet it is clear that not every possible contingency has been provided for, even for the convalidation of marriages in danger of death. For the experience of many will bear witness to the fact that cases will arise in which one of the parties will refuse to submit to the formality of renewing consent, even when that has been made as easy as possible through a dispensation from the juridical form. The final answer, of course, could come only from the Holy See itself and one can do little more than suggest some possible explanations for the exclusion of this widest of all dispensatory powers, radical sanation.

It cannot be denied that it might be expected that this power should have been granted in these canons, if the Church wished to provide for the most extreme cases. On the other hand, there may be less cause for wonder at its exclusion, when it is recalled that the powers which actually are conferred in these canons were granted for the first time only some fifty years ago. This fact might indicate that the Holy See does not feel that the time is yet ripe for the concession of any greater powers than the ones which have already been granted. For it was only after many urgent petitions from local Ordinaries throughout the world and after the most careful deliberation that the Holy See finally departed from its traditional rigid policy and granted broader dispensatory powers for urgent cases.

A second reason that might be suggested is the fact that the Holy See considers that it has granted sufficient powers for the normal run of cases, and that a further concession of power might lead eventually to a certain degree of laxity on the part of those who would receive the power. In other words, if the Holy See were to concede the power to grant sanation for the extreme cases, it might easily lead to a situation where these extraordinary powers would be used too readily for cases which could be otherwise cared for if the dispensing authority used sufficient diligence. For it must be remembered that the powers granted to local Ordinaries are also granted to pastors and confessors in the same circumstances when timely recourse to the local Ordinary is cut off.

A third reason that might be proposed is that when these canons were being formulated, the Holy See had in mind to grant extensive faculties to local Ordinaries whereby they could grant radical sanation. In view of this fact, it undoubtedly felt that it was making ample provision for the few extreme cases in which one party would obstinately refuse to renew consent and that, even if some delay were entailed in petitioning the local Ordinary for the favor of sanation, it would ultimately represent a greater good to risk the delay rather than to make a too general concession of power in the common law.

CHAPTER VII

THE PROCEDURE IN RADICAL SANATION OF MARRIAGES

The subject matter of the preceding chapters indicates that in radical sanation the Church has done her utmost to provide for the most extreme cases of invalid marriages. But this great zeal and generosity on the part of Holy Mother the Church would be of little value if those to whom the care of souls is entrusted were not equally zealous and generous in their pastoral work. This is especially true in reference to the invalid marriages among the faithful in their parishes. For more often than not, these souls are not only among those in greatest need of zealous care, but are also among the most difficult and trying persons that priests are liable to encounter. In view of this fact it would be following the easier course if one were to neglect such persons entirely, or to take the attitude that there is no solution for their problem, since they are willing to do so little for themselves. But such an attitude would not be in conformity with the mind of the Church which has made every possible provision for the convalidation of marriages just as long as at least one of the parties is willing to cooperate.

It is one thing, however, to be willing and anxious to do all that is possible to bring about the convalidation of these marriages, but it is quite another thing to be certain that it is done according to the law. In the first place, the very important thing to be borne in mind at all times in reference to invalid marriages is that it is the mind and wish of the Church that these marriages be convalidated, if that is at all possible. Even when a marriage is attacked as invalid because of defect of consent, defect of form or a diriment impediment, the law prescribes in Canon 1965, that the ecclesiastical judge should strive in every possible way to reconcile the parties and to procure the convalidation of the marriage. Although this admonition is restricted to the ecclesiastical judge only, it applies in equal manner to any pastor, confessor or other priest who may be aware that the parties are contemplating a suit for nullity. This is especially important in marriages of which children have already been born, for in the event of a declaration of nullity, they would be the ones to suffer the greatest harm. For their sake, then, if for no other reason, it is certainly imperative that the convalidation of the marriage be procured.

Once it has been ascertained that a marriage is invalid, the natural question arises concerning the best method of procuring the convalidation. If the parties themselves, or at least one of the parties, be aware of the invalidity of the marriage, there can be no question of dissimulation, that is, of leaving them in good faith. On the other hand, if both parties are unaware of the nullity of their marriage, three ways of acting suggest themselves. The first is to inform the parties of the nullity of the marriage. The second is to leave them in good faith, which is equivalent to allowing them to live in material sin and without the benefit of the sacrament of matrimony. The third is to secure radical sanation. Returning to the case in which one or both parties are aware of the invalidity of the marriage, there are three courses of action The first is to proceed according to the norms of simple convalidation. This is not merely desirable, but also mandatory, for this is the ordinary and normal means provided by the Church. The second course of action—in the event of the first means proving of no avail—is to procure the radical sanation of the marriage. This is, of course, the extraordinary mode of convalidation, but it is by no means so extraordinary that priests should hesitate to seek it or that others should hesitate to grant it, provided they have the necessary faculties and are assured that all the conditions are fulfilled. There is, undoubtedly, a great hesitancy on the part of many, either to seek this favor or to grant it because of its extraordinary character. This hesitancy seems not to be well-founded in view of the readiness with which the Holy See has granted faculties for this favor. The third course of action that may be followed in these cases—if the other two fail—is to attempt to bring about a separation of the parties. But this is, of all courses of action, one to be resorted to only in extreme cases because of the seriousness of the matter.

In the event that it proves possible to procure the convalidation of the marriage either by simple convalidation or by radical sanation, there are certain preliminaries that must be observed. In a general way, these preliminaries are the same for the convalidation of a marriage as they are for the contracting of marriage. In other words, the pre-nuptial investigation is just as important for the convalidation of a marriage as it is for a marriage just being contracted. Therefore, above all things, it is necessary to determine the freedom of the parties from any prior existing bond. If a prior bond is found to exist the entire case should be turned over to the Chancery Office. In the interim the parties should be urged to separate, if this is at all possible, or at least to live as brother and sister through a partial separation *a toro*. If no prior bond is found to exist, the investigation should then be centered around the question of impediments and especially the impediment of crime, for this is easily overlooked, especially when there has been a previous marriage which has been dissolved by death. If any impediments of the divine law are found to be present, there can be no convalidation of the marriage. If the marriage to be convalidated began during the existence of a prior bond, there can be simple convalidation if the prior bond has ceased, or is dissolved legitimately, but there can not be any radical sanation. Yet even in such cases, if simple convalidation cannot be procured, it will be perfectly correct to submit the case to the Sacred Penitentiary, which might be moved to grant the favor of a radical sanation if the circumstances warranted it. Generally, however, it will be best not to place much hope in obtaining the favor even from the Sacred Penitentiary. In marriages involving the impediments of mixed religion or disparity of worship, the diocesan laws pertaining to pre-nuptial instructions should be observed as well as the general laws on the giving of the pre-nuptial promises. In cases involving radical sanation it will scarcely ever be possible to conform to the laws regarding the instructions or even to those concerning the giving of formal promises by the non-Catholic, but in any event, it is absolutely necessary that there be moral certitude concerning the attitude of the non-Catholic on the question of the Catholic baptism and education of all the children already born or yet to be born of the marriage.

Once the preliminary investigations have been made and it has been determined which mode of convalidation is to be followed, it is necessary to conform to the laws and regulations governing either method. Therefore, if simple convalidation can be used, the norms of Canons 1133-1137 must be observed according to the case in question. Thus, if the marriage is invalid only because of defect of form, the parties should renew their consent in the form prescribed by Canon 1094. If the defect of form resulted from an attempt at marriage before a non-Catholic minister, particular attention should be paid to the question of the censure attached to this act. On the other hand, if it is necessary to have recourse to radical sanation for one reason or another, the laws governing the application for rescripts and their subsequent execution must be carefully observed, lest there arise any question as to the validity either of the rescript or of its execution. In general, rescripts from local Ordinaries are granted in the *forma gratiosa,* which is to say that they do not require an executor, and the parties need only to be informed. But when rescripts are obtained from the Holy See, they may require an executor, and in this case it is of the utmost importance that one who is named executor attend to the careful observance and fulfillment of those things which are prescribed in the various clauses of the rescript. Perhaps not all of these items are demanded for the sake of validity, nevertheless, for peace of mind and certainty of valid sanation, everything should be done as prescribed. For this reason it will be useful to review the canons dealing with rescripts.

The following formulas will serve as examples of petitions to the Holy See or the local Ordinary. Several things, however, should be noted once more concerning the specific procedure to be followed in relation to sanation. The first of these is that if application is made to the local ordinary or to the Sacred Penitentiary for the internal sacramental forum, the names of the parties are not to be given. If the rescript is granted in the sacramental forum, it is to be destroyed at once and if the impediment becomes public later on, petition should be made in the external forum. If the rescript is granted in the non-sacramental internal forum, at least a full notation of it should be kept in the secret marriage record of the episcopal curia. If the impediment later becomes public, there will be no need of a further sanation in the external forum. If the rescript is granted in the external forum, a record should be made not only in the marriage register of the parish, but also in the baptismal records of the parties. The second thing to be noted is that if the local Ordinary has faculties sufficient to cover the case in question there will be little need of petitioning the Holy See for this favor. For this reason it will be proper to petition the local Ordinary first, and then, if he has not sufficient faculties, he in turn will forward the request to the Holy See. It is to be noted that the local Ordinary can send his petitions to the Sacred Consistorial Congregation, which will forward them to the proper Congregation. If, however, there is an urgent reason for keeping the petition even from the knowledge of the local Ordinary, the petition can be sent directly to the Sacred Penitentiary, observing the rule concerning the names of the parties. That is, if it is for the sacramental forum, the real names are omitted; if it is for the non-sacramental forum and it will be necessary for the Sacred Penitentiary to record the sanation because the Ordinary cannot be informed of it, the real names and addresses of the parties will have to be given. If it is necessary to petition the Holy See in the external forum, because the local Ordinary does not have sufficient faculties, it will be expedient to obtain a letter of approbation from the Ordinary or let him forward the petition. The third thing to be noted is that in petitioning either the Holy See or the local Ordinary it is considered the better policy to write in Latin. However, in petitioning the Holy See, Italian, French, Spanish, German, and English are admitted.

CONCLUSIONS

The following items seek to set down in a summary manner the conclusions that have been reached in the present study of radical sanation.

1. The Roman Law system did not have a remedy for the convalidation of marriage and the legitimation of children that could be identified in any way with that which is called radical sanation in Canon Law. Cf. P. 15-19.

2. The claims of Giovine and Perrone, who assert that the earliest traces of radical sanation are found in certain conciliar enactments of the sixth century, are based on uncertain interpretations of those enactments and cannot be accepted as conclusive. Cf. P. 20-22.

3. All evidence seems to confirm the fact that radical sanation first came into use in 1301 during the reign of Boniface VIII. Cf. P. 23-28.

4. At first radical sanation was regarded primarily for its value as a mode of legitimating children. Cf. P. 23.

5. The assertion that Pope Gregory XIII denied that he could grant radical sanation must be rejected as an argument against the Papal power, Cf. P. 31-32.

7. The phrase *"sanatio in radice"* was first used in pontifical documents in the year 1788. Cf. P. 36.

8. The history of radical sanation is marked by little change or development in the legislation governing it from its origin up to the Code. Cf. 36-42.

9. Children born before their parents exchanged a true marital consent cannot be legitimated by the radical sanation of their parent's marriage, but will be legitimated in virtue of the provisions of canon 1051. Cf. P. 62.

10. Contrary to the expressed opinions of Payen and Cappello, and contrary to the implied opnions of others, it is concluded that children legitimated by radical sanation are held by the exceptions of canon 1117. Cf. P. 67-71.

11. The Sacred Congregation of the Propagation of the Faith has competency to grant faculties for dispensation and sanations in the territories committed to it. Cf. P. 124-125.

12. Contrary to the opinion of Wernz-Vidal it is concluded that the Sacred Congregation of the Propagation of the Faith must have recourse to the Holy Office for the sanation of marriages involving the impediments of mixed religion and disparity of worship. In other words, this Congregation is not, of itself, competent in this matter. Cf. P. 125.

13. The opinion of Blat that the Sacred Congregation for the Oriental Church has competency in matters pertaining to the impediments of mixed religion and disparity of worship is not well-founded and cannot be held. Cf. P. 128-129.

14. Local Ordinaries in the United States are empowered to grant radical sanation for a marriage between a Catholic and a Jew in virtue of their quinquennial faculties. Cf. P. 154-155.

15. Local Ordinaries in the United States are empowered to grant radical sanation for a marriage that is invalid because of the impediment arising from solemn profession. Cf. P. 156-157.

16. Ordinaries cannot grant radical sanation in virtue of Canon 81. Cf. P. 166-171.

17. Ordinaries cannot grant radical sanation in virtue of Canons 1043 and 1045. But the reasons advanced by Gasparri and Vromant for this fact do not offer a correct explanation for the exclusion of this power from these canons. Cf. P. 171-177.

APPENDIX I

The intent of the following schema is to indicate in a summary way the points of similarity and difference between simple convalidation and radical sanation, considered first in regard to their respective mode of operation and second in relation to the effects produced by each.

I.—*Mode of Operation*

RADICAL SANATION	SIMPLE CONVALIDATION
1. Perfect radical sanation dispenses from the renewal of consent (Canon 1138, § 1).	1. Always requires the renewal of consent (Canons 1133-1137).
2. If marriage is invalid because of defect of form, radical sanation always dispenses from the observance of the form for convalidation (Canon 1138, § 1).	2. If marriage is invalid because of defect of form, form must always be observed for convalidation (Canon 1137).
3. If marriage is invalid because of an impediment, R. S. dispenses from the impediment and from prescribed form (Canon 1138, § 1).	3. If marriage is invalid because of an impediment, a dispensation from the impediment accompanied by a renewal of consent is required (Canons 1133-1135).
4. If the marriage is invalid because of a defect of consent, which was later remedied, partial sanation can be granted. If consent was never supplied, there can be no sanation of the marriage (Canon 1140, §§ 1, 2).	4. If marriage is invalid because of a defect of consent, it is convalidated by the giving of consent by one or both parties according to the nature of the defect (Canon 1136).

II.—*Effects*

1. Convalidates marriage from the moment it is granted (Canon 1138, § 2).	1. Convalidates marriage from the moment consent is validly renewed according to the norms of the law (Canon 1081, § 1).
2. Contains a retrotractive force in respect to the canonical effects of the marriage (Canon 1138, § 1).	2. Contains no retrotractive force in respect to canonical effects (Canon 1116).
3. Perfect radical sanation always legitimates children *ex tunc*, that is, from the moment parents exchanged consent (Canon 1138, § 1).	3. Does not always legitimate children; when it does, legitimation takes effect from time consent is renewed if child is spurious; takes effect *ex tunc* if child is a natural child (Canons 1051, 1116).
4. Can effect legitimation without convalidation of the marriage, if death or insanity prevent convalidation. This is sanation improperly so called.	4. Never effects legitimation unless it also produces convalidation of the marriage.

APPENDIX II

The following formulas are intended to serve as illustrations of petitions to the Holy See, the Apostolic Delegate or the local Ordinaries for the favor of radical sanation. Names of persons and places have been inserted merely as an indication of the form to be used in such petitions.

1. *Petition for the radical sanation of a marriage invalidly contracted by two Catholics or by a Catholic and a non-Catholic.*

A. To The Holy See

Beatissime Pater:

Ordinarius *Renensis* suppliciter petit a Sanctitate Vestra sanationem in radice matrimonii (civiliter initi), *vel* (invalide initi ob impedimentum *disparitatis cultus*) inter *Joannes T. Smith,* Catholicus (Acatholicus) et *Alicia R. Ainsworth,* Catholica (Acatholica non-baptizata). Orator (oratrix)................................ ....conscientiae suae coram Deo consulere exoptat; altera vero pars absque gravi periculo de matrimonii invaliditate et de renovationis consensus necessitate moneri nequit. Consensus maritalis utriusque partis perseveret et nullum periculum divortii adest.

Et Deus, etc.

Patritius J. Connor,
Vicarius Generalis.

B. To the Apostolic Delegate or Local Ordinary

Your Excellency,

James Brown of this parish attempted marriage (before a civil officer) (in the presence of a non-Catholic minister) with *Regina Brennan.* a Catholic, (a baptized, unbaptized non-Catholic). *James Brown* is now penitent and sincerely desires to have his marriage convalidated. *Regina Brennan* refuses to renew her consent in the presence of a priest, *or Regina Brennan* cannot be induced to give the formal promises and furthermore refuses to renew her consent in the presence of a priest, but she will not impede the Catholic Baptism and education of all children, of both sexes, born or yet to be born of this marriage. The prior marital consent of both parties is still persevering and there is no indication that there will be a future divorce. Begging Your Excellency to grant this petition, I am,

Respectfully Yours in Christ,

James B. Empey,
Pastor.
St. Paul's Church, Uniontown, Nev.

2. *Petition for the radical sanation of a marriage null because of an impediment discovered after the marriage had been contracted in the prescribed form.*
Illme ac Revme Dne,

Joannes Ryan et *Maria Paige,* paroeciani mei, pratermissis publicationibus, quin ullum detectum fuerit impedimentum, matrimonium, in facie Ecclesiae contraxerunt, (ac successive consummarunt, prole exinde susepta).

Obstat vero impedimentum consanguinitatis in tertio aequali gradu lineae collateralis, ut videre est in schemate hic adnexo; quod impedimentum post initum matrimonium tantum innotuit.

Cum vero *Joannes Ryan,* nullo modo ad renovandum consensum coram parocho et testibus induci possit, licet de consensus perseverantia dubitari nequeat, *Maria Paige,* humillime supplicat Dominationi Tuae ut sanationem in radice praefati matrimonii concedere vel a Sede Apostolica procurare dignetur.

Die........... Mensis............... Anni...............

Joannes J. Lambe, parochus.
Paroeciae *Sanctae Teresiae, Reno, Nevada.*[1]

[1] Gasparri, *De Matrimonio,* II, Allegatum V, n. 12. In the foregoing formula substitution can be made according to the nature of the impediment. The word *"concedere"* has been added to the original formula of Gasparri in the present exemplar.

BIBLIOGRAPHY

Sources

Acta Apostolicae Sedis, Commentarium Officiale, Romae, 1909-

Acta Sanctae Sedis, 41 vols., Romae, 1865-1908.

Bullarium Diplomatum et Privilegiorum Sanctorum Romanorum Pontificum, 24 vols., Augustae Taurinorum, 1857-1872.

Bullarii Romani Continuatio Summorum Pontificum, 19 vols., Prato, 1756-1883.

Bullarium Smi Domini Nostri Benedicti Papae XIV, 4 vols., 4 ed., Venice, 1778.

Canones et Decreta Sacrosancti Oecumenici Concilii Tridentini, Romae, 1904.

Codex Juris Canonici, Pii X Pontificis Maximi jussu digestus Benedicti Papae XV auctoritate promulgatus, Romae, Typis Polyglottis Vaticanis, 1918.

Codicis Iuris Canonici Fontes, Cura Emi. Petri Card. Gasparri editi, 6 vols., Romae, 1922-1932; Vol. 7, Cura et Studio Emi. Justiniani Card. Seredi, Romae, 1935.

Collectanea S. Congregationis de Propaganda Fidei, 2 vols., Romae, ex typographia polyglotta, 1907.

Corpus Iuris Canonici, editio Lipsiensis II (Richter-Freidberg), 2 vols., Lipsiae, 1922.

Corpus Iuris Civili, (Kreuger-Mommsen-Schoell-Kroell), 5 ed., 3 vols., Berlin, 1928.

Sacrorum Conciliorum Nova et Amplissima Collectio, Mansi, Joannes, 53 vols., Paris, 1901-1927.

Monumenta Germaniae Historica, Leges, ed. Gregorius Pertz, 5 vols., Hanoverae, 1875-1889.

Pallottini, S., *Collectio Omnium Conclusionum et Resolutionum Qua in causis propositis apud Sacram Congregationem Cardinalium S. Concilii Tridentini Interpretum Prodierunt ab ejus institutione anno MDLXIV ad annum MDCCCLX, distinctis titulis alphabetico ordine per materias digesta,* 17 vols., Romae, 1868-1893.

AUTHORS

Aichner, Simon, *Compendium Iuris Ecclesiastici,* 11 ed., Brixen, 1911.

Ayrhinac-Lydon, *Marriage Legislation In The New Code of Canon Law,* New York, 1932.

Baronii, Caesaris, *Annales Ecclesiastici,* t. 23, 37 vols., Bari, 1864-1883.

Benedict XIV, *De Synodo Dioecesana,* 2 vols., Romae, Typographia S. C. de P. F., 1806. *Opera Omnia,* 17 vols., Aldina, 1847.

Blat, A., *Commentarium Textus Codicis Iuris Canonici,* 6 vols., Rome, Ex Typographia In Instituto Pii IX, 1921-1927.

Böckhn, Placidius, *Commentarium in Ius Canonicum,* 3 vols., Salisburgi, 1776.

Bouscaren, T., *The Canon Law Digest,* 2 vols., Milwaukee, 1934-1937.

Brennan, James H., *The Simple Convalidation of Marriage,* Washington, Catholic University of America, 1937.

Brys, J., *De Dispensatione in Iure Canonico Praesertim apud Decretalistas et Decretistas usque ad medium saeculum decimum quartum,* Brugis-Welteren, 1925.

Buckland, W. W., *A Textbook of Roman Law from Augustus to Justinian,* 2 ed., Cambridge, University Press, 1932.

Cappello, Felix, *Tractatus Canonico-Moralis de Sacramentis,* 3 ed., 3 vols., Vol. III, *De Matrimonio,* Rome, Marietti, 1933.

Carberry, J. J., *The Juridical Form of Marriage,* Washington, Catholic University, 1933.

Cerato, P., *Matrimonium A Codice Iuris Canonici Integre Desumptum,* 4 ed., Patavii, 1929.

Chelodi, Joannes, *Ius Matrimoniale iuxta Codicem Iuris Canonici,* 3 ed., Tridenti, 1921.

Cicognani, A. G., (Brennan-O'Hara), *Canon Law,* Philadelphia, Dolphin Press, 1935.

Claeys-Bouuaert-Simenon, *Manuale Iuris Canonici,* 2 ed., 3 vols., Wettern, 1926. *Manuale Iuris Canonici,* 3 ed., 3 vols., Gandae, 1930.

Cleary, J. F., *Canonical Limitations On the Alienation of Church Property,* Washington, Catholic University, 1936.

Corbett, Percy E., *The Roman Law of Marriage,* Oxford, 1930.

Corradus, Pyrrhus, *Praxis Dispensationum Apostolicarum,* Coloniae Agrapinae, 1697.

De Angelis, P., *Praelectiones Iuris Canonici et Methodum Decretalium Gregorii IX exactae,* 4 vols., Rome, 1877-1887.

De Becker, Julius, *De Sponsalibus et Matrimonio,* 2 ed., Louvain, 1903.

Declareuil, J., *Rome the Law-giver,* New York, 1926.

De Justis, Vincentius, *De Dispensationibus Matrimonialibus,* Luca, 1726.

De Smet, A., *De Sponsalibus et Matrimonio,* Brugis, 1909.

Devoti, J., *Ius Canonicum Universum,* 3 vols., Romae, 1837.
Dictionnaire De Droit Canonique, Paris, 1928.
Dodd-Tierney, *Church History of England,* 5 vols., London, 1839-1943.
Duskie, John A., *The Canonical Status of the Orientals in the United States,* Washington, Catholic University, 1928.
Esmein, A., *Le Mariage En Droit Canonique,* 2 ed., Paris, 1929.
Fagnanus, Prosper, *Commentaria In Quinque Libros Decretalium,* 4 vols., Venetiis, 1696.
Farrugia, P. Nicolaus, *De Matrimonio et Causis Matrimonialibus, tractatus canonicomoralis juxta Codicem Iuris Canonici,* Rome, 1924.
Feije, Henry, *De Impedimentis et Dispensationibus Matrimonialibus,* Louvain, 1885.
Ferraris, F. L., *Bibliotheca Canonica, Iuridica, Moralis, Theologica necnon Ascetica, Polemica, Rubricistica, Historica,* ed. novissima, 9 vols., Romae, Ex typographia Polyglotta S. C. de Prop. Fide, 1891.
Freisen, J., *Geschichte des canonischen Eherechts,* Paderborn, 1893.
Gasparri, P., *Tractatus Canonicus De Matrimonio,* 3 ed., 2 vols., Paris, 1904. *Tractatus Canonicus de Matrimonio,* ed. nova, 2 vols., Vaticanae, 1932.
Genestal, R., *Histoire de la Legitimation des Enfants Naturels en Droit Canonique,* Paris, 1905.
Giovine, Petrus, *De Dispensationibus Matrimonialibus,* 2 vols., Neapoli, 1863.
Gonzalez Tellez, E., *Commentaria Perpetua in Singulos Textus Quinque Librorum Decretalium Gregorii IX,* Lugduni, 1725.
Hinschius, Paul, *System des katholischen Kirchenrechts,* Berlin, 1883.
Hostiensis, H., *Summa Aurea,* Venice, 1570.
Kearney, Raymond A., *The Principles of Delegation,* Washington, Catholic University, 1929.
Konings-Putzer, *Commentarium in Facultates Apostolicas,* New York, 1898.
Kubelbeck, Wm. J., *The Sacred Penitentiaria and Its Relations to Faculties of Ordinaries and Priests,* Washington, Catholic University, 1918.
Laurentius, Jos., *Institutiones Iuris Ecclesiastici,* Friburgi, Brisgoviae, 1903.
Leage, R. W., *Roman Private Law,* MacMillan, London, 1932.
Leitner, M., *Lehrbuch des Katholischen Eherechts,* 3 ed., Paderborn, 1920.
Lydon, P. J., *Ready Answers In Canon Law,* New York, 1934.
Manning, J. J., *Presumptions of Law in Marriage Cases,* Washington, Catholic University, 1935.
Martin, Michael, *The Roman Curia,* New York, 1913.
Mothon, J., *Institutions Canoniques,* 2 vols., Bruges, 1924.
Motry, Louis H., *Diocesan Faculties According to the Code of Canon Law,* Washington, Catholic University, 1922.
Moyle, *Imperatoris Justiniani Institutiones,* 5 ed., Oxford, 1923.
Navarrus, *Opera Omnia In Sex Tomos Distincta,* Venice, 1618.
Nimkoff, M. F.-Ogburn, W. F., *Family Life,* New York, 1934.
Nodlin, H., *Summa Theologiae Moralis Iuxta Codicem Iuris Canonici,* 3 vols., 19 ed., Ratisbonae, Pustet, 1929.

Ojetti, B., *Synopsis Rerum Moralium et Iuris Pontificii*, Romae, 1899.
O'Keefe, Gerald M., *Matrimonial Dispensations, Powers of Bishops, Priests and Confessors*, Washington, Catholic University, 1927.
O'Mara, William A., *Canonical Causes for Matrimonial Dispensations*, Washington, Catholic University, 1935.
O'Neill, William H., *Papal Rescripts of Favor*, Washington, Catholic University, 1930.
Payen, G., *De Matrimonio in Missionibus*, 3 vols., Zi-Ka-Wei, 1929-1936.
Perrone, J., *De Matrimonio Christiano*, 3 vols., Leodii, 1861.
Petrovits, J. J. C., *Church Law on Matrimony*, Philadelphia, 1919.
Pichler, Vitus, *Ius Canonicum Secundum Quinque Decretalium Titulos Gregorii IX*, 2 vols., Venice, 1741.
Pirhing, H., *Ius Canonicum Novo Methodo Explicatum, Omnibus Capitulis Titulorum Promiscuae et Confuse Positis, in ordinem doctrinae digestis*, 4 vols., Delingae, 1722.
Putzer, Jos., *Commentarium in Facultates Apostolicas*, 4 ed., New York, 1897.
Ramstein, Matthew, *The Pastor and Marriage Cases*, New York, 1936.
Reiffenstuel, A., *Ius Canonicum Universum*, 7 vols., Paris, 1864-1870.
Rigantius, J. B., *Commentaria in regulas, constutiones et ordinationes Cancellariae Apostolicae*, 4 vols., Coloniae Allogrogum, 1751.
Robinson, W., *Elementary Law*, ed. nova, Boston, 1910.
Roby, *Roman Private Law*, 2 vols., Cambridge, 1902.
Roelker, Edward G., *Principles of Privilege*, Washington, Catholic University, 1926.
Sanchez, Thomas, *De Sancto Matrimonii Sacramento Disputationum Libri Sex*, 3 vols., Lugduni, 1669.
Santi, F., *Praelectiones Iuris Canonici Iuxta Ordinam Decretalium*, 2 vols., Ratisbon, 1892.
Scherer, R., *Handbuch des Kirchenrechts*, 2 vols., Gran, 1898.
Schmalzgreuber, F., *Ius Ecclesiasticum Universum*, 6 vols., 1843-1845.
Sebastianelli, W., *Praelectiones Iuris Canonici*, 2 ed., Rome, 1905.
Scott, *The Civil Law*, (A translation of the Corpus Iuris Civilis of Justinian), 17 vols., Cincinnati, 1932.
Sherman-Robinson, *Readings in Roman Law*, New York, 1933.
Simier, Jules, *Curie Romaine*, Paris, 1909.
Sipos, Stephanus, *Enchiridion Iuris Canonici*, Editio altera, Pecs, 1931.
Steigler, M. A., *Dispensation, Dispensationswesen und Dispensationsrecht im Kirchenrecht geschichtlich dargestellt*, Mainz, 1901.
Tanquerey, Ad., *Synopsis Theologiae Moralis*, 11 ed., 3 vols., Desclee, Paris, 1930.
Timlin, Thomas, *Conditional Matrimonial Consent*, Washington, Catholic University, 1934.
Van Espen, Bernardus, *Ius Ecclesiasticum Universum*, 5 vols., Lovanii, 1753.
Vecchiotti, S., *Tractatus Canonicus de Matrimonio*, Taurini, 1868.

Vlaming, Th. M., *Praelectiones Iuris Matrimonii,* 3 ed., 2 vols., Brussum in Hollandia, 1921.

Vromant, G., *Ius Missionariorum,* 5 vols., *De Matrimonio,* vol V., Louvain, Museum Lessianum, 1931.

Wernz, Franciscus, *Ius Decretalium,* 6 vols., Prati, 1911-1913.

Wernz-Vidal, *Ius Canonicum,* 6 vols., *Ius Matriomoniale,* vol. V., 2 ed., Rome, Apud Aedes Universitatis Gregorianae, 1928.

Winslow, Francis J., *Vicars and Prefects Apostolic,* Washington, Catholic University, 1924.

Woywod, S., *A Practical Commentary on the Code of Canon Law,* 3 ed., 2 vols., New York, 1932.

Zitelli, Z., *De Dispensationibus Matrimonialibus,* Rome, 1887.

PERIODICALS

Apollinaris, Rome, 1928-

Le Canoniste Contemperain, Paris, 1881-1926.

Periodica de re canonica, morali, liturgica, Brugis, 1927-

ALPHABETICAL INDEX

BIOGRAPHICAL NOTE

Robert Joseph Harrigan was born on July 26, 1909, at Springfield, Massachusetts. He received his elementary and secondary education in Catholic schools of that City and entered the Maryknoll Preparatory College at Clark's Summit, Pennsylvania, in 1925. His studies in Philosophy and Theology were made at the Maryknoll Seminary, Maryknoll, New York, and at St. Mary's Seminary, Baltimore, Maryland. At the latter institution he received the degrees of A.B., M.A., and S.T.B. He was ordained to the priesthood June 10, 1933. In the fall of 1935 he enrolled in the School of Canon Law at the Catholic University of America and received the degree of J.C.B. in 1936 and that of J.C.L. in 1937.

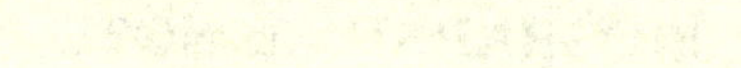

CANON LAW STUDIES

1. Freriks, Rev. Celestine A., C.PP.S., J.C.D., Religious Congregations in Their External Relations, 121 pp., 1916.
2. Galliher, Rev. Daniel M., O.P., J.C.D., Canonical Elections, 117 pp., 1917.
3. Borkowski, Rev. Aurelius L., O.F.M., J.C.D., De Confraternitatibus Ecclesiasticis, 136 pp., 1918.
4. Castillo, Rev. Cayo, J.C.D., Disertacion Historico-Canonica sobre la Potestad del Cabildo en Sede Vacante o Impedida del Vicario Capitular, 99 pp., 1919 (1918).
5. Kubelbeck, Rev. William J., S.T.B., J.C.D., The Sacred Penitentiaria and Its Relations to Faculties of Ordinaries and Priests, 129 pp., 1918.
6. Petrovits, Rev. Joseph, J.C., S.T.D., J.C.D., The New Church Law On Matrimony, X-461 pp., 1919.
7. Hickey, Rev. John J., S.T.B., J.C.D., Irregularities and Simple Impediments in the New Code of Canon Law, 100 pp., 1920.
8. Klekotka, Rev. Peter J., S.T.B., J.C.D., Diocesan Consultors, 179 pp., 1920.
9. Wanenmacher, Rev. Francis, J.C.D., The Evidence in Ecclesiastical Procedure Affecting the Marriage Bond, 1920 (Printed 1935).
10. Golden, Rev. Henry Francis, J.C.D., Parochial Benefices in the New Code, IV-119 pp., 1921 (Printed 1925).
11. Koudelka, Rev. Charles J., J.C.D., Pastors, Their Rights and Duties According to the New Code of Canon Law, 211 pp., 1921.
12. Melo, Rev. Antonius, O.F.M., J.C.D., De Eexemptione Regularium, X-188 pp., 1921.
13. Schaaf, Rev. Valentine Theodore, O.F.M., S.T.B., J.C.D., The Cloister, X-180 pp., 1921.
14. Burke, Rev. Thomas Joseph, S.T.D., J.C.D., Competence in Ecclesiastical Tribunals, IV-117 pp., 1922.
15. Leech, Rev. George Leo, J.C.D., A Comparative Study of the Constitution "Apostolicae Sedis" and the "Codex Juris Canonici", 179 pp., 1922.
16. Motry, Rev. Hubert Louis, S.T.D., J.C.D., Diocesan Faculties According to the Code of Canon Law, II-167 pp., 1922.
17. Murphy, Rev. George Lawrence, J.C.D., Delinquencies and Penalties in the Administration and Reception of the Sacraments, IV-121 pp., 1923.
18. O'Reilly, Rev. John Anthony, S.T.B., J.C.D., Ecclesiastical Sepulture in the New Code of Canon Law, II-129 pp., 1923.

19. Michalicka, Rev. Wenceslas Cyrill, O.S.B., J.C.D., Judicial Procedure in Dismissal of Clerical Exempt Religious, 107 pp., 1923.
20. Dargin, Rev. Edward Vincent, S.T.B., J.C.D., Reserved Cases According to the Code of Canon Law, IV-103 pp., 1924.
21. Godfrey, Rev. John A., S.T.B., J.C.D., The Right of Patronage According to the Code of Canon Law, 153 pp., 1924.
22. Hagedorn, Rev. Francis Edward, J.C.D., General Legislation on Indulgences, II-154 pp., 1924.
23. King, Rev. James Ignatius, J.C.D., The Administration of the Sacraments to Dying Non-Catholics, V-141 pp., 1924.
24. Winslow, Rev. Francis Joseph, A.F.M., J.C.D., Vicars and Prefects Apostolic, IV-149 pp., 1924.
25. Correa, Rev. Jose Servelion, S.T.L., J.C.D., La Potestad Legislativa de la Iglesia Catolica, IV-127 pp., 1925.
26. Dugan, Rev. Henry Francis, A.M., J.C.D., The Judiciary Department of the Diocesan Curia, 87 pp., 1925.
27. Keller, Rev. Charles Frederick, S.T.B., J.C.D., Mass Stipends, 167 pp., 1925.
28. Paschang, Rev. John Linus, J.C.D., The Sacramentals According to the Code of Canon Law, 129 pp., 1925.
29. Pointek, Rev. Cyrillus, O.F.M., S.T.B., J.C.D., De Indulto Exclaustrationis necnon Saecularizationis, XIII-289 pp., 1925.
30. Kearny, Rev. Richard Joseph, S.T.B., J.C.D., Sponsors at Baptism According to the Code of Canon Law, IV-127 pp., 1925.
31. Bartlett, Rev. Chester Joseph, A.M., LLB., J.C.D., The Tenure of Parochial Property in the United States of America, V-108 pp., 1926.
32. Kilker, Rev. Adrian Jerome, J.C.D., Extreme Unction, V-425 pp., 1926.
33. McCormick, Rev. Robert Emmett, J.C.D., Confessors of Religious, VIII-266 pp., 1926.
34. Miller, Rev. Newton Thomas, J.C.D., Founded Masses According to the Code of Canon Law, VII-93 pp., 1926.
35. Roelker, Rev. Edward G., S.T.D., J.C.D., Principles of Privilege According to the Code of Canon Law, XI-166 pp., 1926.
36. Bakalarczyk, Rev. Richardus, M.I.C., J.U.D., De Novitiatu, VIII-208 pp., 1927.
37. Pizzuti, Rev. Lawrence, O.F.M., J.U.L., De Parochis Religiosis, 1927. (Not printed.)
38. Bliley, Rev. Nicholas Martin, O.S.B., J.C.D., Altars According to the Code of Canon Law, XIX-132 pp., 1927.
39. Brown, Mr. Brendan Francis, A.B., LL.M., J.U.D., The Canonical Juristic Personality with Special Reference to Its Status in the United States of America, V-212 pp., 1927.
40. Cavanaugh, Rev. William Thomas, C.P., J.U.D., The Reservation of the Blessed Sacrament, VIII-101 pp., 1927.

41. Doheny, Rev. William J., C.S.C., A.B., J.U.D., Church Property: Modes of Acquisition, X-118 pp., 1927.
42. Feldhaus, Rev. Aloysius H., C.PP.S., J.C.D., Oratories, IX-141 pp., 1927.
43. Kelly, Rev. James Patrick, A.B., J.C.D., The Jurisdiction of the Simple Confessor, X-208 pp., 1927.
44. Neuberger, Rev. Nicholas J., J.C.D., Canon 6 or the Relation of the Codex Juris Canonici to the Preceding Legislation, V-95 pp., 1927.
45. O'Keefe, Rev. Gerald Michael, J.C.D., Matrimonial Dispensations, Powers of Bishops, Priests and Confessors, VIII-232 pp., 1927.
46. Quigley, Rev. Joseph, A.M., A.B., J.C.D., Condemned Societies, 139 pp., 1927.
47. Zaplotnik, Rev. Johannes Leo, J.C.D., De Vicariis Foraneis, X-142 pp., 1927.
48. Duskie, Rev. John Aloysius, A.B., J.C.D., The Canonical Status of the Orientals in the United States, VIII-196 pp., 1928.
49. Hyland, Rev. Francis Edward, J.C.D., Excommunication, Its Nature, Historical Development and Effects, VIII-181 pp., 1928.
50. Reinmann, Rev. Gerald Joseph, O.M.C., J.C.D., The Third Order Secular of Saint Francis, 201 pp., 1928.
51. Schenk, Rev. Francis J., J.C.D., The Matrimonial Impediments of Mixed Religion and Disparity of Cult, XVI-318 pp., 1929.
52. Coady, Rev. John Joseph, S.T.D., J.U.D., A.M., The Appointment of Pastors, VIII-150 pp., 1929.
53. Kay, Rev. Thomas Henry, J.C.D., Competence in Matrimonial Procedure, VIII-164 pp., 1929.
54. Turner, Rev. Sidney Joseph, C.P., J.U.D., The Vow of Poverty, XLIX-217 pp., 1929.
55. Kearney, Rev. Raymond A., A.B., S.T.D., J.C.D., The Principles of Delegation, VII-149 pp., 1929.
56. Conran, Rev. Edward James, A.B., J.C.D., The Interdict, V-163 pp., 1930.
57. O'Neill, Rev. William H., J.C.D., Papal Rescripts of Favor, VII-218 pp., 1930.
58. Bastnagel, Rev. Clement Vincent, J.U.D., The Appointment of Parochial Adjutants and Assistants, XV-257 pp., 1930.
59. Ferry, Rev. William A., A.B., J.C.D., Stole Fees, V-135 pp., 1930.
60. Costello, Rev. John Michael, A.B., J.C.D., Domicile and Quasi-domicile, VII-201 pp., 1930.
61. Kremer, Rev. Michael Nicholas, A.B., S.T.B., J.C.D., Church Support in the United States, VI-136 pp., 1930.
62. Angulo, Rev. Luis, C.M., J.C.D., Legislation de la Iglesia sobre la intencion en la application de la Santa Misa, VII-104 pp., 1931.
63. Frey, Rev. Wolfgang Norbert, O.S.B., A.B., J.C.D., The Act of Religious Profession, VIII-174 pp., 1931.

64. ROBERTS, REV. JAMES BRENDAN, A.B., J.C.D., The Banns of Marriage, XVI-140 pp., 1931.
65. RYDER, REV. RAYMOND ALOYSIUS, A.B., J.C.D., Simony, IX-151 pp., 1931.
66. CAMPAGNA, REV. ANGELO, Ph.D., J.U.D., Il Vicario Generale del Vescovo, VII-205 pp., 1931.
67. COX, REV. JOSEPH GODFREY, A.B., J.C.D., The Administration of Seminaries, VI-124 pp., 1931.
68. GREGORY, REV. DONALD J., J.U.D., The Pauline Privilege, XV-165 pp., 1931.
69. DONOHUE, REV. JOHN F., J.C.D., The Impediment of Crime, VII-110 pp., 1931.
70. DOOLEY, REV. EUGENE A., O.M.I., J.C.D., Church Law on Sacred Relics, IX-143 pp., 1931.
71. ORTH, REV. RAYMOND CLEMENT, O.M.C., J.C.D., The Approbation of Religious Institutes, 171 pp., 1931.
72. PERNICONE, REV. JOSEPH M., A.B., J.C.D., The Ecclesiastical Prohibition of Books, XII-267 pp., 1932.
73. CLINTON, REV. CONNELL, A.B., J.C.D., The Paschal Precept, IX-108 pp., 1932.
74. DONNELLY, REV. FRANCIS B., A.M., S.T.L., J.C.D., The Diocessan Synod, VIII-125 pp., 1932.
75. TORRENTE, REV. CAMILO, C.M.F., J.C.D., Las Processiones Sagradas, V-145 pp., 1932.
76. MURPHY, REV. EDWIN J., C.PP.S., J.C.D., Suspension Ex Informata Conscientia, XI-122 pp., 1932.
77. MACKENZIE, REV. ERIC F., A.M., S.T.L., J.C.D., The Delict of Heresy in its Commission, Penalization, Absolution, VII-124 pp., 1932.
78. LYONS, REV. AVITUS E., S.T.B., J.C.D., The Collegiate Tribunal of First Instance, XI-147 pp., 1932.
79. CONNOLLY, REV. THOMAS A., J.C.D., Appeals, XI-195 pp., 1932.
80. SANGMEISTER, REV. JOSEPH V., A.B., J.C.D., Force and Fear as Precluding Matrimonial Consent, V-211 pp., 1932.
81. JAEGER, REV. LEO A., A.B., J.C.D., The Administration of Vacant and Quasi-vacant Episcopal Sees in the United States, IX-229 pp., 1932.
82. RIMLINGER, REV. HERBERT T., J.C.D., Error Invalidating Matrimonial Consent, VII-79 pp., 1932.
83. BARRETT, REV. JOHN, D.M., S.S., J.C.D., A Compartive Study of the Third Plenary Council of Baltimore and the Code, IX-221 pp., 1932.
84. CARBERRY, REV. JOHN J., Ph.D., S.T.D., J.C.D., The Juridical Form of Marriage, X-177 pp., 1934.
85. DOLAN, REV. JOHN L., A.B., J.C.D., The Defensor Vinculi, XII-157 pp., 1934.
86. HANNAN, REV. JEROME D., A.M., S.T.D., LL.B., J.C.D., The Canon Law of Wills, IX-517 pp., 1934.

87. LEMIEUX, REV. DELISLE A., A.M., J.C.D., The Sentence in Ecclesiastical Procedure, IX-131 pp., 1934.
88. O'ROURKE, REV. JAMES J., A.B., J.C.D., Parish Registers, VII-109 pp., 1934.
89. TIMLIN, REV. BARTHOLOMEW, O.F.M., A.M., J.C.D., Conditional Matrimonial Consent, X-381 pp., 1934.
90. WAHL, REV. FRANCIS X., A.B., J.C.D., The Matrimonial Impediments of Consanguinity and Affinity, VI-125 pp., 1934.
91. WHITE, REV. ROBERT J., A.B., LL.B., S.T.B., J.C.D., Canonical Ante-Nuptial Promises and the Civil Law, VI-152 pp., 1934.
92. HERRERA, REV. ANTONIO PARRA, O.C.D., J.C.D., Legislation Ecclesiastica sobra el Ayuno y la Abstinencia, XI-191 pp., 1935.
93. KENNEDY, REV. EDWIN J., J.C.D., The Sprecial Matrimonial Process in Cases of Evident Nullity, X-165 pp., 1935.
94. MANNING, REV. JOHN J., A.B., J.C.D., Presumption of Law in Matrimonial Procedure, XI-111 pp., 1935.
95. MOEDER, REV. JOHN M., J.C.D., The Proper Bishop For Ordination and Dimissorial Letters, VII-135 pp., 1935.
96. O'MARA, REV. WILLIAM A., A.B., J.C.D., Canonical Causes For Matrimonial Dispensations, IX-155 pp., 1935.
97. REILLY, REV. PETER, J.C.D., Residence of Pastors, IX-81 pp., 1935.
98. SMITH, REV. MARINER T., O.P., S.T.Lr., J.C.D., The Penal Law For Religious, VII-169 pp., 1935.
99. WHALEN, REV. DONALD W., A.M., J.C.D., The Value of Testimonial Evidence in Matrimonial Procedure, XIII-297 pp., 1935.
100. CLEARY, REV. JOSEPH F., J.C.D., Canonical Limitations on the Alienation of Church Property, VIII-141 pp., 1936.
101. GLYNN, REV. JOHN C., J.C.D., The Promoter of Justice, XX-337 pp., 1936.
102. BRENNAN, REV. JAMES H., S.S., A.M., S.T.B., J. C. D., The Simple Convalidation of Marriage, VI-135 pp., 1937.
103. BRUNINI, REV. JOSEPH BERNARD, J.C.D., The Clerical Obligations of Canons 139 and 142, X-121 pp., 1937.
104. CONNOR, REV. MAURICE, A.B., J.C.D., The Administrative Removal of Pastors, VIII-159 pp., 1937.
105. GUILFOYLE, REV. MERLIN JOSEPH, J.C.D., Custom, XI-144 pp., 1937.
106. HUGHES, REV. JAMES AUSTIN, A.B., A.M., J.C.D., Witnesses in Criminal Trials of Clerics, IX-140 pp., 1937.
107. JANSEN, REV. RAYMOND J., A.B., S.T.L., J.C.D., Canonical Provisions for Catechetical Instruction, VII-153 pp., 1937.
108. KEALY, REV. JOHN JAMES, A.B., J.C.D., The Introductory Libellus in Church Court Procedure, XI-121 pp., 1937.
109. MCMANUS, REV. JAMES EDWARD, C.SS.R., J.C.D., The Administration of Temporal Goods in Religious Institutes, XVI-196 pp., 1937.

110. MORIARITY, REV. EUGENE JAMES, J.C.D., Oaths in Ecclesiastical Courts, X-115 pp., 1937.
111. RAINER, REV. ELIGIUS GEORGE, C.SS.R., J.C.D., Suspension of Clerics, XVIII-249 pp., 1937.
112. REILLY, REV. THOMAS F., C.SS.R., J.C.D., Visitation of Religious, XI-195 pp., 1938.
113. MORIARTY, REV. FRANCIS E., C.SS.R., J.C.L., The Extraordinary Absolution from Censures, 1938.
114. CONNOLLY, REV. NICHOLAS P., J.C.L., The Canonical Erection of Parishes, 1938.
115. DONOVAN, REV. JAMES J., J.C.L., The Pastor's Obligation in Prenuptial Investigation, 1938.
116. HARRIGAN, REV. ROBERT J., M.A., S.T.B., J.C.L., The Radical Sanation of Invalid Marriages, 1938.

www.ingramcontent.com/pod-product-compliance
Lightning Source LLC
LaVergne TN
LVHW050241080826
844660LV00012B/576

* 9 7 8 0 8 1 3 2 2 3 0 5 6 *